The City of Capital

For Clyde, Scarlet and
Seamus

The City of Capital

LONDON'S ROLE AS
A FINANCIAL CENTRE

*Jerry Coakley and
Laurence Harris*

Basil Blackwell

First published 1983
Basil Blackwell Publisher Limited
108 Cowley Road, Oxford OX4 1JF, England

British Library Cataloguing in Publication Data
Coakley, Jerry
    The city of capital.
    1. Financial institutions – London (England)
    I. Title   II. Harris, Laurence
    332.1'09421'2   HG186.G7

    ISBN 0-631-12805-0
    ISBN 0-631-13363-1 Pbk

Typesetting by Oxford Verbatim Limited
Printed in Great Britain by
Billing and Sons Ltd, Worcester

Contents

Preface

This book is intended for the non-specialist who, recognising that Britain's financial system is a major power in the land, wishes to understand how and why this is, and what the problems are that surround its institutions and functions.

We are economists, but we have avoided using the jargon of our trade or the more snappy jargon that the financial operators themselves use, for we believe that something as important as the City should be accessible to anyone whose own jargon is plain English. Similarly we have avoided giving academic economists' theories of financial institutions a central place. Models of banks' optimising behaviour and of the principles of financial intermediation have their uses, but they are not very useful for understanding the City as a whole. Apart from anything else they have little bearing on the changes and development of the financial system, on its special institutional structure, or on the power that financial operations confer, and these are the aspects that concern us here.

We have written the book while engaged on a research project investigating the changes in bank lending to industry. Part of it reflects that research quite directly and we are grateful to the Research Committee of the Open University for their financial assistance toward the project.

We have benefited enormously from the comments of friends and colleagues. Discussions of financial issues with our colleagues Martin Croasdale and Trevor Evans in the Open University's Financial Studies Research Group have had a marked effect on our way of thinking. In addition, Alison Johnson, Ute Kowarzik, Marjorie Mayo and Richard Minns have each read part or all of the text and saved us from our worst sins in pedagogy, literary style, and substantive errors. Iris Manzi, Debbie Curtis and Sandie Millar have slaved heroically over typewriters and photocopiers to reconcile our impossible scrawls with impossible deadlines. We need hardly say how grateful we are to them all. We hope they will think the final product is good enough to have made their efforts worthwhile.

Jerry Coakley
Laurence Harris

Introduction:
The City's £562 Billion Treasure

The Square Mile of the City of London is a different world. Its exclusive concern is money and finance, and its workers, commuting from the suburbs, earn the wherewithal to set themselves apart from white-collar employees elsewhere. A *Financial Times* columnist reported the bewilderment shown by the head of a medium-sized manufacturing company he had met in Leeds in 1982: 'It's those figures you print every now and then, showing what people get paid in London banks. They seem hardly credible up here, like news from another world' (*Financial Times*, 23 September 1982, p. 33). Indeed, with the average reported rate for the general manager of a City bank at £56,250 at that time and having shown an increase of 33 per cent while manual workers were settling for figures around 5–7 per cent, the City must seem quite bewildering to anyone in industry – or formerly in industry but now on the dole.

The other-worldliness of the City makes it a closed book to many people, but at the same time there is a widespread feeling that it is somehow important to all our lives and livelihoods; that perhaps it should be regarded with some suspicion or kept at a distance, but that one should know more about it. This book sets out to make the City more accessible and understandable to anyone who recognises themselves in that description of the intelligent person eyeing the City.

The curious thing about the City's other-worldliness is that it does have real ties with the more familiar parts of the economy. Industry and trade could not survive without the finance and financial dealings it provides, and the City could not make profits unless the real economy were profitable. Its difference and opaqueness arise because while those ties are real they are indirect, so that its financial operations have acquired great independence. At times it appears that money itself creates money, and that the connection with trade and industry is superfluous.

One of our principal aims in this book is to explore the connection between the country's financial centre and other sectors of the economy and to make this connection explicit, for otherwise it is impossible to understand the City's role. In fact, the links are never far below the surface, for their historical relics crop up in the most striking places. For example, the hall in which the Directors of the Bank of England meet has an architectural elegance and a richness of furnishing that epitomise money-making-money: its luxury, deep within the Bank's buildings, appears completely cut off from the world of chimneys and trade. But high on one wall there is a needle that pivots. It is not the hand of a clock but a pointer connected to a wind vane on the roof, which indicates the wind's direction. Nowadays it may simply distract the less attentive directors, but it was originaliy installed because the bankers needed to know when ships could enter and leave port. Their business was tied to the physical movement of the exports and imports they financed: the weather-cock indicated the direction of bills of exchange and cash as well as the wind. More relevant to the modern City's connection with industry and trade is the fact that, when the economy is in crisis and factories close in bankruptcy, financiers whose money seemed safely embedded in money find that, after all, it is jeopardised by the fraility of industry and trade. At the start of 1981, for example, Massey-Ferguson, one of the world's great manufacturing companies, was close to bankruptcy: if it had collapsed five British banks would have lost £70 million, with Barclays alone standing to lose £23 million from this encounter with industrial reality.

The City of London is a small territory within London – 'the Square Mile' – possessing its own local authority, police and ethos. But it is at the centre of Britain's whole financial system, and in large measure of the world's financial system, and it therefore stands as the embodiment of that system. When people talk of 'the role of the City' they mean the role of finance, and we do the same. The concentrated, frenetic activity of making money that goes on within this area is what we are interested in, but it is a shorthand for the system as a whole. The 'Square Mile' has a circumference of thousands of miles. The banks with headquarters there have branches in every British High Street and many overseas High Streets; the major building societies all have branches throughout Britain and usually have their headquarters outside the City, as, too, do some of the insurance companies and pension funds that are so crucial to the financial world. And yet the City remains the centre around which the whole financial system revolves. There *are* other financial centres in Britain; Edinburgh bankers and fund managers would be particularly incensed if it were suggested that they were subordinate to the City of London, for they do have a distinct identity and Scottish finance has a partial autonomy, but in truth, even for the Scottish financial companies, London is their ultimate centre.

What goes on within the financial system that revolves arould the City? There are two distinct types of operations; (a) dealing, and (b) borrowing and lending. This book is concerned principally with the latter but it touches on the former to some extent.

Dealing is the work of the City's markets. Some, such as the London Metal Exchange, organise the purchase and sale of commodities; on the Baltic Exchange shipping contracts are bought and sold; Lloyds of London deals in insurance and reinsurance contracts. Others deal in money; cash, bank deposits and bills of exchange. The foreign exchange market, for example, buys and sells national currencies and determines their exchange rate. The stock market trades in bonds and shares.

All of these markets are crucial to the City; they are at the core of the financial system of banks, building societies, insurance companies and so on. But, with the exception of the foreign exchange and stock markets, the following chapters concentrate exclusively upon the other side of the City's work, its borrowing and lending.

Borrowing and lending are connected with dealing in many ways; bonds, which are the records of loans that have already been advanced to companies, governments and other bodies (and bills and deposits, which are liquid loans), are themselves traded. But borrowing and lending – the creation of new credit – is a much more sophisticated operation. It makes the City a genuine centre of *finance*, rather than merely a glorified market, and it gives the City its special position *vis-à-vis* industry and trade.

Both finance and dealing have two dimensions, international and national. The City finances and is financed by British industry and ordinary people; but it also borrows, lends and deals on a world scale. Indeed, it has been, is, and intends to continue to be, one of the world's leading centres of international finance. The City is the world's leading centre for international lending and borrowing even if a large proportion of this business is transacted by the City offices of overseas banks. And the City's stock exchange ranks second to New York only. Accordingly, in Part I (chapters 1–4) we examine this international business of finance, for it has a fundamental effect upon the City's role. In Part II we set out its domestic position, its connection with British industry and people, and we do so by looking at the rather distinct borrowing and lending operations of the four leading types of financial institutions; pension funds, insurance funds (chapter 5), banks (chapter 6) and building societies (chapter 7). Between them these institutions command a position in the economy to which enormous potential power attaches: that power, its effect on policy, and what could be done about it are the subject of Part III. The nature of that power, and whether its potential is realised, emerges in the course of the book and is not readily reducible to the amount of money they control. But the sheer size of the treasure controlled by these institutions is an indicator of their position, and its composition tells us a lot about the nature of their business.

Carving up the treasure

City institutions have at their disposal the massive treasure of some £562 billion, or just over £10,000 per head of the 1981 British population. To place this in perspective, £562 billion is roughly double the 1981 annual domestic produce (as measured by GDP) of the UK or more than 28 times that of the Third World country, Colombia. Note that we say that the City has this amount *at its disposal*: it does not necessarily own it. Rather, it represents mainly the sums of money that individuals, companies and public authorities have placed with City institutions in the form of various deposits, insurance and pension contributions. And of course it is not only the British who contribute to this treasure and who make decisions on its disposal. As much as half the funds of banks and insurance companies originate from overseas residents or institutions and most of the world's leading financial institutions have offices in the City.

Although City institutions do not own most of the £562 billion, the fact remains that, within some constraints, they exercise the power to dispose of it as they please: in other words, City institutions *control* the movements of these vast sums of money. They decide on the directions in which these funds are invested as between different sectors of the economy, as between British and overseas investments, and as between short-, medium- or long-term investments. From this perspective City institutions possess an enormous degree of power; it contrasts sharply with the economic theorists' view of such institutions as mere financial *intermediaries* acting as neutral agents channelling funds between various sectors of the economy and between different national economies.

If the City as a whole has great financial power, how powerful are different types of institutions within the City? A partial answer is given in table 1, which shows the market value of leading institutions' funds at December 1981. It is immediately obvious that banks as a group predominate among financial institutions,

TABLE 1   DIVISION OF THE £562 BILLION, DECEMBER 1981

	£ billion	%
Banks	331.7	59.8
Insurance companies	74.3	13.0
Building societies	62.3	11.0
Pension funds	63.8	10.9
Trusts	16.1	2.8
Other	13.8	2.5
Total	562.0	100

Source: Financial Statistics (London: HMSO).

accounting for 60 per cent of the City's funds, while insurance companies (the next most significant group of institutions) hold only 13 per cent. The group of banks includes not only the familiar High Street clearing banks but also a range of other British and overseas banks. The domination of the banks is part of the pattern of the general preponderance of deposit institutions within the City. These deposit institutions supply various types of credit or loan finance and include, in addition to banks, building societies and hire purchase and finance companies (included in the 'Other' category). Together, deposit institutions account for almost three-quarters of the City's treasure. The remaining quarter of the funds *nominally* lies at the disposal of what are traditionally known as 'the investment institutions', although, as we explain in chapter 5, much of this is *de facto* under banks' control. The investment institutions comprise insurance companies, pension funds and various forms of trusts such as investment trust companies and the more familiar unit trusts. When people speak of 'institutional domination' of the City's capital markets (for it is largely in these long-term markets that the institutions invest) they mean domination by insurance companies, pension funds and trusts.

Banks, building societies, insurance companies and pension funds are our concern, for together they dominant finance in Britain. At this stage let us briefly look at the 'giant four', the largest British representatives of each of these types of financial institution.

Among *banks*, Barclays Group stands head and shoulders above its competitors. Indeed, in terms of assets it is the leading British financial institution. At the end of 1981 Barclays had total assets of some £48.8 billion (£59.05 billion in 1982), which at that time equalled the annual product of Switzerland. This meant it ranked sixth in the world, behind the two largest US banks (Bank America and Citicorp) and the three largest French banks (BNP, Crédit Agricole and Crédit Lyonnais), all of which have major offices in the City.

Barclays' business is to borrow and lend, but like other banks, and like the banker in a card game, it also deals – buying and selling for a turn, rather than dealing the pack. Its borrowing consists almost entirely of the deposits that firms, individuals and other bodies place with it. These made up 88 per cent of the liabilities side of its balance sheet (in 1981). They comprise many distinct types of deposits, from the few hundred pounds in your current account and the deposit account in which individuals build up nest eggs to the huge deposits made by companies and other banks. It uses this money to acquire assets, and the greatest of these – 74 per cent of its total assets in 1981 – are loans to industry, individuals and governments.

The terminology of balance sheets is strange. If people had placed £59.05 billions worth of deposits with us we would count ourselves fortunate, blessed with a great asset; but accountants and bankers, being pessimistic, count deposits as a bank's *liability* because they have to be paid back. That is despite the fact that Barclays' whole existence and that of all banks, rests on the assumption that deposits will *not* have to be repaid: certainly, some depositors will be withdrawing money at any one time, but others will be putting money in, so that deposits as a whole will not have to be repaid. Because of this assumption, banks feel confident in lending out the sums deposited with them but, nevertheless, deposits are called liabilities. On the other hand, loans from banks are always called *assets*, although with the fear that has swept the banking community in recent years over the soundness of their borrowers, they could be forgiven for wondering, 'with assets like that, who needs liabilities?'

Barclays is not only the largest banking group, it exemplifies British banks' international orientation. Of its gross profits of £616 million in 1981 no less than 39.3 per cent came from its international division. (Politicians, church leaders and public bodies have seen its international orientation from another angle, claiming that parts of the Barclays Group have given support to the South African economy and regime.) While London banks have an international orientation, banks all over the world have an orientation towards London; by the end of 1982 no less than 427 overseas banks had either a full branch or a representative office in London, or they were indirectly represented in London through owning a stake in a consortium bank (*Banker*, November 1982).

Banks like Barclays are in fierce competition with other British banks, and all British banks have to compete with foreign ones; but the keenest British competition for UK banks as a whole comes from the *building societies*. These, like banks, are deposit institutions, for most of their money – their liabilities – consists of deposits, although they go under various names (such as 'share account' deposits). The building societies compete with banks for deposits, particularly for the savings deposits of the stereotypical British householder, but they are not in the same league. The dominance of banks as a whole is paralleled by the difference between the leading bank, Barclays, with assets of almost £60 billion, and the leading building society, the Halifax, with assets of £11.9 billion in January 1982 (£14.1 billion 1983). But the importance of building societies is denoted by the fact that, despite that discrepancy, the Halifax is Britain's largest non-bank financial institution, with 977 branches and 1824 agencies in January 1983.

The assets of the Halifax consist principally of mortgages to individual households, which comprise some 80 per cent of the total. In this building societies contrast strongly with banks, whose loans are to individuals, firms and states, and are sometimes unsecured. Building societies' loans are to individuals and secured on the value of the mortgaged property. The banks themselves made inroads into house mortgage lending at the start of the 1980s, but the building societies' concentration on this type of lending continues to mark them out. During its 1982 financial year the Halifax lent £1 million more to house purchasers than did any other financial institution.

The remaining two types of financial institutions covered in this book are *insurance companies* and *pension funds*. Rather than collecting short-term deposits, these investment institutions collect long-term savings in respect of life assurance and pensions, out of which they pay current claims while accumulating the surplus in a fund. The Prudential Corporation is Britain's largest insurance company, with assets of £10.9 billion at the end of 1981 (£13.5 billion in 1982). This level of total assets would have enabled the Prudential to purchase all shares of the General Electric Company (GEC) and about 50 per cent of those of British Petroleum (BP), Britain's two largest companies by market valuation in mid-1982. The liabilities side of the Prudential's balance sheet is straightforward, the money the companies collect consisting of insurance premiums and contributions alone. Its assets, however, consist of stocks and shares (£4.1 billion), real estate and property (£3.3 billion), government securities (£1.6 billion), and other bonds (£1.1 billion) and other investments (£0.8 billion). Unlike banks and building societies, which specialise in various forms of credit, the Prudential's money is spread across a wide range of assets. And the Prudential's activities are highly international: at the end of 1981, 28 per cent of its life business premiums were overseas, while the proportion of overseas general premiums was higher still, at 58.3 per cent. During 1981 one third of its net new investments went overseas and this more than doubled to a figure of 70 per cent during 1982.

In terms of total assets, the pension schemes of public sector employees dominate the world of pension funds. At March 1982 no less than seven of the top ten British pension funds were for public sector employees, the largest being the Post Office Staff Superannuation Fund with assets of some £5.2 billion. These assets, ultimately owned in a legal sense by Post Office employees, would have been sufficient to purchase 98 per cent of shares in Royal Dutch Shell (Britain's third largest company in mid-1982).

The Post Office Fund's investments follow the same broad pattern as the Prudential's, being spread between shares, bonds and property in the main; but shareholdings represent a greater proportion of its assets (43 per cent) than the Prudential's (38 per cent). The fund's overseas investments accounted for some 10 per cent of these assets, but, in contrast with the Prudential, all of the Post

Office Fund's liabilities (its pension contributions) originate in Britain.

From these asset portfolios, then, deposit institutions, banks and building societies seem to lord it over the City in terms of the amount of funds at their disposal. Given these institutions' predominance, it is not surprising to find that banks like Barclays dwarf all other British City institutions. The dominance of banks is additionally reinforced to the extent that they manage, and effectively have at their disposal, funds on behalf of pension funds and moneyed individuals. It would none the less be wrong to conclude from this that banks are the sole or even the principal target of the critics' historical preoccupation with the City. As we shall see, the issues of major concern to the critics, and those that continue to be raised over the years, tend to be ones that relate to the role of the City as a whole.

At the crossroads

Describing the institutions' balance sheets and the facts of their business serves a purpose, but it is not our real aim in this book. We are more interested in analysing the institutions in depth, attempting to go behind them to discover the relations between the City and the rest of the economy, and in assessing the City's power. We do so because the country's economic difficulties have placed the City at something of a crossroads. Having survived many crises in the course of its long history, the City's future now has to be judged in the context of Britain's overriding economic problem, the task of generating new growth on a new basis.

The issues have been raised most forcibly by left-wing criticisms of the financial system; minds have been concentrated by the possibility, however remote, that left-wing arguments will lead to nationalisation of, or penalties on, the City.

The City has been the bogey of the Left, probably rivalling only the public schools as the supreme example, in left-wing polemics, of anachronistic but none the less dangerous class rule in Britain. But distrust of money and the power of the moneyed classes has from time to time influenced populists far removed from socialism, and has even found echoes in the centre ground of British politics. This may be due, as the Fabian economist G. D. H. Cole thought, to the apparent complexity of finance, to the fact that '[o]rdinary intelligent people are apt to be frightened about monetary problems, because at the first approach everything seems to be topsy-turvy', but it is more likely due to their perception of the financial system's actual history.

The age of the City institutions is impressive, making them a potential tourist attraction if nothing else. The Bank of England was created by a Tonnage Act in July 1694, making it the world's fourth oldest central bank; the Royal Exchange (the home of the recently established London Financial Futures Market) opened in 1571, and the origins of the London Stock Exchange can be traced back to coffee house meetings in the late seventeenth century. Its age gives an impression of maturity and strength, but this is deceptive, for the City lives on innovation and hence is always at the mercy of unskilled adventurers. The secondary banking crash of 1973 to 1975 was the result of both the ambitious new banks and the big old established banks – and even the Crown Agents – risking all on ventures of which even the Mafia's financiers would have been wary. The small, new operators (such as Cornhill Consolidated Group, whose short life was characterised by 'reckless trading, persistent window dressing of accounts, circular loans, lies and contempt of boardroom procedure' (*Financial Times*, 31 December 1980)), were the extreme, but they could exist only because the City is in perpetual need of such adventurers; they are the source of many of the innovations that are its life-blood.

City scandals occurred as long ago as 1721, with the bursting of the South Sea Company's bubble (and, with it, the financial ambitions of royalty and politicians) and continue today, with the most dramatic recent scandals occurring among members of the Stock Exchange and Lloyd's of London. But they are relatively unimportant in the long run. The real issues that stem from the City's history are its role in the economy – its links with industry and trade – and its concentrated power, rather than its scandals and adventurers. These are the grounds on which the Left has pitched its criticisms of the City, and they are the problems that have to be solved as the City stands at the crossroads.

The questions that the Left has asked are real, and they have increased in urgency as Britain's general economic malaise has turned into an intractable crisis with human resources and physical plant going to waste, fodder only for the compilers of statistics on unemployment and insolvency. After three postwar decades of unprecedented prosperity, the bewilderment of mass unemployment has generated an intense search for explanations, and while 'Thatcherism', a world crisis and the militancy of British workers are all popular candidates, 'the City' keeps entering the lists.

Three main problems have to be faced in assessing the future of the financial system: (1) can the City provide the finance needed for the regeneration of Britain's 'real economy'? (2) will the City be brought down by the weakness of the real economy, industry and commerce, in Britain and many other countries? and (3) is it possible to restrict the City's power to constrain and determine government policy? These three questions run through the whole of this book.

Can the City provide the finance?

The dominant, but often rather non-specific, accusation of the City's modern critics has been that the financial system has failed industry and commerce; it has starved them of appropriate funds for modernisation or the adoption of new products and techniques. The fact that Britain's economic crisis did not come out of the blue but is the culmination of a long process of 'de-industrialisation' (in which employment in manufacturing industry has shrunk by 38 per cent between 1960 and 1983) has highlighted the complaint.

The 'financial starvation' thesis has been linked with the argument that the City has had inadequate funds to lend to industry because it has diverted money to other 'unproductive' uses. The £562 billion treasure has been increasingly directed into overseas investment and investment in land and real estate, uses that have been given priority over industry because of their high, if risky, profitability.

These arguments are weighty and serious, but there is little hard evidence to support them. The cumbersomely named 'Committee to Review the Functioning of Financial Institutions' was established under Sir Harold Wilson principally to examine the overall question of whether there was a shortage of funds for industry. The 1980 Report of this Wilson Committee was a weak document from any point of view, but its rejection of the 'financial starvation' view has not been refuted. When it comes to the alternative uses, there is no dispute about the fact that overseas investment has comprised an increasing proportion of the City's investments especially since 1979; but there is no reason to think that there is a fixed pool of funds the availability of which for industry has been reduced by this outflow, and there is no factual knowledge of whether it has affected industry through more complex channels.

The historical record does not carry a clear message. However, the question of whether the City can provide the finance needed for economic regeneration is a question concerning the future, and the past can yield only indirect lessons. While the book as a whole looks at the past and current position, the final chapter explicitly looks to the future.

Will the City crash?

The questions about the provision of finance concern the City's ability to underpin industry. A question that several pundits, in the City and outside it, consider to be more urgent is whether the 'real economy's' underpinning of the financial system has become so weak that banks and other City houses will crash, bringing losses to many and so disrupting the delicate balance of the economy that the slump is intensified.

The issue has been put on the agenda by two types of phenomena. First, the failure and near-failure of several major corporations and a large number of smaller ones has forced banks to make large provisions for bad debts. Second is the virtual short-term bankruptcy of countries such as Poland, Mexico, Argentina and a host of others with heavy debts to the international banking system in which the City's banks are leading actors.

The sovereign states' near-defaults on their international loans are causing the greatest concern. During the 1930s depression more than three-quarters of Latin American countries' debts had gone into default by the middle of the decade; and the difficulties experienced by Mexico, Argentina, Brazil, Ecuador, Chile, Cuba, Uruguay and Venezuela between August 1982 and March 1983 led many to think that history could repeat itself with nasty consequences for the City. So concerned was one *Financial Times* journalist over the banks' inability to face the danger that his article was headed 'Of profits and imprudence', and claimed 'Bankers and auditors are fiddling while the banking edifice threatens to burn.'

Can the City's power be restricted?

Where the City goes from here is not simply a question of whether it provides finance for the economy or whether it survives the risk of a crash: it is a question of whether it retains its status as an independent centre of economic power in Britain.

The City's critics have claimed that its international operations have given it a direct power over industry and a direct influence over governments and their economic policies. The power of the City can be examined only by looking at the position of finance and at the City as a whole; its standing in a critical position within the structure of the economy is the only possible source of such power. We have taken that approach in this book, both examining the position of the whole City within the economy and also tracing its power through the various institutions that comprise it, for we judge that understanding the City's power is crucial to assessing the financial system, but this aspect is often neglected.

Underlying much left-wing criticism of the City is, of course, fear of its power: fear of the bankers' ramp. Whereas the Wilson Committee, and the 22 official investigations that were its fore-runners since Walpole, have been concerned with reforming the financial system and improving its efficiency, today's socialist critics are inevitably concerned more with its power than with its efficiency. The various committees in the Labour Party and labour movement that have produced the Alternative Economic Strategy, the plan for a state-directed expansion, turn their attention to the City because of their fear that its power could undermine the power on which their plans depend – that of the state. Whether the City is effectively beyond state control, whether its operations seriously limit the state's freedom of actions, whether it is more powerful than the state, are therefore questions that this book cannot avoid. The power relations that connect with the City – the City and industry, the City and the state – are the background against which the book examines the details of the financial operations. In the end, the conclusion we reach in the final chapter appears inescapable: if a Labour government is to implement its Alternative Economic Strategy, the City's major institutions will have to be nationalised.

PART I

THE CITY INTERNATIONAL

The City's international business has affected its whole development, and this business itself has changed over time. Chapters 1 to
3 deal with the changes that have occurred while London has
maintained its leading position in the world's financial system. The
final chapter in Part I examines the widespread fear that international finance could succumb to a crisis, a financial crash,
emanating from any of the countries that are bound up with it.

1

Is the City Undermining British Sovereignty?

The title of this chapter poses a stark question, but it is one that arises whenever people encounter the City's international role. Are the City's banks and financial institutions a threat to Britain's sovereignty?

At times of crisis and doubt the British have a tendency to identify foreign threats to British sovereignty working through economic warfare. When Ramsey MacDonald cut spending in 1931 and broke his Labour government, it was seen to be at the instigation of the bankers of Europe and New York; when Harold Wilson's government lost control of the economy in the 1960s the attack on Britain had come, people were told, from the Gnomes of Zurich; when the Labour administration of James Callaghan and Denis Healey embraced monetarism and cuts in government spending after the 1976 slide in the exchange rate, the blame was laid at the door of the IMF's Washington headquarters; and when British factories shut their doors, creating dole queues of three million people, an invasion of commodities marching from the Far East was blamed as often as the incompetence of British governments, managements or workers.

Radicals of various hues, however, have identified a different threat to our sovereignty: the City itself, either as a traitor or as a Trojan horse within our own walls. The image is a powerful one, with the same dramatic element as the Philby to Blunt spy stories: that of secret betrayal by those in the establishment who epitomise Britishness, betrayal by the bankers of the Square Mile balancing the subversion of the Whitehall and Palace men.

But is it an accurate image? This and the following two chapters examine the City's international role, the activities that are in some way its essence, and in doing so we look at that question from several angles.

Immediately the question, 'Does the City undermine British sovereignty?' is posed, however, its ambiguities become evident, since for each reader the words 'British' and 'sovereignty' have a different significance. In their popular usage they conjure an image of the British state having the powers, if only the City would let it, to act unfettered in the interests of the British people as a whole; but such a conception of 'British sovereignty' has no pertinence. For the British people can not be classified 'as a whole' and are never all affected by an event or situation in the same way. To take only the broadest and most obvious economic divisions, the interests of multinational firms running factories in Britain are distinct from those of firms whose whole base is British; financial capitalists differ from their industrial counterparts; and the conflicts between capitalists and workers infuse our whole society. Thus, the question of whether the City undermines British sovereignty has usually turned on whether the City has harmed particular sectors, and most frequently, on whether it has undermined the strength of industry. Even socialists pose the problem in terms of the City's effect upon industrial capital; for, while never claiming that what's good for the Engineering Employers' Federation is good for the workers, the Left recognises that when industrial growth has faltered the working class has suffered. The question has become one of whether the City's international activities have undermined industry, or, in terms of 'sovereignty', whether they have prevented the state from pursuing the industrial growth policies that the French, Japanese and other governments have, in their different ways, successfully applied since the Second World War.

'Overseas alliance' versus 'enclave' theses

The claim that the international role of the City has harmed industry has come to the fore several times in recent history. The most notable example was the City's insistence through the mid-1960s on maintaining the exchange value of the pound at $2.80 while Keynesian economists claimed, with some justification, that a lower exchange rate was needed in order to improve industry's sales and profits. The rationale for the City's rigidity has many elements – there is nothing that leads one to think the City has an essential and permanent interest in maintaining high fixed rather than flexible exchange rates – but one aspect was undoubtedly the belief among many of its representatives that cutting the exchange rate would deal a heavy blow to the City's international business because it would inflict losses on all those foreign investors, government and private, who held sterling deposits and investments in London. This was a belief that was characteristic of the last years of the Sterling Area, the financial relic of Britain's attempts to remain an imperial power; and when eventually in 1967 the bitter pill was forced down and the decision taken to devalue sterling to $2.40, the event, though traumatic for the City, marked the beginning of a new and uniquely fruitful international position. At the time, however, the City's stand against devaluation was taken in pursuit of its then-perceived interests, and it did harm industrial capital; the puzzle is why the City should pursue international policies that weaken the industrial base in Britain.

It is a puzzle because banking and finance depend ultimately upon industry for their profits; their revenue in interest and fees come from the surplus created in industry, so policies that harm industry also inflict damage ultimately on the financial system itself. That is true in a general sense, but the puzzle becomes soluble once we look at the specific divisions that exist within industry and the variety of channels through which the financial system can obtain its profit: ultimately the City's reward comes from the profits generated by many countries' production rather than from those activities located on our shores.

Writers on the City's role in British capitalism have offered two distinct solutions to the puzzle. One is the thesis that British industry is fundamentally divided between nationally restricted, locally based capital on the one hand and the merchants and industrialists whose operations, partly deriving from Empire days, are international in character on the other. On this thesis, the City pursues its international operations as the financial arm of the latter group, so that the international policies it adopts may harm production within Britain but, instead of harming industry as a whole, will benefit industrialists whose London head offices rest upon foreign foundations. There is, it is argued, an alliance between the City and the international wing of British capital: the thesis is that of an *'overseas alliance'* to explain the City's role in events like those preceding the 1967 devaluation.

The alternative thesis is that the City's international operations are not principally undertaken as the financial arm of any segment of commercial and industrial capital; although they do service those sectors, the most important characteristic of the City's world activities is that they are truly supra-national. According to this thesis, the '*enclave*' thesis, the fact that the financial institutions are physically situated within the borders of the United Kingdom is a geographical, spatial, fact which is insignificant compared to their economic location as part, probably the most important part, of a world-wide financial system of banks and other institutions whose freely moving billions hardly know national boundaries. According to the enclave thesis, then, the City's international work has a truly international logic to it, is world-wide in its own right, and does not reflect or work in alliance with the international aspirations of British commercial and industrial houses.

In fact, both the 'overseas alliance' and the 'enclave' theses go a long way towards explaining the City's international work and policies over the past century or more. The City has been the financial arm and ally of British commerce and industry as it built export markets, raw material sources, transport systems and factories across the world, and it has also been an independent entity at the centre of a world financial system whose operators make their money from moving funds around and care nothing for the particular interests of one segment of Britain's commerce and industry – or any other country's, for that matter. Although both aspects have co-existed, their relative weight has varied over the years. Today, the international role of the City is dominated largely by its 'enclave' aspect; in terms of one of its most successful economic operations, the Square Mile is international or foreign territory, just as the Soviet Union's London embassy is in terms of its political operations. But the significance of the enclave aspect did not happen automatically; it was constructed during the 1960s and early 1970s, and the battle over the 1967 devaluation was a turning point, for it was the last instance when the City set out to defend its international role as part of the 'overseas alliance'.

Examining the debate and events around the 1967 devaluation will illuminate what is meant by the two aspects – the 'enclave' and 'overseas alliance' aspects – of the City's world role. The election of a Labour government in 1964 was followed by three years when foreign exchange crises dominated the economic life of the country. In 1966 in particular, there was intensive selling of sterling which would have pushed its price (its exchange rate) in terms of dollars well below the $2.80 that prevailed until then; to ensure that the exchange rate did not in fact fall, the government spent quantities of dollars ('foreign exchange reserves') buying sterling to offset the bankers' and industrialists' sales, and it tailored its domestic economic programme to reassure these speculators that holding money in pounds as deposits in London banks and money markets was better than selling them. The question was whether the government *should* have defended the $2.80 exchange rate, or whether it should have devalued so that the pound could be bought for $2.40 or some other relatively low price.

The academic and industrial lobby arguing for devaluation rather than defence of the pound marshalled two particularly powerful arguments: first, that once foreign exchange market operators had decided the price of sterling was too high they could not ultimately be convinced that the government would maintain it at $2.80 so would sell until their prophecy was fulfilled by the government's having insufficient reserves to continue the defence; and, second, that industry would in any case benefit from a lower exchange rate. The argument, 'industry would benefit' is significant only if it means that profitability would increase, but in fact it was presented as the different argument that the value of industry's *sales* would rise. A lower price for the pound in terms of the dollar would mean that foreigners could buy our produce more cheaply in terms of their currency so industry would sell more exports, while British firms and consumers would find foreign goods more expensive and would, instead, increase their demand for British goods. This increase in sales value would increase industry's profits, it was argued, particularly if the real value of wages were held back through an incomes policy.

The City's arguments, put by the Bank of England, against devaluation partly touched on the same question of the profitability of industry, taking a different perspective on it. They argued that, although devaluation would increase sales and the short-term profitability of industry, it was a soft option; it could be no substitute for a discipline that would yield a more lasting increase in profitability. Defending the exchange rate was, on this view, necessary because it would force British industry to cut its own domestic costs if it was to keep prices down and compete with foreign firms instead of having a reduction in the price of sterling do the job for it. Thus, the discipline of a high exchange rate would force firms to improve productivity and firmly resist wage increases. But this was not the prime consideration in the City's defence of the exchange rate; above all, devaluation was rejected because it was thought that it would damage the City's own international business.

The 'Sterling Area'

Until the 1960s the City's international business was dominated by its links with British commercial and industrial expansion abroad. Its finance of export and import trade in the early stages of the Industrial Revolution gave birth to the Bill on London (a short-term IOU that enabled sellers to get their money from the bank before their ship reached the buyer's port), which was central to the growth of the London banking system and money market through the nineteenth century. And the City provided the channels through which Victorian industry exported its surplus capital in foreign investments; the growth of the Stock Exchange between the Napoleonic Wars and the First World War was founded largely on the financing of foreign ventures.

The shaping of this international business paralleled the formation of the British Empire and the whole group of countries, whether within the Empire or not, that comprised the politico-economic system of the Pax Britannica. Capital was exported to, and profits repatriated from, this world system through the City, but the capital was owned by British industry and commerce (being generated from their domestic and, particularly, their overseas operations), and after deducting the City's take the profits went to those industrial firms and their commercial partners. A crucial feature of the system was that the administrations of the overseas territories and nations themselves held their treasure in London one way or the other; effectively, they were lending their money to the City or to the British state and British industry via the City.

From 1931 to the 1970s this system was regularised, to a degree that changed as historical circumstances changed, in the arrangements known as the 'Sterling Area'. The nature of the Sterling Area is discussed in the next chapter. The important thing about it for our present purposes was that its existence was founded upon the 'overseas alliance' between the City and the externally oriented part of Britain's industrial and commercial capital. It developed from the trading and investment relations between the 'workshop of the world' and her overseas Empire and related countries; and, even as the overseas members developed towards varying degrees of economic and political independence, privileged access to the London capital markets (or, looked at from the other end, unimpeded channels for the export of British capital) remained central to it.

An outcome of this Sterling Area arrangement was that countries such as India and Egypt, and they especially, came out of the Second World War holding large deposits in London. Attitudes towards these, 'The Problem of the Sterling Balances', influenced the international policies of the City and British governments for the ensuing quarter-century and were instrumental in the City's opposition to the 1967 devaluation. Looked at from one angle, these sterling balances had been payment for the raw materials that Britain imported for the war effort (although, given the opposition of the militant independence movement in India against helping the British war without Indian independence, it would distort history to say the money was payment for India's voluntary support for the war effort); looked at from the other angle, the sterling balances were loans of foreign exchange to the British state and British economy from countries that desperately needed the foreign exchange themselves and that, since they held sterling instead, had to import manufactured goods from the factories of Birmingham, Lancashire and Scotland rather than Pittsburgh and Detroit. As well as the official holdings of sterling balances by the authorities of the overseas sterling area, private sterling balances were held by the overseas firms and financial institutions which were linked with the trading and investment system whose centre was Britain.

In the postwar period the ability of all these official and private holders to exchange their sterling for foreign exchange was restricted, for sterling was not legally convertible (although there were loopholes that could be and were taken advantage of); but from 1958 sterling balances did become officially convertible, and over the next decade or 15 years the City and, under its tutelage, the British state were preoccupied with persuading rather than forcing the overseas holders to continue to hold sterling. They had to maintain 'confidence' in the City and in the British economy whose trade and investment underpinned the City's role in the Sterling Area if the calamity of foreign holders selling their sterling balances for dollars was to be avoided. That possibility was seen to be a calamity because it would have overturned London's pivotal role as the supplier of capital and financier of British capital's foreign investment; it would have swept away the 'overseas alliance' that until then had been the strongest of the two helix-shaped international strands in the City's genetic make-up. But that danger was not what dominated public discussion. The perception of events, even as presented in the City's representatives' statements on the issue, was that the exchange rate itself was at stake rather than the future of the City in the overseas alliance.

With hindsight, however, it is clear that the defence of the $2.80 pound was a means rather than the ultimate end. If the pound had been devalued, it was thought, the holders of the sterling balances who would, of course, find their wealth thereby devalued would 'lose confidence' in the City; and the delicate balance by which they had held sterling and the City's finance had been the centre of their world for trade and investment would collapse. The Governor of the Bank of England spoke of shame and moral issues when the pound was eventually devalued, but what had been at stake were the very material interests of the City's overseas alliance.

The banker to the dollar

The 1967 devaluation did, indeed, mark the end of an era, and initiated a period when the City's international character has been marked by the profits made in its 'enclave' function. In the event, the devaluation did not lead to a total and irreversible decline in foreign holdings of sterling, but those who held pounds ten years after 1967 did so for quite different reasons and as part of a totally different system from their equivalents in the earlier postwar years. And the City's profits within that system were no longer predicated basically upon the trade and investment of British industry that bound the old Sterling Area and sterling balances to London. Now the City's profits and its remarkable post-1967 rate of growth were marked by its role as the banker to the dollar, its achievement in becoming the world's leading centre for the international borrowing and lending of dollars. These were dollars that the City both borrowed from and loaned to sovereign governments and multinational corporations around the whole world; they were not the money transfers of British industry's trade and investment. To put it in an extreme form, the City of London came to act as the intermediary between the rest of the world's borrowers and lenders, and could, in principle, have carried out that function whether British factories and merchants continued to exist or not, although British industry did not pack up and the City's old functions continued to bring it significant profits as industry increased rather than decreased its international trade and investment after 1967.

The City's 'enclave' business of dollar deposits and loans came to be known as *Euro*dollar business to capture the fact that the dollars were based on the European side of the Atlantic instead of being deposits held in bank accounts in America itself. For a similar reason, this Eurodollar business is known as 'offshore banking', since its handling of dollars took place geographically outside United States territory (partly in order to be free of American banking regulations). Although the most important centre of offshore dollar operations was London, the adjective could almost refer to the fact that the City of London had, in terms of its economic functions, become in large measure offshore from the 'real economy' of Britain – the humming factories, the desolate factories, the expanding TV and hi-fi-shops and the increasingly busy dole and supplementary benefit offices.

The City's activities acquired their 'offshore' character in the same sense as the other offshore growth industry of the 1970s, North Sea oil – in the sense, that is, that its activities did not depend upon the 'real economy' of onshore Britain. But in both cases there was a strong effect in the other direction. Just as the 'pirate' pop radio ships of the 1960s were unaffected by the British authorities but had a strong effect upon the British culture and its laws, so both North Sea oil and the City's Eurodollar business have directly and indirectly affected the conditions under which British industry has operated and the British people have lived their lives. In particular, both have affected conditions through their effects upon the financial markets: they lay behind a sharp rise in the exchange rate in 1979–81 at the critical moment when factories operating in Britain needed some protection to enable planned regeneration instead of the fierce competition that the high pound brought in the form of cheap imports and dear exports; and the Eurodollar markets' existence encouraged the historically high interest rates that existed at the same time and hit industry squarely in its pocket.

The interests of the City

Two aspects of the City's international activities are explored in the following two chapters. Chapter 2 examines the connection between the City's and industry's international roles in the context of the 'overseas alliance', while chapter 3 elaborates the City's modern 'enclave' role at the centre of the world Eurodollar markets. Nevertheless, it should not be thought that these two aspects are simple and completely distinct from each other; it is not true that when one exists the other cannot, nor is it true that they can exist side by side without affecting each other. The two functions are analytic categories, which in practice co-exist and in doing so affect each other: the City was important as an intermediary between third parties even when its predominant function was connected to British industry's Empire, and the growth of its modern offshore activities has not only co-existed with the functions it performs for British industry's international connections, but has also affected the nature of those functions.

In the following chapters we shall return to the question of whether the City's two international roles undermine British sovereignty. If they did so in any meaningful sense, what could be the channels for or the *modus operandi* of this effect, and in whose interests would it be pursued. At one level, it is not necessary to look further than the Square Mile itself to understand the City's interests, for in reality its international (and other) operations are conducted with an eye fixed firmly upon the profits of the operators themselves.

Different operators derive their profits in different ways, and therefore look beyond their immediate operations and profits to differing extents; but however much they may be concerned with external developments, their concern emanates only from the connection that exists between them and the financial institution's own profits. A foreign exchange dealer surrounded by communications equipment and connections to markets around the capitalist world, buying, selling and deciding at a frenetic pace, has a direct influence on all our lives; for it is such sales of sterling that can push down the sterling exchange rate, thereby raising the cost to British workers of imported food and consumer goods while perhaps helping to raise industry's exports, employment and profits. But the dealer's actions are not taken in order to produce such effects; the sale of sterling occurs simply because the dealer thinks a profit can be made from it.

The dealer has to look forward, to form expectations of the exchange rate's behaviour in the near future, because that will influence whether or not the deal yields a profit; but this forward look is not likely to cover the long period it would take for workers' consumption decisions, imports and exports to be fully affected by the exchange rate. And if the dealer were concerned with those effects, it would be not because of the benefit or harm they bring to the interests of workers or some fractions of British capital, but because they are relevant to the profitability of the foreign exchange deal itself.

At the other extreme, a banker advising a pension fund to invest a proportion of funds abroad instead of in British shares (as they did on a large scale as soon as foreign exchange controls were completely lifted in 1979) *is* taking a long-term view about the prospects for the profitability of British capital; but even in that case the advice to invest abroad is not designed with the aim of starving British factories of funds: it is designed to profit the pension fund and the bank itself in the light of the banker's view of the future. The interests of the City's institutions and operators are, then, simply the pursuit of their own profits. At times this may harm British workers or capital operating here or abroad or may benefit some section; it may even lead the City to form an alliance with the internationally oriented section of British capital, the 'overseas alliance', to pursue similar policies over long periods. But whatever the alliances and coincidence of interests that exist at various times, the continuing theme is the financial institutions' pursuit of their own short-term or long-term profits.

As to *how* this pursuit of the City's interests operates, clearly, it is not in all respects channelled and coordinated through the conscious organisation and leadership of any committee or group of financiers, nor do the interests of different institutions always coincide, as we shall see in chapter 7. Many of the most important developments in financial markets affecting the 'real economy' are the results of thousands of operators buying and selling foreign exchange, bonds or bills for short-term gain, and in that way causing changes in exchange rates (or interest rates) that affect the whole economy. Such events, rather than conspiracies or coordinated policies, have been behind some of the most significant foreign exchange crises or interest rate fluctuations this century. Nevertheless, there is in addition leadership, guidance and policy. Despite the fact that the different City operators have different sources of profit and hence sometimes conflicting views (or, rather, because of it), the Bank of England has acted as the City's leader, formulating policy in relation to its interests, and on one hand regulating and influencing the anonymous operations of the City's markets while on the other speaking for the City to influence government policy towards it and towards the economy as a whole.

Since its nationalisation in 1946 (and, in a more general sense, for three-quarters of a century before nationalisation), the Bank of

England has formally been in the anomalous position of being an arm of the state and the instrument for the state's supervision of the financial system while also being the voice of the financial system in trying to force its policies on the state. The very existence of the latter role means that, if successful, it must predominate over the former, since the Bank will find itself executing policies it has formulated, and a crucial lever for these policies has always been the City's international operations.

It was the City and the Bank of England that demanded Ramsay McDonald's cuts in government spending in 1931. It was demanded at the same time as the anonymous forces of the foreign exchange market brought about a run on sterling, but nevertheless it was a consciously formulated demand supported by the considered arguments of government-appointed committees dominated by financiers (such as the May Committee), and the cuts were finally forced on the government by the Bank reporting to the Cabinet what the foreign exchange dealers and foreign central banks would 'stand for'. That is the classic example of the City's leadership formulating a government policy on foreign exchange that can affect the whole economy. Another is its success until 1967 in persuading the 1964 and 1966 Labour governments to stake the whole economy on the defence of the pound.

Less publicised, but equally important, has been the Bank of England's success in the last two decades in persuading the government to leave international banking in London less regulated than in many other financial centres and thereby to encourage its growth as the world centre for Eurodollar banking and the best location for branches of foreign banks engaged in it.

The City, then, does have interests, and pursues them both in a spontaneous manner in its day-to-day operations and in a coordinated way under Bank of England leadership. It is significant for our present concerns that the City's international operations are central to the pursuit of its interests, and for two reasons: first, the institutions' and markets' functions of trading in foreign exchange and in lending and borrowing to and from foreign operators in foreign currencies are a major source of the City's profits; and, second, their influence over the exchange rate and, in relation to their foreign business, over interest rates gives the City power over the two prices – of foreign exchange and of credit – that affect the whole economy. If British sovereignty is being undermined by finance, it is not a plot from abroad – Gnomes of Zurich, or the IMF furthering US capital's hegemony – that is doing the tunnelling: it is the operations of the City of London pursuing its interests, particularly in respect of international money and capital. But the relevant issue is not British sovereignty *per se*: it is whether the direction of the economy and the formulation of economic policy are subject to those interests.

2

The Export of Capital

To say that the City of London is at the centre of the world's financial system is not to imply that it is merely an 'offshore' centre, an enclave or device for channelling money from one foreign country to another. The City is also in the business of investing *British* money abroad (regardless of whether, as some would maintain, the funds should have gone into industry at home). This export of British capital is one side of the City's international role. It has dominated City life since the earliest days, but its nature and role have changed dramatically as the other international and domestic activities of the City have changed.

The characteristic that distinguishes the export of capital from the transactions connected with the City's 'offshore' role is that its funds are derived from the profits generated within British industry. But that begs the question instead of answering it. For one thing, profits flowing from British factories located in Britain do not come wholly from the production that takes place there; a factory's profitability is affected by the efficiency of the factories from which it buys supplies and to which it sells, and in the case of Britain those are as likely to be abroad. Moreover, when we talk of profits 'generated within British industry', do we mean industry located in Britain or industry owned by British firms?

To answer these questions we need to disentangle the various forms of overseas investment and make sense of the balance of payments data from which they are derived. The first possible source of confusion is that overseas investment denotes net out-flows of money and capital for the purposes of *investment*, rather than for the actual building of factories and installation of plant or machinery. Because 'overseas investment' is synonymous with overseas *financial* flows, and the City necessarily plays a central role in the process whereby capital is exported, this raises the issue

mentioned above of whether the funds exported could or should
have been employed instead to finance real investment in Britain.

The second difficulty is that there are two kinds of overseas
investment, *portfolio* and *direct*. Portfolio investment is the more
straightforward of the two concepts: if a British financial institution
buys shares or bonds in a foreign firm or overseas government
bonds, the purchase is a portfolio investment. Direct investment
is by industrial and commercial companies rather than financial
institutions. It includes the net financial investment by British
merchants and industrialists in their overseas activities. More
specifically, it includes the UK parent company's share of retained
profits from its overseas operations, that company's net purchases
of overseas shares and bonds, and changes in overseas (inter-
company and branch) indebtedness to the UK head office.

In brief, portfolio investment involves City financial houses buying overseas shares and bonds, property and other investments,
while direct investment entails overseas spending by UK industry
and commerce, financed by overseas retained profits and by loans
raised from City and other institutions. Table 2.1 shows the
relative magnitudes of both direct and portfolio investment over
the 1971–81 period.

The City's overseas heritage

The export of capital has meant different things to the City and to
the British economy at different times. In the half-century before
the First World War, foreign loans had been one strand in the
system that linked three elements: (1) foreign trade, (2) the
multilateral financing of foreign trade and credit (the City as the
centre of a world system with funds entering from different parts of
the world and being loaned out again), and (3) the export of capital
from Britain itself. It was a multilateral system that had grown on
the basis of expanding trade in the nineteenth century, and this has
led some to assume that the City had the pursuit of free trade at its
heart. But it came increasingly to be constructed around spheres of
influence as the industrialised countries competed for markets.
Within that period the export of capital came to be instrumental in
dividing the world into British, as opposed to German, French or
other, spheres of influence. Nevertheless, during the whole period
the export of capital from Britain was part of a single world financial system, with London at its centre and sterling as its dominant, if
not quite its sole, currency apart from gold.

TABLE 2.1 UK PRIVATE INVESTMENT OVERSEAS, 1971–1981 (£ million)

	1971	1972	1973	1974	1975	1976	1977	1978	1979	1980	1981
Direct	−676*	−737	−1631	−1575	−1171	−2145	−1885	−2740	−2788	−3491	−5157
Portfolio	−45	−604	+276	+725	−59	+90	+12	−1073	−909	−3147	−4100
Other†	−139	−61	−415	−298	−137	−214	−461	−821	−2858	−1566	−1380
Total	−860	−1402	−1760	−1148	−1367	−2269	−2334	−4634	−6555	−8204	−10637

* A negative sign implies a net outflow of investment
† Oil companies and miscellaneous investment
Source: *United Kingdom Balance of Payments* (London: HMSO).

At the outbreak of the First World War in 1914, long-term investment abroad by British firms and people constituted 41 per cent of the total foreign investment in the world. Although the foundations for this had been laid in the 30 years before 1880 with loans to foreign governments and for railway construction, the outflow continued until the war destroyed the old order, so that in the final years of Edwardian tranquility, 1905–1913, foreign investment was 6.8 per cent of gross national product (some writers put it as high as 9 per cent). And the interest and profits yielded by this wealth accounted for one-tenth of national income. These flows were mostly portfolio investment; the typical picture is of financial institutions buying the interest-yielding bonds of foreign governments, railway companies and public utilities while the middle classes – the rentiers and 'widows and orphans' – of southern England made similar investments through them and drew the interest to pay the school fees.

By contrast, foreign investment in mines, plantations and agricultural and manufacturing enterprises was a relatively unimportant component in the outflow of capital from Britain in the early twentieth century; portfolio investment had come to be seen as an alternative to the extension of British industry abroad and to industrial investment at home. By 1913, 30 per cent of British overseas investment in securities comprised loans to governments and municipal authorities (of which the majority were to the dominions and colonies), 40 per cent were to railways (especially in the United States) and 5 per cent were to public utilities. Only 16 per cent was invested in commerce, industry or enterprises producing raw materials. Nevertheless, in some areas control over production itself was a crucial element in foreign investment and worth fighting for: one element in the background to the Boer War was the need to retain control over the British investments in the Rand's gold mines and growing commerce.

For more than a decade after the First World War, Britain's bankers and entrepreneurs struggled to restore the *status quo ante*. The reconstruction of a world system where sterling, linked to gold, was the dominant trading currency, where London was central to the financing of a multilateral web of world trade, and where the City was the principal source of long-term investment capital was an objective to be attained at any cost. The Cuncliffe Committee, in 1918 and 1919, proposed a return to the gold standard and matching economic and financial policies without questioning the ability of the postwar world to replicate the prewar.

The economic crises of the 1920s and 1930s, however, forced an objective reappraisal. The rivalry between different countries' economic interests, between one set of industrialists and another, between one set of bankers and another, was killing free trade. Tariffs and quotas on imports were being raised and currencies devalued to cut imports. The City, whose capital exports before the war had been linked to its pre-eminence in providing world-wide short-term finance for free trade, found itself at the centre of a more restricted trading and financial system.

Thus it was that, after the disruptions of the war and the false starts that followed, a new system based on London – the Sterling Area – came to be established in the 1930s, a system that lasted, in varying forms, effectively until the late 1970s. Instead of encompassing the world, it comprised a bloc – a large and powerful bloc, but in many senses a defensive one – within which free trade and the export of capital could take place, with sterling at the centre of a multilateral credit and payments system. But the export of capital to the rest of the world was relatively restricted by a ring around the Sterling Area that was, at times, very tight indeed. In 1979, however, all such restrictions were abolished, and foreign investment, now subordinate to the City's new world-wide multilateral role as an offshore centre, grew dramatically as British funds were invested via City institutions throughout the globe.

The Sterling Area is one of those economic phenomena that most people have heard of, although few are quite sure what it is or why it was so important. Its significance lay in the fact that the countries that belonged to it kept their foreign exchange reserves in Britain and were able to obtain long-term investment funds from the City. Since the Overseas Sterling Area (to give those countries the official title with which they came to be endowed) kept reserves in London, they were, effectively, lending to Britain on a short-term basis, but with a degree of permanence. It was like a customer's relation with a bank: the customer's deposit can be withdrawn at short notice, but the bank knows that it can rely on a pool of deposits whose total is fairly stable. In return for this, the members of the Sterling Area had privileged access to the long-term capital exports of the City, and at times this was a valuable privilege indeed. They also kept their currencies tied to sterling, so that the exchange rate between any two of these countries – Australia for example and Britain – remained fixed even when sterling was devalued against the dollar; and when trade throughout the world was subject to restrictions, some Sterling Area countries enjoyed relatively (but by no means completely) free access to each other's markets. Apart from the United Kingdom itself, the members of the Sterling Area included the dominions and colonies (except for Canada, which was integrated into the United States' dollar bloc), and, at first, the Scandinavian countries, Argentina and a few other countries that had developed close links with Britain.

The Sterling Area was not formed like the European Economic Community, by a treaty, or ever formalised around a constitution at a definite point in time. It grew and changed as circumstances altered. A major impetus to its establishment was Britain's abandonment of the gold standard in 1931, which heralded a period of instability in exchange rates. It was this period of uncertainty that led the Sterling Area countries to tie their currencies to sterling at a fixed rate and to place their reserves in London; and it was largely as a consequence that overseas holdings of sterling doubled (from £411 million to £808 million) between the end of 1931 and the end of 1937. In return, Sterling Area countries received favourable treatment when the authorities tried to control the amount of funds that overseas borrowers could raise by issuing bonds in London. Until 1936 the Bank of England exercised discreet control by issuing guidance to the merchant banks who handled such fund-raising; after that date informal control was exercised through the Foreign Transactions Advisory Committee; but throughout, members of the Sterling Area had privileged access.

In some ways this was merely a continuation of the situation that had existed previously; even at the turn of the century the Empire and a few countries within Britain's economic sphere of influence (such as Argentina) had been the major recipients of British foreign investment: the only real change was that now the boundary around them was being defined.

During the Second World War this boundary became a rigorous one, forming the members of the Sterling Area into a single tightly integrated economy. Within it, India effectively loaned Britain enormous sums by selling goods to Britain and receiving payment in sterling which was held as India's reserves in London; and other less developed countries, particularly Egypt and Sudan, did the same. This accumulation of the 'sterling balances' caused nightmares for postwar politicians, trying to manage the economy and ever-fearful that the holders of the balances would withdraw their money and push down the pound's exchange rate. As an incentive to maintain these short-term deposits, throughout the postwar years overseas borrowing in London was restricted by exchange controls designed to conserve Britain's foreign exchange treasure. In consequence, Britain's exports of capital concentrated on the Overseas Sterling Area, reaching more than £300 million in 1965.

Even though the rationale for the existence of a Sterling Area weakened from the mid-1950s onwards, the privileged access of its overseas members to London as a source of long-term capital continued. The Sterling Area was the focus for the City's export of capital, and for its international role as a whole, until well after the rationale for this focus had disappeared. In chapter 1 we pinpointed 1967 as the turning-point at which the City's most prominent international activity shifted from exporting capital to acting as a multilateral offshore centre; it was at that point that the City ceased to regard itself as the centre of the Sterling Area.

The tensions and intense debates that led up to the 1967 devaluation of the pound, which the City strenuously opposed, arose precisely because the City clung to this image of itself as centre of the Sterling Area, after the seeds of a more integrated world financial system (in contrast to one divided into blocs) had begun to germinate throughout the world. The City opposed devaluation largely because it regarded a high and stable value for the pound as essential to its ability to win international business, in particular to compete with New York; and it believed that a strong pound was a necessary condition for success because devaluation would harm the residual holders of the sterling balances (whose reserves, held in sterling, would be reduced in value at one stroke by devaluation), who would then finally break with their tradition of channelling their borrowing, lending and other financial transactions through London.

Devaluation, however, proved to be an experience the City could live with; more than that, it broke the City's fixation with the Sterling Area and its imperial heritage. Not only was the City now able to concentrate upon its multilateral, 'offshore' centre role; but also, the next burst of overseas investment, which started in 1979, was of a different character and was not directed towards the ghost of the Empire.

Opening the foreign investment floodgates

At the end of the 1970s the financial institutions of the City began to lobby quite forcefully for the abolition of the exchange controls that had restricted overseas investment for decades. It was not the lending of foreign currencies borrowed *as foreign currencies* (the 'enclave', 'offshore', or 'Eurodollar' side of the banks' business) that had been restricted – indeed, it was actively encouraged – but the ability of British firms, people or institutions to exchange sterling for dollars or other foreign currencies in order to invest the money abroad. Dollars could be obtained for these purposes, but they were special dollars existing in a pool set aside for overseas investment: if overseas assets were sold, the dollars acquired were added to the pool, and if a firm wished to acquire dollars for overseas investment it had to buy them from this pool and, because of its limited size, pay a premium – the 'dollar premium' – over the normal exchange rate. The lobby for abolition of these exchange controls and dollar pool arrangements was a lobby for freedom to export capital to whichever areas of the world were most profitable, unrestricted by any focus on the old Sterling Area. In 1979 Mrs Thatcher's government responded by abolishing all such exchange controls.

No one could predict how the pension funds, life insurance companies, unit trusts and investment trusts – the institutions that controlled long-term investment funds – would react. They had not previously abstained totally from investing abroad, and some particularly held substantial assets in the USA – the National Coal Board's pension fund, for example, had a stake in the Watergate office block in Washington, which at the start of the 1970s featured in the events that led to Richard Nixon's resignation – but they had been limited by the exchange controls. Would their lifting lead to an immediate outflow of funds, and, if so, would the outflow be a short burst or would it last a long time? Most significantly, if there were a long-lasting outflow of funds, what effect would that have on the availability of finance for the restructuring of British industry?

In the event, the initial response was relatively slow. Pension funds and the other institutions of long-term finance did not immediately catch up with long-missed opportunities to invest abroad. This was partly because the opportunities had not been missed as much as the lobbyists had implied: about 15 per cent of the shares owned by Imperial Chemical Industries' pension fund were foreign before exchange controls were lifted, about 8 per cent in the case of Unilever's pension fund, and 6 per cent in the case of the Prudential Corporation. The slow start was also partly because investing in assets denominated in foreign currencies while having an obligation to pay out pensions and life policies in sterling adds one more element to the risks that always threaten to jeopardise the public's trust in the institutions: in addition to the risk that shares or property in which they invest may drop in value, overseas investment carries the risk that, when the time comes to convert the foreign income they yield into sterling, the foreign currency's exchange rate may have fallen so that each dollar or yen is worth fewer pounds.

Nevertheless, the institutions did take the opportunity to increase their overseas investments. Comparing the half-year shortly before the abolition of controls with that shortly after, whereas pension funds and insurance companies made net new investments of £148 million in overseas equities in the first six months of 1979, they invested over four times as much in this way (£663 million) in the first half of 1980. They also shifted the geographical pattern of their overseas investment, directing the outflow particularly towards the stock markets of Tokyo, Hong Kong, Singapore and Australia. As an illustration of this, one of the banks' packages of overseas investments designed to channel pension funds' money toward Japan (Fleming's Japanese Exempt Fund) increased its business nearly seven-fold, from £11 million to £70 million, between the end of 1979 and the end of 1980, whereas another such fund oriented towards investment in the United States (County American Exempt Fund) only doubled over the same period.

The lifting of exchange controls on overseas investment did lead to a substantial outflow of funds in the first two years, and in some months the purchase of foreign shares by the institutions exceeded their purchases of British shares. Within two years of the abolition of exchange controls, the proportion of pension funds' wealth held overseas (measured at market values) had risen from 6 to 9.5 per cent, while life insurance companies' had risen from 3.1 to 4.9 per cent and investment trusts' from 32 to 41.5 per cent.

These outflows were occurring at the same time as attention was being focused upon the adequacy of the financial institutions as suppliers of finance to British industry, and they seemed to provide a prima facie case for the argument that the City was putting its overseas operations before its financing of the domestic economy; to confirm the critics' view that the City would always channel British funds abroad instead of into employment-generating channels at home if given the opportunity; and to strengthen the opinion that it should not be given the opportunity. The outflow did not necessarily mean this, however; for it could be argued, and it was strongly argued by the City's advocates at the time, that the outflow of capital was a once-and-for-all adjustment towards a sensible balance between overseas and home assets that had previously been thwarted by exchange controls. Subsequent years have showed that argument to be wrong, however. The proportion of their new funds that pension funds and life insurance companies invested abroad remained at historically very high levels at the end of 1982 and showed no sign of dropping. Table 2.2 shows they accounted for 28 and 22 per cent respectively of net investment.

The boom in overseas portfolio investment that followed the removal of exchange controls in 1979 coincided with the worst economic crisis Britons have experienced for half a century. The remarkable purchase of foreign shares has been accompanied by a slump in investment in plant and machinery in Britain to the point where, in 1981, it accounted for only 12.9 per cent of gross domestic product. In this respect the third quarter of the twentieth century begins to appear to have parallels with the end of the nineteenth (especially if we interpret the latter in the generous sense of ending with the outbreak of the First World War). Then, three major booms in portfolio investment abroad occurred, in 1870–73, 1880–90 and 1904–13, and each coincided with a decline in domestic investment in fixed capital. At that time, the inverse relationship led to complaints by industrialists (especially in iron and wool) that foreign investment was a drain on the economy.

Today, similar opinions are voiced and demands are made for controls over foreign investment and for institutions' funds to be directed towards the financing of investment in new plant and new industries in Britain. This time the criticism comes from the labour movement rather than business, and that is partly a reflection of the fact that the power in British industry lies with that sector – the multinational corporations – that itself invests heavily overseas. The boom in portfolio investment overseas at the beginning of the 1980s has to be seen against the background of a steady accumulation of direct investment abroad throughout the postwar period by multinational corporations with headquarters in Britain. Britain is second only to the United States in the number of multinational corporations that are operated from the country, and, as shown in table 2.3, their direct investment abroad has been a continuous feature of the economy. The leaders of British industry, having themselves been investing heavily overseas, were not in a position to argue for controls to prevent an external drain of investment resources.

TABLE 2.2 NET INVESTMENT BY PENSION FUNDS AND INSURANCE COMPANIES, 1976–1982

	1976	1977	1978	1979	1980	1981	1982
Pension funds (£ million)							
UK public sector securities	1272.8	1115.3	1276.7	2284.6	2070.8	1868.7	1297.1
UK company securities	1022.5	1234.7	996.8	1511.2	2204.2	1906.7	1993.2
Overseas company securities	96.3	180.5	319.7	452.8	1423.9	1565.4	1734.7
Other UK investments*	611.1	677.4	1092.8	1280.4	847.5	1406.1	1540.3
Other overseas investment	−31.3	−29.3	32.1	28.5	71.0	78.2	186.4
Total pension funds	2971.4	3178.6	3718.1	5557.5	6617.4	6825.1	6751.7
Overseas investments as % of total	2.2	4.8	9.5	8.7	22.6	24.1	28.5
Insurance companies (£ million)							
UK public sector securities	1864.3	2384.6	2688.4	3037.5	2732.5	2935.8	1957.9
UK company securities	316.0†	639.8†	811.2†	829.1	910.3	1363.6	1896.3
Overseas company securities				195.6	617.2	806.0	982.0
Other UK investments*	798.1	803.6	1182.5	1498.1	1496.1	2269.5	1321.3††
Other overseas investments	50.4	78.1	173.8	148.1	142.3	114.4	478.4
Total insurance companies	3028.8	3906.1	4855.9	5708.4	5898.4	7489.3	6635.9††
Overseas investments as % of total	n.a.	n.a.	n.a.	6.0	12.9	12.3	22.0

* Other UK investments include overseas property investment which cannot be separately identified. This implies that the overseas investments percentages are *underestimates*.

† For these years insurance companies' overseas company securities cannot be identified.

†† Figures for agents' balances not available.

Source: *Business Monitor MQ 5.* (London: HMSO).

TABLE 2.3 UK PRIVATE DIRECT INVESTMENT OVERSEAS, 1971–1981 (£ million)

	1971	1972	1973	1974	1975	1976	1977	1978	1979	1980	1981
Unremitted profits of subsidiaries	−329*	−465	−840	−851	−879	−1454	−1292	−1259	−1636	−1646	−2184
Net purchases of shares and bonds	−229	−197	−563	−380	−309	−485	−473	−993	−1303	−1719	−2296
Other transactions	−118	−75	−278	−344	+9	−206	−126	−488	+151	−126	−683
Total	−676	−732	−1627	−1575	−1171	−2145	−1885	−2740	−2788	−3491	−5157

* A negative sign implies a net outflow of investment.
Source: United Kingdom Balance of Payments (London: HMSO).

An overseas drain on investment?

Whether the labour movement or business puts forward the argument that overseas investment is at the expense of domestic investment, and whoever promotes the policy that foreign investment should be curtailed in order to stimulate the regeneration of British industry, the validity of these views is not a foregone conclusion. Does a rise in foreign investment cause a reduction in investment in Britain? This is not an easy question, and cannot be answered quickly by reference to the data, but on the whole it seems that such a relation has not existed under the present financial and industrial system. If we are to assess the question carefully, the first thing to note is its asymmetry, for although it uses the word 'investment' for both foreign and domestic activities, the first concerns the transfer of money abroad and has no necessary element of purchasing plant and machinery (since the whole of overseas portfolio investment and much direct investment involves purchasing shares and bonds), whereas 'investment in Britain' means the purchase of real assets in the form of buildings, plant and machinery. Thus, if foreign investment has inhibited domestic investment two things must have occurred: first, the use of the money abroad must have restricted the supply of funds that was available for the finance of investment in new plant, etc., in Britain; second, it must have been the case that, if those funds had been available to domestic industry, industry would have taken them up and used them to finance new investment. There is some doubt about both of those elements, although the reasons are not quite the same for direct investment overseas as for portfolio investment.

For multinational corporations' *direct* investment the two elements merge into one: if they had not financed investment in plants abroad, perhaps because they were not allowed to obtain foreign exchange, would they have invested in plants in Britain? For the typical multinational the question is purely academic, since exchange controls would not have been able to prevent the movement of investment funds. A large proportion of their profits financing their foreign investment are generated abroad and no exchange controls could have forced them to bring the funds back into Britain to finance investment here – and in any case, the multinationals' ability to switch funds from one country to another through accounting devices such as transfer-pricing means that even profits that are not generated abroad can make their first appearance there. If, despite the difficulties a greater proportion of multinationals' funds were forced to remain in Britain, there is no reason to think that they would be used to finance their own investment in productive facilities in this country. Multinationals' investment decisions are made on the basis of long-term plans concerning the world-wide pattern of their operations; this phenomenon of 'world-wide sourcing' became well established in the 1970s and has been described as:

- establishing subsidiaries abroad with the explicit purpose of supplying the markets of the host country to only a limited extent, if
  at all, but exporting mainly or exclusively to third countries *and* to
  the country which the parent companies used to call their home;
- organizing veritable business empires with complex logistical
  networks among their affiliates;
- implementing in a world-wide context a centrally planned business strategy based on a 'global outlook' and availing themselves
  of their 'global scanning capacity'. [Adam, 1975, p. 90]

Thus, multinationals' decisions on whether to increase their production facilities in Britain depend on their world-wide strategy, and the extent to which they are constrained to keep funds in Britain is only a minor element in their global assessment. It is more likely that restrictions on the disposition abroad of any profits generated in Britain would have affected their global strategy more by discouraging investment here than by encouraging it. That is not to say that nothing should be done to direct multinationals' investment toward Britain: it implies only that a very radical system of control of their activities would be needed, and that success could not be expected from exchange controls alone being imposed.

What of *portfolio* investment abroad? If pension funds, for example, were restricted in their ability to buy yen or dollars to invest on foreign stock exchanges, would the money have generated new productive capacity in Britain? The money would not necessarily have gone directly into industrial projects, for pension funds have not operated in that manner. The domestic assets into which they have put their money have been government bonds, real estate and company shares. And the latter have been predominantly existing shares rather than new shares issued by firms to finance expansion; in the 1970s new issues accounted for only a small proportion of external funds to industry, but this was not because the pension funds were investing abroad on a large scale.

Again, then, it seems that exchange controls restricting the export of capital would not have significantly affected industrial investment in Britain. But this, too, is based on the assumption that pension funds operate in the same manner as in the past; more radical measures to change pension funds' *modus operandi* could succeed in directing into industrial expansion money that is prevented from going abroad.

We have been asking the counter-factual question, 'what would have happened in the past if exchange controls had prevented the export of capital?' and on that basis concluded there is no reason to think that the export of capital has restricted industrial expansion at home, although more radical policies in the future could ensure that 'domesticated' funds are used fruitfully. The same conclusion is reached if we approach the problem from another angle and ask ourselves how the export of capital that Britain has experienced in recent years fits into the logic of the international economic system. Looked at from the perspective of the world as a whole, the portfolio investments and direct investment abroad that have emanated from Britain cannot be categorized as 'export of capital', for the phrase implies a one-way process. In fact, the flows of finance out of Britain have been just one element in a mass of complex transfers of capital between the world's economies. As British capital has been invested in the United States, so American portfolio and direct investments have flowed into the United Kingdom; more generally the postwar has been characterised by the development to unprecedented levels of mutual investments between the advanced capitalist countries. It is not a question of a drain of capital, but of the building of interconnections between the economies, the internationalisation of economic activity in which the world-wide sourcing of the multinational corporations is an important element. The capital employed in economic activity, whether it takes the form of financial wealth or factories as going concerns, is internationalised; in consequence, the loans that finance any country's industry come from many countries (or the stateless international pool), and the work that produces a 'British' car, say, is carried out by a multitude of factories across the globe completing parts of the process within the one multinational corporation. In quantitative terms, the symptom of this interrelationship is that net inflows of investment to the United Kingdom counterbalanced the outflows over the period 1971–77, but since

1978 net outflows have predominanted. The 'export of capital' is
not simply offset by these 'imports of capital': each is one side of the
same coin, and when the balance is calculated the net outflow of
funds is smaller than would be implied by the cry 'the export of
capital has starved British industry of funds', even if net outflows
accelerated in 1981. These quantities are summarised in table 2.4.

The fact that investment abroad has as its inextricable counterpart
foreign investment in the UK weighs against one of the standard
arguments for controlling the export of capital, the claim that it has
simply drained funds from investment in Britain. It fits in with the
other reasons for doubting that the export of capital through the
City has generated a financial scarcity that underlies Britain's long
de-industrialisation. But what conclusions can be drawn from this?
What are the implications for policy?

It does not mean that controls over the export of capital are
undesirable – quite the contrary. What it does mean is that they
have to be seen as part of a wider policy to change the nature of the
City and the working of economic policy. The export of capital has
not been an isolated phenomenon, a simple cause producing a
shortage of funds and industrial decline, so its prevention alone
 cannot be expected to act as a panacea. Exchange controls can
have an impact, but only in the context of a strategy that orients the
banks and investment institutions towards providing the finance for
a major re-investment programme in British industry and alters the
circumstances and perspectives of industrial management itself.

In addition to the allegation that the export of capital starves
British industry of finance, another argument is brought in support
of exchange controls, and it is this argument that is most likely to
carry weight when a government next re-imposes controls. This is
 the view that stemming the outflow will be necessary in order to
protect the balance of payments or prevent a decline in the
exchange rate. Since exchange rate crises have been at the centre of
the City's power over government policy throughout this century,
that argument for controlling the outflow does have great attractions, particularly for socialists who wish to curb the City's
undemocratic power. It does have an undesirable side to it, for
closing the gates to protect Britain's treasure has a rather miserly,
autarkic and inward-looking characteristic; but that is not the only
way to look at it.

Socialists see controls over the export of capital as a means of
regulating and controlling the flow of capital instead of shutting the
door absolutely tight against it. Since in the present pattern flows of

TABLE 2.4 NET OVERSEAS INVESTMENT, 1971–1981 (£ million)

	1971	1972	1973	1974	1975	1976	1977	1978	1979	1980	1981
Overseas investment in UK	1015	772	1497	2204	1514	2091	4399	1908	4361	5243	3356
UK investment overseas	−860	−1402	−1760	−1948	−1367	−2269	−2334	−4634	−6555	−8204	−10,637
Balance*	155	−630	−263	1056	147	−178	2065	−2726	−2194	−2961	−7281

* A negative sign implies a net outflow of investment.
Source: United Kingdom Balance of Payments (London: HMSO).

capital in all directions are associated with the reorganisation of the world's economy, a changing division of labour between different economies, and a change in the nature of each economy, socialists see controls over capital flows as a way of intervening in that process. Again, for them it comes down to a question of democracy and power. Control over capital flows, exercised through a democratic government, is an attempt to influence the shape of the world economy or, at least, to influence Britain's position in it. And democratic control is contrasted with the blind and unaccountable forces of competition and the market that direct capital movements at present.

3

London, the Offshore Banker

For centuries, London has been an international market-place for trade in commodities and finance that is not directly connected with British industry. The London Metal Exchange is a world centre for trade in metals between foreign buyers and foreign sellers as well as British ones; the Baltic Exchange trades shipping charters world-wide; similarly, London is the centre in which foreign purchases and sales of commodities as diverse as gold and cocoa are brought together. To a dealer or broker, money is a commodity little different from coffee beans, copper or peanuts in its ability to turn a quick profit for the sharp-witted; so London also became the world centre for buying and selling currencies. When pounds are sold for dollars in London's foreign exchange markets, the transaction may stem from a British industry buying the dollars it needs to pay for imports from America, but the purchase and sale orders are just as likely to result from firms, banks or individuals anywhere in the world placing an order in London.

These transactions mark the City as an international trading centre which is geographically in the United Kingdom but economically may just as well be in international waters or in orbit. Indeed, one reason that London has retained its dominance as the centre for foreign exchange markets, despite the strong challenge from New York at the end of the 1970s, has been that, like a satellite with a well-chosen orbit, its dealers and brokers are, within the space of a working day, able to communicate with Hong Kong and Japanese markets before they close (London's morning), New York when it opens (London's afternoon) and Zurich, Paris and Frankfurt all day. Its strength has little to do with British industry's foreign exchange business resulting from its imports and exports of goods and capital.

Buying and selling commodities and money (foreign exchange)

is one thing; lending money is rather different, and it is borrowing
and lending – credit – that are at the heart of the City's economy.
The truly remarkable phenomenon of the 1960s and 1970s, however, has been the City's rapid expansion of types of borrowing and
lending that, like its trading functions, are international or even
stateless, in the sense of having no essential connection with British
industry. In this case the orbiting satellite's business is borrowing
and lending *Eurodollars*, a form of money comprising dollars held
outside the USA that came into the world in 1958. Eurodollars are
a special type of bank deposit and are as much money as is a
cheque account with a High Street bank. Like ordinary bank
deposits, Eurodollars are a type of money that has never been
consciously created or validated by any government; it grew, at first
without the conscious design of any party, from the interactions of
governments, banks and multinational corporations going about
their business. Nevertheless, governments throughout the world
are enmeshed with banks and financial institutions seeking to
borrow Eurodollars from them (if they are Eurodollar-rich, as the
Arab oil producers have been) or to lend to them (if they are the
Mexicos, Brazils or Argentinas of the 1970s). London is not the
only city in which the vast Eurodollar credits are arranged, but it is
the main one. The City set out to become the leading centre for
Eurodollar credits; and with the help of British governments' non-
intervention in its business and other governments' regulation of
their banks, it succeeded.

Why is Eurodollar lending and borrowing so peculiarly international, so completely dissociated from the British economy in the
midst of which it is located? Eurodollars are a form of money that
arose from attempts to escape the US government's regulation of
its banks. That flight from regulation was the initial impetus; it gave
Eurodollars their essential character, so that, despite many ingeni-
ous innovations in the techniques of borrowing and lending this
form of money, non-regulation of the banks involved in it has
remained the *sine qua non* of its continued existence. Thus, the
essence of this money is its international freedom, so that a bank
handling it can do so only if it is part of an international rather than
a national system. Ideally, the bank should be orbiting or moored
in international waters; but since working in such conditions would
hardly suit the lifestyle of bankers, the next best thing is to locate it
on a piece of land with a congenial environment and a territorial
government that leaves it relatively free so as to approximate, as
nearly as possible, the bank moored in international waters. The

UK authorities, adopting the perspective of the Bank of England, have done just that, and the City has flourished, nurtured by and nurturing its Eurodollar business.

The importance of non-regulation to the growth of the Eurodollar business cannot be doubted; when President Reagan was persuaded by New York interests that that centre should compete with London in attempting to capture Eurodollar business, the method chosen was to permit, from December 1981, a special enclave of de-regulated banking business – International Banking Facilities – on the US mainland. The only cloud over its prospects when it was established was whether it was unregulated enough to compete with London. In fact, the traditional distrust of bankers in American society meant that the IBFs could not be as free as banks in London and it initially failed to compete successfully but by 1982 285 foreign banks were represented there.

To say that Eurodollars are a form of money that is by nature unregulated gives their essence, but what are they exactly? And how did Eurodollar banking, and the City's involvement in it develop up to 1982? Those are the questions to which we turn now. The purpose is not to establish the facts for their own sake – they are well known – but to provide the basis for evaluating the effects of these credit operations upon everyday life. We, in common with a growing school, judge that these effects include two that should be a major cause for concern.

(a) the Eurodollar credit system greatly reduces the power of democratically elected governments;
(b) it multiplies the risk of a banking crash, which would bring down industry with it.

By the end of this chapter we shall have set out the reasoning behind these conclusions.[1]

The growth of Eurodollars

Eurodollars are, first, a form of money – a particular type of bank deposit – and, second, an entity that is borrowed and lent and is

1 Although we refer to Eurodollars, deposits and loans of Deutschmarks, Sterling, French Francs and other currencies outside their home country have also acquired the Euro prefix and some of the same characteristics. Eurodollars are by far the most important of these Eurocurrencies and our discussion focuses on them as the exemplar.

characterised by particular types of loans. These two aspects are
inextricably linked, just as in ordinary banking deposits (which are
a form of money) are what a bank borrows from the account-holder
and then lends onwards.

If you ask a banker what Eurodollars' special character is as
money, what distinguishes a Eurodollar bank deposit from a non-
prefixed dollar deposit in a US bank, the answer will be that, unlike
the latter, it is a deposit of US dollars held in a bank located outside
the United States. That is an accurate definition as far as it goes, but
from our point of view its emphasis on geographical location is just
an expression of the Eurodollar accounts' freedom from the control of the American state (and others). Both ways of looking at it
are illustrated by the origins of the system.

In the 1950s US dollars were in great demand by European
governments and firms desperate for a secure way to hold their
reserves ('as good as gold') and for the means with which to buy
imports of American and other goods. From 1958 the position
changed; the scarcity of dollars was eased as the United States
began to run a balance of payments deficit, paying out more than it
was receiving and doing so in dollars. The dollars that came into
European hands both before and after the turnround could have
been deposited by their European holders in bank accounts in New
York. That would, in a sense, have been the 'normal' thing to do in
the new era of the dollar's supremacy in international affairs: after
all, in the earlier age of sterling's supremacy, foreign owners of
pounds held them as bank accounts in London. But now the dollar
owners used them to open accounts – dollar accounts – in banks in
Europe and other centres 'offshore' from the United States, and
the new form of money was thereby created. Why did they deposit
their dollars in Europe rather than New York? Because European
banks were not under the jurisdiction of the US government and
monetary authorities; specifically, they were free from US political
jurisdiction and from US control over interest rates.

Freedom of European banks from US political jurisdiction was
especially important to the countries of the Soviet bloc, whose
deposits, it is believed, initiated Eurodollar banking. Wishing
to ensure that their precious holdings of dollars could not be
impounded by a US government instruction to American banks as
a move towards check-mate in the cold war, they deposited them in
accounts in the more independent European centres. Looking
back during the years of *détente*, their caution may have appeared
to be excessive and based on an overestimation of America's

willingness to use economic weapons; but 1979 demonstrated that bank accounts and other investments in the United States could, indeed, be counted as fair game in a diplomatic conflict. In that year, President Carter's administration used its Emergency Economic Powers Act to impound, among other assets, the dollar deposits of Iran in US banks in its conflict with Ayatollah Khomeini's regime. Whether wise or not, the Soviet bloc governments' early attempt to keep their dollars from American jurisdiction and find them a European home was an important beginning.

Even more important in sustaining the growth of Eurodollar deposits was the desire of dollar-holders to earn the maximum interest on them by placing them in banks that were free from US controls over the rate of interest payable on deposits. The Federal Reserve restricted in two ways the rate of interest that banks in New York and other American cities could pay to depositors: first, its Regulation Q directly set the maximum payable interest rate; second, by requiring banks to hold a proportion of their assets in the form of reserves on which they could not earn interest, their ability to pay interest on the money they received – deposits – was diminished. The European banks attracted dollar deposits by, quite simply, being able to pay more for them.

From the earliest days, London's banks were a major attraction as a home for Eurodollar deposits. Their business continued to expand with the growth in this form of money. Table 3.1 shows the main phases in its broad growth; it refers to total gross Eurodollar deposits in banks within the Bank for International Settlements reporting area. Two things stand out: the exceptional rate of growth of these deposits from 1970, and their acceleration following the rise in the price of the Organisation of Petroleum Exporting Countries (OPEC) oil in 1973. That event was the most significant in shaping the Eurodollar system that the Western world inherited as it entered its major economic crisis in 1980, and it is worth examining it in some detail.

The rise in the price charged for their oil caused some oil exporting countries (OECs),[2] outstandingly Saudi Arabia (but also Kuwait, United Arab Emirates and Qatar), to acquire huge flows of dollars from their sales; their income was much greater than the sums they spent on imports of equipment to develop their countries or luxury items desired by their elites. In consequence, those oil

---

2 The oil exporting countries (OEC) as here defined comprise the 13 members of OPEC together with Trinidad and Tobago, Bahrain, Brunei and Oman.

TABLE 3.1 EUROCURRENCY MARKET SIZE, 1970–1980 ($ billion)

	1970	1971	1972	1973	1974	1975	1976	1977	1978	1979	1980	1981	1982
Gross size	110	145	200	315	395	485	595	740	950	1235	1525	1860	2015
Net size	60	85	110	160	220	255	320	390	495	590	730	890	940
Eurodollars as % of all Eurocurrencies	81	76	78	74	76	78	80	76	74	72	75	78	81

Source: *World Financial Markets* (New York: Morgan Guaranty).

exporters built up financial wealth that could be invested overseas; indeed, it had to be, for it was only Europe, America and Japan that had financial institutions and markets able to provide bonds, bank accounts and other interest-yielding homes for large funds. In the event, the great bulk of these funds went to Europe, especially London, and of greatest significance for our story is the fact that a surprising proportion of these funds went into bank deposits (rather than bonds, shares or property) in Europe: as dollars deposited in banks outside the United States, this represented a vast accumulation of Eurodollars. It was surprising, and is still not satisfactorily explained, because if the oil-rich had invested a larger proportion in government bonds and corporate bonds and shares in the industrialised countries, they would, at the cost of some liquidity and flexibility, have earned greater profits; instead, by lending to (depositing with) the Eurocurrency banks, they enabled them to lend to governments and corporations and build their own profits. Whatever the rationale, the OEC petro-dollars swelled the coffers of the Eurodollar banks. Figure 3.1 shows the total amounts of new funds the OEC countries had available to invest in international financial markets between 1973 and 1982. It shows the sharp rise that occurred after both price rises and the equally sharp drop that occurred as the oil-producers' surpluses declined toward the end of the period.

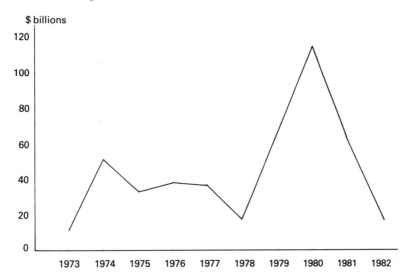

Figure 3.1   Oil-exporting countries' total net cash surplus, 1973–1982
Source: Bank of England data.

Table 3.2 is more interesting. It shows the channels in which these funds were invested and highlights the fact that, in 1974, 1979 and 1980 (the years following and associated with the two OPEC price rises), the oil producers invested as much as 54, 74 and 48 per cent respectively of their new-found dollar wealth in bank deposits instead of higher-yielding bonds or other assets. And, most significant from the point of view of our subject, out of these bank deposits, most could be identified as Eurocurrency deposits, of which as much as 100 per cent was deposited in banks in London in 1981 and around 45 per cent over the period as a whole.

Syndicated credits and Eurobonds

At the beginning of this section, however, we said that Eurodollars are not only a form of money, but also a special type of bank deposit; more important is the fact that they are borrowed and loaned under credit arrangements that have been devised for them and are quite different from, say, the typical loan that a British bank makes in sterling to a British firm. Therefore, to gain a full understanding of the City of London's new international role we have to examine the character and development of these credits.

Eurodollars are loaned to governments, government-backed corporations and multinational corporations, and two distinct categories are used: syndicated medium-term credits, and Eurobonds. For years, each Monday's *Financial Times* contained a half-page or so summarising developments in the Euromarkets, one half of which examined the credits and the other half the bonds, and although there are intermediate types of lending to such borrowers those categories are basic. (In addition, short-term, for example overnight, loans, called inter-bank loans, of Euro-currencies are made from one bank to another and are also made by multinational corporations.) *Syndicated dollar credits* are loans of dollars from banks located outside the United States and, since 1981, from the IBFs.They are medium-term in the sense that the governmental or corporate borrower contracts to repay them during a fixed period, which may be anything from three to ten years, and they are syndicated in the sense that a group of banks club together a loan larger than any one individual bank could handle. If a bank wants to get its money back before the date specified in the contract it cannot, and in that respect a syndicated credit (or any fixed-term bank loan) is quite different from a

TABLE 3.2 DEPLOYMENT OF OIL EXPORTERS' CASH SURPLUSES, 1974–1982 (£ billion)

	1974	1975	1976	1977	1978	1979	1980	1981	1982
United Kingdom									
Sterling bank deposits	1.7	0.2	-1.4	0.3	0.2	1.4	1.4	0.4	1.3
Eurocurrency bank deposits	13.8	4.1	5.6	3.1	-2.0	14.8	14.8	7.8	-9.4
Treasury bills	2.7	-0.9	-1.2	-0.2	0.2	—	-0.1	—	-0.1
Portfolio investment	0.5	0.3	0.4	0.4	0.1	0.4	—	—	—
Other	2.3	0.6	1.1	0.2	-0.3	0.6	1.5	1.1	-1.0
Total UK	21.0	4.3	4.5	3.8	-1.8	17.2	17.6	9.3	-9.2
United States									
Bank deposits (mainly $)	4.1	0.6	1.7	0.4	0.8	4.9	-1.1	-2.0	4.4
Treasury bills	5.3	0.5	-1.0	-0.9	-1.0	3.3	1.4	-0.5	0.4
Portfolio investment	1.3	3.2	3.0	3.1	1.6	1.0	4.7	4.6	-0.4
Other	1.0	5.3	8.4	6.5	-0.2	-0.3	9.1	14.2	8.6
Total USA	11.7	9.6	12.1	9.1	1.3	8.9	14.1	16.3	13.0
Bank deposits* in other countries	9.0	5.0	6.5	7.5	5.0	18.7	26.2	-5.1	-12.8
Other transactions	11.5	16.3	12.7	13.1	8.9	9.0	28.6	29.0	12.7
Total† deployed cash surplus	53.2	35.2	35.8	33.5	13.4	53.8	86.5	49.5	3.5

* These bank deposits are largely Eurocurrency deposits.
† This total represents the total *identified* deployment of cash surpluses, and differs from the total surpluses shown in figure 3.1 by a residual of unidentified items.
Source: Bank of England.

Eurobond. A *Eurobond* is an IOU raised by the borrowing state or corporation in order to raise Eurodollars from institutions such as banks, pension funds and insurance companies that buy them; like any bond or share, those investors are able to resell the IOU to others if they wish to recoup their cash or switch investments before the IOU matures. An additional difference between bonds and credits is that the former's maturity – the number of years before the borrower has to repay the IOU – is not restricted to the medium term.

Both syndicated credits and Eurobonds have grown as the lending side of Eurodollar banking has expanded concomitantly with the deposit side; but they have grown at uneven rates, and the fluctuations in each type of lending have not been synchronous. The most notable phenomenon is that lending by banks through syndicated credits has accounted for a far higher amount of Eurodollar lending than have the bonds – approximately three times as much. Syndicated credits were the distinguishing feature of Eurodollar lending in the 1970s (although they have not always been and will not necessarily be so in the future, for in 1982 and early 1983 the relative importance of Eurobonds increased when bankers found some of their favourite syndicated credits turning into bad debts). We shall discuss these credits again, for they significantly changed the face of banking in London.

Equally as significant a characteristic of Eurodollar lending as syndication is the destination of the loans and the relations between the lending banks and the borrowers. As table 3.3 indicates, 51.5 and 45 per cent of new Eurodollar credits between 1970 and 1982 comprised loans to industrialised and developing countries respectively, principally to their governments ('sovereign loans') or to enterprises where borrowing was covered by government guarantees. The remaining 4.5 per cent was loaned to communist-ruled states.

Borrowing dollars in large amounts from the banking system changed the face of politics and development plans in these Third World and communist countries: it underpinned the industrialisation and the growth in the purchase of consumer goods in oil- and gas-rich Indonesia, Algeria and Mexico and in countries such as Brazil, Argentina and South Korea; and it financed the cash for modernisation in Poland under Mr Gierek while proving to be a major influence on the political struggles that occurred in 1981 when the plan collapsed. In part, the impact of Eurodollar syndicated credits upon these countries arose from the relationship

TABLE 3.3 PUBLICLY ANNOUNCED EUROCURRENCY BANK CREDITS, 1970–1982 ($ billion)

	1970	1971	1972	1973	1974	1975	1976	1977	1978	1979	1980	1981	1982
Industrialised countries	4.2	2.6	4.1	13.8	20.7	7.2	11.3	17.2	29.0	27.2	39.1	86.0	42.7
Developing countries	0.5	1.3	2.4	7.3	13.2	11.1	15.0	21.0	37.3	48.0	35.1	45.3	41.4
Communist countries	0	0.1	0.3	0.8	1.2	2.6	2.5	3.4	3.8	7.3	2.8	1.8	0.8
Total*	4.7	4.0	6.8	21.9	29.3	21.0	28.9	41.8	70.2	82.8	77.4	133.4	85.1

* The totals differ from the sum of the three types of sovereign loans by a small residual equal to lending to international organisations.
Source: World Financial Markets (New York: Morgan Guaranty).

they implied between the bankers and the borrower. The banks held definite views on which countries were suitable borrowers, the degrees of risk involved in each and the rate to be charged; but, once having decided to lend to a country, they themselves imposed no conditions on how the economy should be run or which countries they should trade with (although in the weak cases they would lend only if conditions had been imposed on the country by the International Monetary Fund). In this, the banks differed from other lenders – the IMF, the World Bank and individual governments in bilateral agreements – and even from domestic banks which, lending to industrial firms, may monitor their customers' operations. Eurodollar *credits'* unconditional nature *vis-à-vis* national economies, the freedom they appeared to offer sovereign borrowers, was the other face of the characteristic freedom of Eurodollars as *money*.

The City of London's role as the centre of the growing Eurodollar business in the 1960s and, especially, in the 1970s was signalled, with a clarity that leaves no room for doubt, by the manner in which the interest rate on syndicated loans is calculated. Banks in the syndicate charge the borrower, in addition to fees for arranging the loan, an interest rate calculated as 'LIBOR plus the spread'. The jargon is meaningless to an outsider but is easily explained. 'LIBOR' represents (but does not always equal) the interest that the banks have to pay on the deposits they have received; the 'spread' is the margin of interest they add to it in charging the borrower; from the latter, plus the fees, the banks derive their profits. Now, LIBOR is the rate banks have to pay when they borrow (for short periods of three or six months) deposits from other banks; its name is an acronym of 'London Inter-Bank Offer Rate', because, wherever the Eurodollar business is transacted, London so dominates the field that the cost of funds to the bank is calculated as the price that obtains on the loans from one bank to another in London. (It is significant that, as New York attempted to challenge London's pre-eminence in 1981, the same Eurodollar loans were experimentally based on New York banks' rate ('prime rate') instead of LIBOR; the experiment was adopted because it appeared to offer some profit advantages, but the failure of New York to supplant LIBOR is a symbol of the continued dominance of London.)

Before leaving the subject of LIBOR, it should be noted that its existence stems from loans of Eurodollars from one bank to another (inter-bank loans and deposits), and that form of lending as distinct from loans to governmental and corporate borrowers is a major element in the lending and borrowing of Eurodollars. The total amount of Eurodollar deposits in advanced countries and offshore centres is estimated to be $2015 billion in September 1982, but if we deduct the deposits that one bank has made in (in other words, the Eurodollars that one bank has loaned to) another, we would have to subtract $1057 billion or 53 per cent of the gross total (*World Financial Markets*, February 1983). This fact is significant for understanding both the robustness and the risky fragility of the Eurodollar system and, with it, of the City's most dynamic banks; an issue that we consider later in this chapter.

The dominance of Eurodollar business by the City of London, signified by the importance of LIBOR, is matched by the dominance of the City's international business by Eurodollar operations. But one thing should be clear: leadership by the City of London is not the same as leadership by *British* financial operators. ||| N.B. The City's banking business is conducted by branches and subsidiaries of foreign-owned banks as well as by the British banks. The foreign banks moved in to participate in London's Eurodollar business and give its expansion a further upward twist. The presence of their office name plates lining the City's twisting lanes gives tangible expression to the Square Mile's internationalism, the difference between its Eurodollar business and the British economy consisting of factories, offices and shops.

However, to say that the City's Eurodollar business is not based on or essentially derived from the British economy's production and trade is not to say that it has no connection with or effects on them. It is time to qualify the picture we have painted of an international enclave, a plantation whose crop is Eurodollars, cut off from the humdrum rhythm of life in industry.

The connection arises partly from the fact that the export and import of capital now takes place largely through using Eurodollars and other Eurocurrencies. When multinational corporations borrow to finance their British factories or overseas operations or to transfer money abroad, they do it with Eurodollars. This highly sophisticated, very flexible, system of money and credit has become, therefore, the channel through which flows of capital into and out of British production occurs and, by its nature, has greatly facilitated such flows.

A second way in which the 'real' economy in Britain is connected to the Eurodollar markets is through the purely financial operations of borrowing, lending and dealing in currencies to profit from interest rate and exchange rate differences. Although the essence of the City's Eurodollar business is that it borrows foreign currency deposits and lends them on, the flexibility that is at its heart means that those deposits are rapidly convertible into and out of other currencies, one of which is sterling itself. Firms, banks and plain operators may well borrow sterling, use it to buy Eurodollar deposits, and eventually switch back if they expect the exchange rate and the interest rates on sterling and Eurodollars to move in a way that will produce a profit. Or they may do the opposite. Indeed, similar deals are the bread and butter of the Eurodollar business, the mark of the system's universal character, unconstrained by boundaries between national currencies. They have an effect on the British economy because they influence the gyrations of the pound, causing the exchange rate to move quickly in response to conditions in the Eurodollar markets, regardless of what is happening to Britain's balance of payments. But, even though such movements of the exchange rate are not determined by the 'real' economy's trade and investment flows, the cost of imports and exports is affected by them.

Just as the international 'enclave' nature of the Eurodollar business does not mean that it has no connections with the British economy, so too it does not prevent it from having real effects upon Britain. Two are particularly significant: first, the actual constraints that the system imposes on governments' freedom of action and, second, the potential threat of a financial crash to which it has contributed.

A threat to democracy?

Does the existence of Eurodollars, and, particularly, the role of the City as their centre, undermine the power of British governments? Does it mean that the Eurodollar business creates economic conditions that constrain the ability of British governments to choose freely an appropriate policy for the economy? It is an important question for democracy. In 1945 a socialist government with a radical programme of nationalisation and construction of the welfare state was elected with an overwhelming majority. A very important part of its policy was to keep interest rates unusually low (around 2 per cent) and, above all, to keep down the interest the government had to pay on the bonds issued to finance its reconstruction programme. That interest rate policy was pursued by the government as a reflection of the British people's choice of a socialist path for reconstruction.

Would it be possible now? If a socialist government (or a non-socialist one, for that matter) chose to adopt a policy of low interest rates in order to stimulate economic growth and employment or reduce the cost of financing public expenditure, could it do so without changing the City's international role? To put it another way, would the continued existence of the world's Eurodollar system prevent a British government from implementing its independent interest rate policy? The answer to those three versions of the question is no, no, and yes, respectively.

Those can't be conclusive answers, but there is considerable evidence to support them. The underlying reasoning connects London's interest rates, the sterling exchange rate and the huge volume of internationally mobile funds that exist in the Eurodollar banking system, as follows. If interest rates on sterling bank deposits in England, or on sterling assets such as short-term British government IOUs (Treasury bills), were pushed below the interest rates obtainable in New York or on Eurodollar deposits outside America, the latter would be moved from sterling bank deposits into dollar deposits to gain the higher yield, or from British bills to American, and the result would be two-fold. The reduction in demand for (withdrawal or funds from) the sterling deposits and bills would push their interest rate upward, away from the low level at which the government was aiming. And the switch of funds away from sterling would involve selling increased amounts of sterling for dollars and thereby lowering its price, the exchange rate. Could the government hold out against these pressures and keep interest rates low? The answer is that it could do so only if it was willing to relinquish control over the exchange rate; if it was willing to allow the low interest rates, in driving funds abroad, to push the exchange rate down.

A socialist government could not permit the exchange rate to be determined in this way by speculators' movements of funds, for it is a key price affecting the cost of imported food, consumer goods and raw materials and also the competitiveness of exports; but if it tried to have both low interest rates by international standards and control over the exchange rate it would fail. To keep control over the exchange rate the government would have to buy pounds for dollars (or other currencies) as fast as they are being sold in the rush to invest in Eurodollars. If there are vast footloose sums moving, the government has to have equally vast amounts of dollars and foreign exchange to offset them. The volume of such restless funds invested in sterling is not known, but the existence of the Euro-dollar banking system means that international finance is founded upon a very large pool of bank deposits whose very nature is defined by their mobility and freedom from regulation, and these funds, when deposited in sterling, move out of it as freely as when they went into it. As a result, it is now generally recognised that the government of a country like the UK cannot control the exchange rate through such methods while simultaneously maintaining interest rates below international levels, because the funds at its disposal in its reserves are not large enough to counterbalance the markets' funds.

It is the *existence* of the Eurocurrency system, rather than the fact that it is centred on London, that gives it this influence over British governments' sovereignty, but the fact that it is London-based imposes further constraints. If a British socialist government did attempt to control the exchange rate it could not do it solely through buying pounds and selling dollars when speculators are doing the opposite; it would also have to control movements of money and money capital into and out of Britain's economy. That would require the imposition of direct controls over foreign exchange movements and over the banks that are active in them. The reason why, in a much less developed financial system, the 1945–51 Labour government was able to keep interest rates low was that there were direct restrictions on foreign exchange and the banking system, restrictions that made sterling non-convertible into foreign currency except with permission from the authorities. The existence of the Eurobanks in London makes the imposition of such controls more difficult; for, even though the controls need not restrict their activity in borrowing and lending dollars or other foreign currencies as such, their activities in switching funds between currencies (into and out of sterling) would be curtailed, and hence the non-regulation on which their presence is based would be problematic. In other words, a socialist government could impose the restrictions its sovereignty implies, but at the cost of weakening the City's Eurodollar role.

Thus, the existence of the Eurobanks in London restricts governments' freedom of action in the most fundamental sense, in that they are entities whose very existence precludes government intervention in their affairs. Apart from the question of control over their foreign exchange activities, governments cannot tax their profits, impose reserve requirements upon them or issue directives concerning their lending activities without eroding the basis of their existence in London.

The ability of governments to regulate and tax any part of the capitalist economy is always circumscribed; within that system a firm engaged in production cannot be taxed and regulated to the point where its motive force – profit – is jeopardised if the system is to be maintained; but the position of the Eurobanks is especially privileged in that respect, and arises because of their very mobility, their international flexibility and relative lack of connection with the British social and economic structure. Their business could be transferred elsewhere, or else their balloon could simply deflate if government regulation and taxation were to increase; this gives them a qualitatively different position *vis-à-vis* the state's sovereignty over them.

The links with financial crises

A fear that has haunted all bankers since the development of capitalism is the prospect of a collapse of the financial system. The bankruptcy of banks and financial institutions brings them the immediate disaster of losing the goose that lays the golden egg (although bankruptcy laws ensure that most of today's bankers would continue to enjoy their personal wealth after the collapse of their houses); it brings them the opprobium of the depositors whose assets have been wiped out; and it also brings the accusation that bankers are responsible for the collapse of production; employment and the 'real' economy. That accusation comes from the popular belief, at times of economic breakdown, that the problems are caused by financial crises.

Whether they are or not, it is certainly the case that the collapse of banks and finance houses has frequently preceded the collapse of production and trade. The failure of the Baring Brothers in 1890 had ramifications throughout the economy, and Milton Friedman has blamed the 1930–33 collapse of a series of American banks for the onset of the disastrous 1930s slump. Today, the principal fear is that banks' Eurodollar business involves risks that could precipitate a financial crisis. At various times during the market's growth fears for its stability have been expressed, and a general pessimism had become pervasive among observers since the end of the 1970s; but since crisis prediction in any field is highly speculative, there has been no shortage of optimists as well as extreme pessimists.

What is the basis for this expectation of crisis and breakdown?

Why are those banks operating in Eurocurrencies particularly at risk? The basic risk is that applying to most banks' operations; they are borrowing money on a short-term basis and lending it for longer periods. This makes them vulnerable to interest rate changes and to unpredictable withdrawals of depositors' funds. If interest rates rise, long-term loans contracted at the lower rates must in the course of their life, as short-term borrowings have to be replaced, be financed by new short-term deposits at the new higher rates of interest, so that banks' profits on the loans fall.

But, unpredictable withdrawals are the greatest danger; the danger from interest rate changes has been reduced by making medium term loans at adjustable interest rates. If depositors, when their short-term deposits mature, wish to withdraw them because they have lost confidence in the bank, the bank cannot repay them by calling in its longer-term loans. The danger of such loss of confidence arising stems from the risks inherent in the types of loans the Eurobanks make, the fact that, during 1976–82, almost half of their new sovereign loans were made to developing countries and a smaller but sensitive proportion (4 per cent) to socialist countries. The fear is that the bankers underestimated the 'country risk', or 'sovereign risk' on those loans; that borrowers will be unable to repay loans and confidence in the lender will therefore collapse.

At the beginning of the 1980s developing countries did cause Eurobankers some sleepless nights. Their governments had borrowed money at high interest rates during the 1970s when high inflation rates made their real cost relatively low and the developing countries needed the money to finance balance of payments deficits after the 1973 OPEC price rise. The reduction of inflation as the monetarist governments in the UK and USA tipped the scales of world recession led to a rise in the real cost of those loans; the prices of developing countries' commodity exports fell faster than the prices of imported manufacturers, and they found themselves acutely short of foreign exchange with which to repay the loans or even to pay the interest on them. One measure of this difficulty is the developing countries' debt–service ratio, the ratio of their outgoings on interest and debt repayment to their total exports. For the 21 major borrowers, this doubled, from 37 to 75 per cent, over 1975–82, and that average conceals several more serious problems in the case of particular countries, for example Argentina, Mexico and Brazil, where the debt–service ratio at the beginning of 1983 was 154, 126 and 117 per cent, respectively.

At the same time the bankers found themselves at risk in loans to socialist countries such as Poland, which had embarked on a development plan that proved to be unsustainable in the context of a world economic crisis; and the risk increased when the 1981 crisis in Poland showed that, contrary to bankers' calculations in lending to Eastern Europe, the Soviet umbrella did not extend to repaying its allies' debts to the banks. These risks have not led to the loss of depositors' confidence in the banks and a withdrawal of funds, but they have led to 25 instances of re-scheduling of loans between 1975 and 1983. 'Re-scheduling' refers to countries that have been unable to meet their repayment obligations on time; such a country is, in effect, in default, but since neither the lender nor the borrower wishes to recognise formally the default, they negotiate a longer period of loan repayment – a 're-scheduling' of the loan. Re-scheduling is a risky business, since the bankers do not know if they are merely throwing good money after bad to postpone the evil day of a formal default; moreover, the negotiations themselves are always at risk from the possibility that one bank (the image of a small mid-Western US bank looms large in City and Wall Street fears) that has participated in the loan may declare a formal default. If that were to happen, the existence of cross-default clauses in loan agreements would lead other banks to declare the borrower in default, and the writing-off of the loan would wreak havoc on banks' balance sheets and depositors' confidence.

Quite apart from the risks they have experienced in the sovereign loans made to Third World and Soviet bloc countries – the 'country risk' involved – the Eurobank system multiplies those risks by the structure of the banking system itself. First, their loans to such borrowers are highly concentrated in a few countries. Of the Eurobanks' publicised loans to Third World countries in June 1982, 84 per cent was accounted for by just 21 borrowers, with Brazil, Mexico, Argentina, Venezuela, Indonesia and South Korea alone accounting for 55 per cent. Political or economic risks in any of those countries would have a disproportionate effect on the banking system because of its concentration on them. In addition, individual banks have concentrated their lending upon particular countries, and they are similarly at greater risk than they would be if they spread their loans between a range of borrowers.

Second, the effect on a bank of default by a borrower depends upon the strength of its capital reserves. If the loans that have to be written off – the extent of the losses, that is – are a small proportion of the bank's shareholders' or equity capital, the bank can survive the default and depositors have no reason to withdraw funds. But the Eurobanks have operated with very low equity capital as a percentage of their total loans. As a result of the expansion of deposits and loans during the 1970s combined with relatively low profit margins prompted by intense competition, the loans have risen to as much as 30 times equity capital.

Third, the risk to any bank is multiplied into a risk to the Eurobanking system as a whole by the interconnections between banks. A high amount of borrowing and lending in Eurocurrencies is from one bank to another; these inter-bank funds are a much more dominant feature of Eurobanking than of ordinary, domestic banking. Their effect is that, if any major bank does suffer losses and go bankrupt with depositors withdrawing funds, the banks that have loaned to it on the inter-bank market will also suffer losses and may also go bankrupt, and there will be similar repercussions all along the inter-bank chain.

The nature of the inter-bank system is that banks lend surplus funds to other banks for a very short period – a day, overnight, or for up to 12 months. It is difficult to estimate the size of these surplus funds exactly, but it was believed to involve Eurocurrency loans of $1000 billion at the end of 1982, and thus to be much larger than the amount of medium-term syndicated credits through which banks had lent to governments and corporations. Its significance, though, stems from the function it performs for the banks, its sensitivity, and the fact that it has come to be used for purposes for which it was not intended. For the banks, its value lies in providing a channel for making a profit on surplus funds, and it also enables them to strike a balance between short-term liabilities and assets: if a bank knows that some of its large depositors are going to withdraw their money in a few days it needs to have some of its money invested in equally short-term loans.

The sensitivity comes from its informality combined with the large sums involved, for its survival depends on all borrowers honouring their huge debts, and upon lenders not panicking and suddenly withdrawing their quickly recallable loans. A London banker quoted in the *Financial Times* (1 March 1983) described its sensitivity and its value to banks in dramatic tones: 'The interbank market must be sacrosanct. It can suffer general contractions without too much of a problem, but if it is not honoured by banks then one can see, mechanically, how the world can come to an end.' The danger of that apocalypse came to be recognised at the end of 1982 and early 1983 because the market *had* ceased to be sacrosanct.

Instead of being a technical device to smooth bankers' balance sheets and soothe their minds, the inter-bank market came to be tapped by countries seeking to finance their balance of payments deficits. Countries such as Mexico and Brazil had decided to supplement their dependence on medium-term syndicated credits by trying to raise money on the inter-bank market. They instructed the London and New York branches of their banks to borrow in their own name as much as possible from other banks. The problems came after Mexico, in August 1982, announced that it would fail to meet its very heavy debt obligations; then, bankers everywhere sought to protect themselves by withdrawing their most easily accessible, most liquid loans – the short-term loans to Latin American countries' banks. The bankers' image of the end of the world loomed large, and it took the shape of a sombrero rather than a mushroom.

The risks attaching to the Eurobanking system are part of the risk of generalised financial crises, and we examine that danger further in chapter 4. For the present, however, it is enough to note that the Eurobanking system brings risks with it. And since Eurobanking is an activity carried out by banks (and other financial institutions) whose activities also include other types of lending, borrowing and money-dealing; since, as we make clear in chapter 5, it is a central activity of the familiar High Street banks, its risks are dangers to the whole structure of banking upon which industry and trade depend.

The Eurobanking system has its centre in London. When, in the final chapter, we look at the policies that should be adopted for the City, the question of whether that role should be discontinued because of its disadvantages has to be faced. The two effects, actual and potential, that the system has on Britain's economy arise from the existence of the Eurobanking system as such rather than from the geographical presence of its headquarters on British soil; but since it is so strongly located in London, a British government has to take much of the responsibility for influencing its future.

4

Financial Crises Past and Future

'Banks Skating on Thin Ice', or 'A Nightmare of International Debts', proclaimed the headlines by the start of the 1980s. In themselves, these two headlines are not remarkable, but the fact that the first came from *Monthly Review*, an American Marxist journal, while the latter was *The Economist*'s title for its 1982 survey of international banking illustrates the new consensus that has emerged regarding the dangers of financial crisis. Writers on the Left and Right vied to publicise their doomsday predictions. *The Guardian* newspaper's financial leader summed up the recent dramas:

> If a writer of financial thrillers had written into his novel continuous debt crises in Eastern Europe and Latin America; the collapse of a government securities broker and an Oklahoma bank which struck at the heart of Wall Street; some of the highest real interest rates in history . . . – it would all have been regarded as too fantastic for words (*Guardian*, 4 January 1983).

The danger of a financial crisis is a real one. Major banks could collapse and savings institutions like pension funds could go under. If it happened, such a crash would be on an international scale rather than confined to London. In some countries small depositors and savers would suffer, although in Britain and the United States it is more likely that the disaster would be felt principally in the curtailment of credit to industry and to governments that need it to keep the wheels turning.

But if it happened, it would not be the first time. The collapse of banking houses and panic on the financial markets were regular occurrences in the nineteenth-century City. The collapse of respected banking names such as Barings in 1890 marked crises that brought the City's expansion to a temporary halt. They had been preceded by a series of bank failures in 1837, 1839, 1842, 1847, 1857 and 1866. During the nineteenth century there were nine financial crises in all, an average of one per decade between 1815 and 1893, and some had dramatic effects on the whole structure of the financial system. For example, the 1815 crisis saw the disappearance of 140 country banks in the United Kingdom (comparing the 1817 total with 1814).

Attempts to stabilize the system, to overcome this apparently endemic accident-proneness, did not achieve any coherence until the view of Walter Bagehot, published in 1873 in his book, *Lombard Street*, came to be accepted. Bagehot argued that the Bank of England should take on the responsibilities of a central bank, not simply in controlling the issue of bank notes (as it did from 1844), but also in supporting or guaranteeing the banking system's ability to borrow and lend. The irredeemable element in any financial crisis, then and now, is that everyone, from depositors to finance houses, wants their money back, and banks or other financial institutions are unable to meet their liabilities out of their assets; they cannot quickly retrieve the cash they have loaned or invested except by incurring a great loss. To prevent the crisis from feeding on itself and the panic from spreading, the central bank, according to the doctrine inherited from Bagehot, has to be ready to lend when no one else will; to act as a 'lender of last resort' – or at least, in its modern version, to persuade others to lend when they would not otherwise have done so.

Twentieth century crises

The history of financial crises and the development of central banks' functions as lenders of last resort pose two puzzles. Are financial crises accidents that arise through banks and finance houses undertaking foolish actions in unpredictable circumstances, or are they endemic to the system? And whatever their nature, can they be prevented by judicious central bank and government policies? These are questions that have to be answered if we are to get any perspective on whether a financial collapse lies around the next corner, or the next. Britain has experienced only two significant financial crashes this century, in 1914 and 1973–75, while the United States went through the very real horror of a financial crash that affected millions of small depositors between 1929 and 1933. We can make some headway towards answering the questions, towards understanding financial crises, by examining those more recent experiences.

The 1973–75 crash came as a shock to the City. The preceding years' growth of a new type of institution, the secondary bank, was brought to a halt by the crash of many of them in those years. The myth that had seemed to be proven fact in the preceding boom – that money could not fail to make money if invested in real estate and asset-stripping – was found to be less than an eternal truth. It was not just the new secondary banks, headed by men like Jim Slater, whizz-kids who seemed to typify the new conservatism of Mr Heath and Selsden Man, that collapsed in the crash: the 1974 crisis directly or indirectly hit at the most blue-blooded firms in the Square Mile. It was even rumoured that National Westminster Bank, one of the Big Four clearing banks, was in a position where it would have difficulty in meeting its obligations, although in the end most such big names had the resources and the backing to weather the calamity (Reid, 1982). The 1973–75 crisis had repercussions on some houses as late as June 1982, when one of the City's top stockbroking firms, Carr Sebag, with roots going back 177 years, collapsed, partly because (according to the *Financial Times* of 5 June 1982) it was finding it difficult to escape the stigma of having enjoyed a close relationship with Slater Walker, the most spectacular failure of 1973–75.

Although the 1973–75 crisis affected the whole City, the secondary banks were at its centre. But what were these banks? And how did the crisis unfold? Before the start of the crisis in November 1973 the secondary banks comprised both the 'Other British banks' of the recognised banking sector and 'Section 123 companies'. The former group included the subsidiaries and associates of British clearing and merchant banks and various other British banks and finance houses. The latter group, 'Section 123 companies', originated with a judgement made in 1966 by Lord Denning in *United Dominions Trust v. Kirkwood*, where he ruled that the court recognised the finance house (United Dominions Trust) as a banker and not a money-lender. The judgement was incorporated into section 123 of the 1967 Companies Act to be administered by the then Board of Trade. By 1973 the number of section 123 companies had risen to no less than 133. Self-made men were now able to discard the three golden balls outside their buildings and turn their offices into banks. Many of both categories of secondary banks had their origins in hire purchase, money-lending or stock market dealing (Reid, 1982).

This may give the impression that secondary banks operated only on the fringes of the City, but in fact they were closely related to established City institutions in at least two respects. On the one hand, the secondary banks were highly 'geared' – a high proportion of their money was borrowed and relatively little came from the owners – so that they were financed by credit from major City banks. On the other hand, some of Britain's biggest bank and insurance companies (including Barclays, Eagle Star, Hambros and the Prudential), not to mention the Crown Agents, owned as much as a quarter of the equity of some leading secondary banks. Bearing this in mind, let us turn briefly to the causes of the 1974 crisis.

That crisis began to unfold late in 1973, but the collapse and near-collapse of secondary banks reached full flood in 1974. The origins of the crisis were two-fold: the implementation of the policies christened 'Competition and Credit Control' (CCC), combined with the dash for growth of Edward Heath's Tory administration. CCC sought to encourage competition between banks by heralding an end to credit ceilings that, during the 1950s and 1960s, had at times restrained the growth of lending by major banks and hire purchase companies. Increased competition between banks in this expansionary environment precipitated an enormous leap in bank lending. Between August 1971 (CCC was introduced in September 1971) and December 1973 sterling bank advances in the UK increased by a factor of over two-and-a-half-times. More critically, the bulk of the increased lending went to finance not British industry and trade, but rather property companies (increase of 519 per cent) and other financial companies, including the section 123 companies (increase of 416 per cent).

Such lending for speculative purposes fuelled the 1971–73 property boom, during which average property prices increased by one-quarter in both 1972 and 1973. The speculative bubble had to burst sooner or later. The collapse was heralded by an increase in what was then the City's key interest rate, its minimum lending rate, to a record 13 per cent in November 1972, by a tough autumn mini-Budget, and by a looming confrontation between the Tories and the miners. Worst hit were the secondary banks, who had to pay significantly higher interest rates for the money they borrowered to finance their property and other speculations. The collapse of the property market followed in spring 1974 when prices of commercial property dropped to between three-quarters and a half their former value, and this collapse of their assets combined with the higher cost of their debts to produce a pincer movement of military precision.

The final phase of the UK crisis resulted from overseas events. The Herstatt Bank collapsed in Germany in 1974 sending shock waves through the Eurobanks, and making all banks anxious to get their money back wherever it was invested, but particularly if it had been lent to the increasingly risky secondary banks. The credit on which they depended vanished.

The 1973–75 crisis began with the Stock Exchange suspending dealings in the shares of London and Counties Securities Group at the end of November 1973, and in those of Cedar Holdings in December 1973. It was the latter's difficulties that gave rise to an unprecedented rescue scheme mounted by the Bank of England in collaboration with High Street banks such as Barclays, Lloyds and the Midland, and which has since become popularly known as the Lifeboat. At its peak in March 1975, the amount of aid advanced under the Lifeboat reached the impressive total of £1285 million. To get some impression of the relative size of this total, it is estimated that in 1974 this would have constituted about 40 per cent of the capital and reserves of English and Scottish clearing banks. Reid (1982) has estimated that, if account is taken of the indirect finance provided by other banks and the investing institutions, the total funds provided to ailing secondary banks under the Lifeboat scheme would reach about £3000 million.

By any standards this amounts to a huge sum expended on what the City would in other circumstances describe as 'lame ducks'. If secondary banks had indeed been confined to the fringes of the City, there seems no material reason why the Bank of England or the High Street banks should have worried unduly about a shake-out in that sector. Ultimately, the sheer scale of the Lifeboat suggests that it was launched to protect the large City banks and institutions, the crew of the Lifeboat, themselves. The Lifeboat also facilitated management shake-outs within the affected firms and enabled the big, old established banks and other institutions later to buy out most of the survivors at knock-down prices.

Reid has analysed the 25 secondary banking firms that directly received aid under the Lifeboat. Of these, 8 went into liquidation, 1 was scaled down and sold off and 14 of the remaining 16 were taken over at some later stage. Table 4.1 shows the way some of the banking companies receiving aid under the Lifeboat changed owners then or subsequently. The table shows that, for 12 out of 14 banks, the new owners are also banks, predominantly British, and generally clearing or merchant banks. It is noticeable that many of the ownership changes have occurred only within the past few years. Reid also analyses a further group of 24 banking and financial companies hit by the 1974 crisis. Of these 5 went into liquidation, a few remained independent, but, again, the majority were taken over. In this case, however, the new owners are a more diverse group than those that took over the banks that were aided directly by the Lifeboat.

To sum up, the 1974 crisis is a contemporary example of a speculative crisis. Although it affected the whole of the City, the

TABLE 4.1   OWNERSHIP CHANGES IN
LIFEBOAT BANKS

Banking company	Assets (end 1973) (£ million)	New owner
Beverley Bentinck	35	Bank of Ireland (1978)
Bowmaker	243	Lloyds Bank (1982)
British Bank of Commerce	59	Grindlays Bank (1974)
Cannon Street Investments	122	Nat·West (1974)
Cedar Holdings	128	Lloyds & Scottish (1979)*
Edward Bates & Sons Holdings†	74	Allied Arab Bank
Keyser Ullman Holdings	433 (Mar 1974)	Bank of England Charterhouse Group (1980)
Medens Trust	11 (June 1974)	Brown Shipley Holdings (1981)
Mercantile Credit	377	Barclays (1975)
Morris Wigram	30	Slavenberg's Bank (1980)
Northern Commercial Trust†	90	Algemene Bank Nederland (1975)
Twentieth Century Banking	62	P & O Group (1974)
United Dominions Trust	896	Trustee Savings Bank (TSB) (1981)
J.H. Vavasseur	52	Mills & Allen International (1978)

* In 1981 Lloyds Bank acquired a majority holding in Lloyds & Scottish.
† Only parts or subsidiaries of these groups were taken over.
Sources: Reid (1982); *Financial Times*.

main casualties were the secondary banks and property companies. The 1974 crisis saw the launch of the Lifeboat, a massive rescue scheme mounted jointly by the Bank of England and the clearing banks. The aftermath of the crisis has witnessed a spate of take-overs within the City by the major banks in particular.

But does that crisis shed any light on the questions posed at the start of this chapter: are financial crises accidental, resulting from imprudent behaviour, or endemic, and can they be prevented by appropriate central bank policies?

The conclusions we must draw at this stage, at least as preliminary conclusions, is that they are not endemic and that they can be prevented by policy. The 1974 crisis was characterised by the wave of speculative activity, by banks in Britain and in other countries. The crisis was not confined to the UK but had an international dimension affecting the United States, West Germany and Italy as well and also having a Euromarkets dimension. And in each case the source of the particular crisis was speculative activities of various types. The Herstatt Bank in West Germany collapsed largely because of foreign exchange and bullion speculation, while both the US and Italian financial systems were affected by the collapse of the Franklin National Bank, part of the empire of Michele Sindona, who is now serving a 25-year jail sentence for fraud. The crisis in the United States was compounded by the collapse of the National Bank of San Diego and of real estate investment trusts. Similarly, in the UK the cause of the 1973–75 crisis was speculation in property, fringe banking and other dubious activity. With its origins in speculative activity and misjudgement, the crisis was susceptible to the authorities' policies: the Lifeboat operation led by the Bank of England *did* halt the slide.

The 1973–75 crisis is one example; another is the US financial crisis that spanned three-and-a-half years from October 1929 to March 1933. Its outcome was quite different – in fact, quite calamitous – but it throws some more light on the question of whether central bank policy can overcome financial crises. The years of crisis covered four particular breakdowns:

(a) the Wall Street stock market crash, October 1929;
(b) the banking crisis, October 1930;
(c) the banking crisis, March 1931;
(d) the banking panic, January–March 1933.

It is important to be aware of these separate elements, since the popular conception of the period, conveyed by the phrase 'the Great Crash', refers only to the first episode and, moreover, to one in which the impact on banks was comparatively light. This is not to underestimate the role of the Wall Street crash, where the decline in the total value of all shares listed in October 1929 is estimated to have been over $15 billion, but the panic on the stock market did not immediately precipitate a banking crisis. The bank crashes of the following years, 1930–33, however, wiped out the wealth of small and large depositors throughout the country; approximately 9000 banks suspended business, and deposits in commercial banks fell by $18 billion, which, at 42 per cent of the total, represents a dramatic shrinkage of the financial system. The shrinkage of deposits was, inevitably, matched on the other side of the balance sheet by the decline in bank loans and investments, which made no small contribution to the 30 per cent decline in US output over the period (although whether the decline in bank deposits was the main cause of the depression or merely one of the many interacting factors is a subject of controversy between monetarist and Keynesian theorists).

Those banking crashes appear to reinforce the tentative lesson of the 1974 crisis: they suggest that central bank action can prevent financial crisis. Milton Friedman and his co-author Anna Schwartz (1963) have pointed to the failure of the US central bank, the Federal Reserve, to adopt Walter Bagehot's principles fully and pump money into the banks as the principle cause of the crashes. And many writers ascribe this failure of the Federal Reserve to an accidental circumstance: the influence of its New York centre in the direction of acting as 'lender of the last resort' to the banking system was on the wane following the death of its forceful leader, Benjamin Strong. The implication, then, is that this financial crisis was not endemic or incurable, but fortuitous, and would have been avoidable if only the central bank had taken the right steps.

But are these appearances valid? As soon as one interrogates more carefully the experiences of 1929–33 or of 1973–75, reasons become apparent for thinking that financial crises are endemic to capitalism and cannot always be prevented by central bank action. Certainly, speculative activity lay behind the 1973–75 crisis in Britain and the 1929 Wall Street crash, but the occurrence from time to time of speculative activity without a real economic base to sustain it is endemic in highly developed Western economies. Certainly, central bank action could have assisted the US banks at the beginning of the 1930s and did provide stabilising leadership in

1974; but the power of the central bank inevitably tends to slip behind.

Are financial crises inevitable?

Speculation involves the buying and selling of bonds, shares, foreign exchange, titles to real estate or commodities and all the other pieces of paper that are traded on financial markets. It has very little immediate connection with the 'real' economy where goods are produced and sold, but it does ultimately depend on it, for the profits that are made in financial trading must have their counterparts in real goods if they are to have any value. The speculators (including millions of ordinary Americans) who saw their shares increase in price in the boom before the 1929 Wall Street crash could not all count this increase as real profit unless there were real assets in the economy – real plant and machinery, and warehouses full of real inventories of raw materials, food and finished goods – to match. In the aggregate, capital gains and interest payments within the financial system have a real basis only to the extent that real profits are being generated and accumulated in production.

However, the essence of modern finance is that its ultimate dependence as a whole upon production's real profits *is* only ultimate; for a substantial period a boom in the prices of shares, real estate deeds or other financial paper can be generated on the basis of optimism alone. The fringe banks at the centre of the 1970s crisis had grown in the preceding years by lending for the purchase of real estate and accepting the property as security. The fact that the property was at historically high prices could not dent the optimism of lenders and borrowers, and the loans themselves helped to keep property prices up. The loans were the hot air that supported the banks' security for the loans. Each supported the other, and the whole contraption was high and rising. This self-reinforcing process, however, was susceptible to any quiver of doubt, for if optimism is a fashion pessimism can easily replace it, just as this year's Paris collections can make the wearers of last year's feel foolish. At the time British industry was generating lower profits than had been seen at any time since the Second World War; thus, when doubts did arise, their rush could not be stemmed by property developers pointing to industry's willingness to pay high rents for their office blocks, the high property prices could not be supported by the revenue that could be extracted by the City from industry's profits.

The twin characteristic of financial markets – their ultimate dependence on the profits of industry and commerce and their ability to generate speculative booms on the basis of optimism without any industrial roots – are what make it inevitable that speculative booms end in crises. Those booms are not only possible but are a perpetual feature of the financial system, for the very heart of the system is its ability to create paper claims whose price is determined by forces of demand and supply on the City's markets, forces that have no direct connection with industrial activity. The financial system lives by creating and trading in certificates and coupons (or their equivalent 'bleep' in the records stored on computers) which promise an income to their owner; but because these claims owe their existence to their ability to be traded in volume at variable prices, speculation is built into their very nature. And the periodic over-expansion of the financial system, over-expansion in relation to the real economic base upon which it ultimately depends, is systemic.

Marxist economists consider that financial crises, occurring with the collapse of speculative booms, serve the function of restoring some balance between the financial and the real economy and correcting the over-expansion of the former. It is apparent nowadays that they additionally serve to force a re-structuring of the financial system itself: the experience of 1929–33 weeded out the weakest American institutions and forced the system towards strengthening the role of the Federal Reserve and creating authorities to supervise and insure elements of the banks' business; while the 1970s British crisis rid the system of its weak, fringe bank component, concentrated power in the more solid financial houses, and stimulated reforms in supervision. This experience contradicts the prognoses of Hilferding, the one classical Marxist economist to carry out a detailed investigation of the financial system. His *Finance Capital*, published in 1910, envisaged that financial crises would become less important as the concentration of banks led them to dominate and control the credit system (and as their integration with increasingly concentrated industry and commerce, in Germany at least, would lead to a reduction in speculation).

In fact, the nature of the financial markets' paper claims has meant that there is always the potential of profiting from innovation, from finding new ways to borrow and lend; thus the financial system has a tendency rapidly to spawn new unstable operators using new techniques, so that the weight and sheer bottom of the great institutions upon which Hilferding placed faith is always able to be subverted.

Drysdale Government Securities is a case in point. A recently formed subsidiary of Drysdale Securities specialising in gilts, with none of the 'track record' that even a casual race course punter would seek in a horse, this firm, with a capital of only $20 million, managed to borrow $4.5 billion (yes, four thousand five hundred million US dollars), a sum twice the size of Jordan's GNP, from the august Chase Manhattan bank and others by operating to the full a relatively novel technique of borrowing and lending. It grew from nothing to that size within the space of a few months, until in May 1982 its speculative dealings misfired and it could not repay its debts. The failure wiped out Chase's first quarter earnings of $116 million, the equivalent of 5 per cent of its shareholders' funds.

Similarly, the failure in June 1982 of the Oklahoma Bank, Penn Square, implied losses of up to $400 million for banks including Continental Illinois, Chase Manhattan and Seafirst, the largest bank in Seattle, which in 1983 became the victim of a takeover bid by BankAmerica. Penn Square's innovation was that it operated an 'energy loan super-market' (selling such loans to other banks), which had boosted its assets from $34 million in 1974 to £525 million in 1981, but the delicately balanced operation soon tripped up. The effect of this failure, one of the largest in US banking history, was to wipe out some of the earnings of the banks affected and, in the case of Seafirst, to wipe out some of its reserves.

The recent collapse of Penn Square in the United States and Banco Ambrosiano in Italy raises questions about the effectiveness of the authorities charged with supervising the banking system. The case of Drysdale was special, since it operated in an area (government securities) that was not subject to any supervision. But Banco Ambrosiano was just another of the estimated 1000 banks engaged in Euromarket activities. Its failure hit the headlines because of the death of its head, Sr. Calvi, in London (officially, by his own hand, but, according to his family, by murder), the death of his secretary, the bank's close links with the Vatican, and the suggestion of a link with a political Freemasons' plot. In the present context, though, it was merely the crash of a bank engaged in the risky business of Eurobanking. While a second inquest and the press speculated over how Sr. Calvi was hung from Blackfriars Bridge, bankers were shocked by central bankers' failure to be responsible for his bank's foreign subsidiaries.

What can cause a crash?

Speculative booms are triggered into financial crises by many factors. It may be a collapse of confidence as inexplicable as the burst of optimism that fuelled the boom. The 1929 Wall Street Crash seems to exemplify that frightening irrationality. It may be the trouble a major finance house brings to itself, and to the other financiers that have lent it money, by losing money on a failed speculation. Or it may be that the financial system's ultimate dependence on the real economy asserts itself by industrial borrowers having to default on their loans. Minsky, a modern Keynesian economist who has promulgated a 'financial instability hypothesis' to explain phenomena such as the stagflation of the 1970s and the risks of crisis, has emphasised the potential significance of industrial borrowers' defaults in triggering financial crises. A rise in interest rates or a fall in profits can push a firm that has borrowed to finance long-term investment projects into a position where its cash flow is not enough to cover even its interest payments. If there has been a period of optimism and expansion in the real economy (apart from a purely financial speculative boom) many industries will have extended their borrowing to a position where they are exposed to such a risk. When it materialises, the losses faced by the banks, insurance companies, pension funds and other institutions that loaned the money can trigger a crisis of the whole financial system.

In fact, there is not much evidence that financial crises have been caused by the default of industrial borrowers. The 1929–33 American crisis and the 1970s British crisis were not sparked in that way, although the weakness of the 'real' economy was the underlying problem. And in the two years up to 1982 the problems that such industrial giants as Chrysler, AEG, International Harvester, Dome and Massey Ferguson had in meeting their financial commitments were borne by the banks without bringing them down even if banks' asset portfolios have become more illiquid as a result. Nevertheless, Minsky's financial instability hypothesis may accurately describe a factor that, in the future, will trigger financial crises.

Whatever does actually trigger financial crises, they occur in circumstances in which the financial system has over-expanded in relation to its base and where several factors have contributed to an underlying weakness. And because of the novelty of the loan operations that characterise each over-expansion, central banks do not have the ability always to prevent the crisis. The truth of these conclusions can be seen by changing the question: instead of asking, as we have, whether the past provides evidence concerning the endemic or accidental nature of financial crises and their avoidability, we can face the question that has confronted all politicians and bankers recently: is a financial crisis about to engulf us in the near future? The answer is yes. No one can be certain, and firm assurances either of disaster or of smoothly continuing banking rituals cannot be accepted. But the balance of probabilities is that a major financial crisis will happen. It is not possible to take a considered view of precisely what will trigger it, or when, but the underlying conditions make it much more likely than not that some event will cause a crisis. These basic conditions are the novel type of expansion – over-expansion – that the British and international banks have pursued since 1974, and the failure of central banks to develop safety-net techniques to match.

In chapter 3 we described the new role that the City and its banks adopted in the 1970s and particularly since 1974, the role of an 'offshore' banking centre channelling funds, in Eurodollar credits, from all over the world to borrowers in any country. The main channels through which the banks operated were innovatory, syndicated, medium-term credits with variable interest rates and the expanded inter-bank market, and a high proportion of these credits and loans were granted to Third World states and Soviet bloc countries. They were not secured by any collateral, by any national assets pledged against the loan – it would have been impossible to effect such arrangements – and the banks' judgements on the borrowers' ability to repay were open to criticism.

By 1982 this bank lending, when added to credit from governments and international agencies (but excluding inter-bank loans), brought developing countries' total international debt to £300 billion, and their ability to pay the interest and repay the debt was coming under increasing strain. This debt–service ratio had increased, for non-oil-exporting Third World countries, from 15 per cent in 1979 to 20 per cent in 1982, and within that average particular countries were in a much more acute position as we saw in the previous chapter. Brazil and Argentina in 1981 had debt–service ratios of over 50 per cent; Mexico, one of the world's largest oil exporters, borrowed so heavily from the banks during the 1970s that by mid-1982 it had debts of £80 billion and a high debt–service ratio. Its oil revenues and political stability appeared to guarantee the banks' returns; but, as the world's bankers and finance officials prepared for that year's meetings in Toronto of the World Bank and International Monetary Fund, Mexico, hit by declining oil revenues, announced its inability to carry on with normal servicing of its huge debt. This was a major shock for the banking system, especially since it followed a series of debt crises from borrowers as diverse as Zambia, Poland and Argentina.

Bank lending to sovereign governments through medium-term syndicated Eurodollar credits led to an over-expansion of borrowing by many countries. Most relevant to our present concern is that it was an over-expansion from the point of view of the banks themselves. The ratio of their outstanding loans to their own equity capital base rose to historically high levels. It did so partly because fierce competition between the banks for the fashionable lending business of syndicated credits occurred even though, for several years, the interest rates they yielded made the loss hardly profitable for the banks and their capital base could not be replenished from accumulated profits. The declining ratio of capital base to loans outstanding has meant that by 1982 banks had become highly susceptible to any losses resulting from defaulting borrowers; for, just as accumulated profits replenish a bank's capital base, money lost through defaults wipes out any part of it and can force a bank into bankruptcy. This weakening of capital ratios is therefore one factor in the basic conditions that make the banks at the heart of the financial system susceptible to sudden shocks.

The strength of British banks' loans has also been weakened on the home front as their industrial borrowers have run into difficulties with low profits and poor liquidity in the recession that began in 1980. In chapter 5 we shall return to the increasing instances of banks putting companies into receivership; in addition, in 1982 Barclays Bank and Midland Bank claimed that some customers who in other times might have been put into receivership were being given special care and nursing by the banks in the hope that their fortunes could be improved. Barclays, for example, claimed to have 600 corporate clients of varying size on its 'sick list'.

These losses and potential losses contribute further to the basic conditions creating a fertile ground for the shocks that trigger financial crisis. The combination of risks on overseas and domestic lending resulted, in 1982, in the Big Four High Street banks having to set aside £962 million to cover bad debts; the damage this inflicted on them is measured by the fact that it amounted to two-thirds of their gross pre-tax profits (of £1.48 billion). Fortunately for the system, depositors did not panic at the news.

The shocks that can come through the banks' commitment to

international lending can come from various sources. Since a 1 percentage point rise in interest rates is estimated to increase the developing countries' annual debt servicing needs by $2 billion, a fall in the value of a borrower's principal export (as in the case of Mexico's oil) or a rise in international interest rates can trigger a major default. And since banks throughout the world are totally interdependent, because they lend to and borrow from each other in vast amounts at every minute and because their international loans to sovereign states are made by groups temporarily joined together as syndicates, a shock to any one bank can be easily magnified throughout the system.

Absence of a world central bank

The danger of a financial crisis in the near future has been widely canvassed and its likelihood is widely recognised, as is the damage it would do to the financial structure upon which today's economic system depends. Surely, it may be asked, governments and central banks have armed themselves with policies to prevent such a crisis: are they not adequate? The policies are not adequate principally because the banking system and its problems have become internationalised whereas the strong monetary authorities have a nationally based authority – the Bank of England, the US Federal Reserve, the Deutsche Bundesbank. The Bank of England in fact emphasised (to the point of exaggeration) the national boundary around its sphere of influence when it objected to the Hong Kong and Shanghai Bank's proposed takeover of the Royal Bank of Scotland on the surprising grounds that it would be controlled by a head office situated abroad and therefore would not be susceptible to the Bank of England's influence.

In the wake of the crash of Herstatt and the 1970s crisis, the central bankers, under the aegis of their own central bank the Bank for International Settlements, came to an agreement in Basle, Switzerland, in 1975. They agreed that each nation's central bank should be responsible for supervising and regulating the operations of banks with head offices in their country, wherever their branches are located, and for branches' obligations in the case of a default. In that way they attempted to overcome the division of responsibility for banks with branches in many countries, but the agreement was only a minor step on the road to overcoming financial crises. Default obligations extended only to branches, and there is no binding commitment to bail out subsidiaries in trouble, to act as a lender of last resort in the full sense. This was highlighted in 1982 by the refusal of the Italian authorities to assume responsibility for the debts of the Luxembourg subsidiary of the failed Ambrosiano bank. Even the minimum supervision and regulation within each central bank's sphere of influence has been slow to materialise: some years after the agreement, for example, the Bank of England devised regulations prescribing the level of cash reserves that banks should hold as a buffer backing various types of banking operations; the banks rejected them with one voice, and it took several more years before a halfway acceptable scheme was formulated.

The Basle agreement was not addressed to the major lacuna in the powers that central banks have to nip financial crises in the bud; the fact that when international borrowers default a large number of banks domiciled in many countries are threatened. When Poland's financial disaster became evident, and banks (like official creditors) had to negotiate the rescheduling of that country's debts, several hundred banks ranging from giants to small provincial ones were represented, and they were based in many countries. When a crisis breaks, central banks concerned with 'their' banks' stability have to cooperate with each other, and there are no formal established mechanisms for such cooperation.

More to the point, there is no international central bank with powers to intervene in and if necessary support the banks of each country. The Bank for International Settlements has no such powers; although known as the central bankers' central bank, its effectiveness is essentially that of a club committee, bringing together, collecting information for, and providing leadership for central banks, especially when there is a need for cooperation between them in international affairs. The International Monetary Fund is often regarded as a potential central bank for the world as a whole; but that mistakes the Fund's essential character, for its members are states, not central banks. The Fund's funds are subscribed by governments, and only governments borrow from it; indeed, one of the driving forces behind its foundation, Henry Morgenthau, the US Treasury Secretary, designed it specifically as a governmental institution to supplant the power of bankers. It does not therefore have formal institutionalised relations with banks, and although throughout the 1970s the Fund's activities have increasingly become articulated, *de facto,* with those of banks and central banks, its separateness from the banking systems has been preserved. To do otherwise would have required transforming the IMF into a completely different type of institution. The shock of Mexico's near default on its international debts in 1982 did concentrate minds, lead to an expansion of the IMF's traditional role, and to proposals for schemes to enable it to bail out the banks, but it is not becoming an international central bank.

The basic circumstances of the banking system, then, make financial crisis likely, and there is no central bank with effective power to halt a crisis of the international financial system. Nevertheless, shocks that would have rocked the nineteenth-century City have been borne by the financial system in recent years without initiating a cumulative crisis. Table 4.2 reproduces the *Financial Times* list of some of the major shocks still felt in August 1982. The shock of Mexico's difficulties in 1982 may have been great, exposing banks to the salutary lesson that their lending

TABLE 4.2　BORROWERS IN FINANCIAL DIFFICULTIES

Country	Extent of difficulty
Mexico	Owes more than $60bn to banks and seeks a moratorium on interest payments
Poland	Owes Western Banks over $14bn and seeks debt rescheduling
Argentina	Poised to re-structure its $36bn foreign debt
International Harvester	Re-structuring part of its $4.2bn debt to more than 200 banks
AEG	Extensive corporate re-structuring of some of its DM 5bn of bank borrowings
Dome Petroleum	Owes banks over C$4.1bn, part of which is being re-scheduled
Massey-Ferguson	Over 200 banks discussing the re-shaping of last year's C$715m refinancing
Grupo Alfa	Seeking refinancing of part of its $2.3bn bank debt
Banco Ambrosiano	Collapse in June left Luxembourg subsidiary owing more than $400m to 200 banks
Drysdale	Collapse in May cost Chase Manhattan $117m
Penn Square	Failure of bank in June results in losses of more than $400m for some US banks; Chase Manhattan, Continental Illinois and Seafirst Corporation particularly hard hit.

Source: Financial Times, 26 August 1982.

to that country was based on a massive misjudgement of its future potential, but it did not lead to a banking collapse. Instead, the main Western countries rapidly put together a loan package and the International Monetary Fund set out the terms for immediate assistance so that Mexico's debts could be rescheduled, or granted more credit. Similarly, Poland's effective, but not formal, default on its debts to banks and governments in 1981 did not cause a banking crash but led to a lengthy process of negotiating what might have appeared to be impossible, a rescheduling of the debts.

Surely the success of the international banking system in escaping, like Harold Lloyd, from one cliff-hanger after another indicates that a financial crisis is not likely? Perhaps Hilferding was right to think that the concentration of finance in the hands of a few big banks would eradicate financial crises, for the big banks have been able to cooperate (and force the smaller ones into line) to avoid default by rescheduling. We think the opposite lesson should be drawn from the banks' recent escapes: instead of solving the problems, they merely intensify them and make a future crisis more difficult to escape. The problem is that by rescheduling borrowers' debts the banks find themselves increasingly locked in; their assets – loans to borrowers – become highly illiquid and effectively take the form of very long-term commitments. They are a recognition that the banks cannot get their money back. The more illiquid a bank's assets, however, the more at risk it is, for its liabilities, the deposits it has borrowed, are essentially short-term and available to be withdrawn; any decline of depositors' confidence in the bank can lead to withdrawals, while the rescheduled loans to bankrupt borrowers cannot be called in to meet such withdrawals.

At the beginning of this chapter we pointed to the sequence of financial crises that hit the City in the nineteenth century; we end it by pointing to the crisis brewing for the 1980s. By the time you read this, it may already have happened.

PART II

THE CITY AND THE UK ECONOMY

The City's international position is crucial – its history, its current role, its problems and its power are all strongly affected by international factors. But a principal foundation of the financial system is the City's link with the industrial and commercial life of the British economy. Chapters 5 to 7 are concerned with the three main types of City business that constitute that link: pension and insurance funds which are central to the flow of long-term capital; banks where loans have a shorter term character but which have a wider role than that; and building societies which dominate the provision of finance for owner-occupied housing.

Nevertheless, it would be wrong to see the City as founded on two separate pillars, its international and its domestic business, for the two are meshed and the City acts as a unique bridge between the two spheres.

The actual and potential disturbances underlying financial crises were, as we argued in chapter 4, both international and domestic. Defaults and near defaults by overseas states (on sovereign loans), by multinational corporations, and by domestically based industries and traders, could precipitate a crisis either separately or in combination, or could worsen a crisis precipitated by an ill-judged financial speculation. Moreover, a crisis which is precipitated by the defaults of industrial and commercial borrowers would be magnified by the interlocking structure of the international financial systems, the 'house of cards' character of the Eurodollar credits and inter-bank loans.

Thus, while the following chapters are concerned with the City's links with British industry and commerce, the connections with its international role are inescapable. The overseas investments of pension and insurance funds are inseparable from their lending policy as a whole. And the banks' practices in lending to industry and commerce have been shaped by the involvement of foreign banks and by developments in 'wholesale' banking promoted by the growth of Eurodollar markets.

5

Pension and Other Funds

In the summer of 1982 Arthur Scargill, the newly elected leader of the National Union of Mineworkers and a man well known for his industrial militancy, turned his attention to the financial world and made what may turn out to have been a historic intervention. As an official trustee of the mineworkers' pension fund (the National Coal Board Superannuation Fund), he broke with precedent and protocol by refusing to endorse its 1982–84 investment plan.

This was the first occasion on which a union trustee had gone to such lengths in rejecting the criteria customarily employed by City investment advisers, but it came in the midst of a mounting left-wing campaign on the issue. Critics of the pension funds argued that their investment overseas, in real estate and in other forms that do not directly provide finance for industry, may maximise financial returns for the pension funds (although Minns, 1982b, casts doubts on their success even in those conventional terms), but that pensioners would fare better if the funds were invested directly in the long-term recovery of British industry. Such a change would mean abandoning the usual investment criteria of the City, but, their critics argue, in that case long-term financial profits would be combined with preservation of jobs.

The pension funds have been under particularly intense discussion, partly because of the weak legal requirements they have been under to disclose information or to be accountable to their members, and partly because the fact that trade unionists are often trustees of the funds covering employees in their industries has made them appear potentially susceptible to pressure from the labour movement. The intensity of the critics' campaign has been fuelled by the very rapid growth of pension funds in recent decades, the realisation that they have become one of the main influences on the stock market prices of shares and bonds, and the belief that part of their great wealth may be directed to investment boards (such as the West Midlands Enterprise Board) under public control. The power of the pension funds, and the degree to which this power has been exercised, is the subject of this chapter.

In respect of their size and investment power, pension funds are not unique; they share certain similarities with the other invest-ment institutions – insurance companies, investment trusts and unit trusts. Each in its special way derives from savers funds generally intended as long-term nest eggs, and invests this money in ways that are supposed to secure income or capital gains for the savers over the long term. In this way they are similar to building societies, but whereas the latter invest predominantly in mortgages, which cannot be traded, pension funds and similar institutions invest in shares, government bonds and other assets that are readily marketed. The pension funds may have a rather anonymous, grey image, but their managers are among the sharpest market operators and come from the same stable as the investment managers of life insurance companies, investment trusts and unit trusts. Moreover, theirs is an incestuous world, with pension funds being managed by insurance companies, investing in schemes run by life insurance companies and investing in investment and unit trusts. In examining the power of the pension funds, therefore, we shall consider them together with the less contentious life insurance companies, although we shall mainly leave the smaller institutions – the investment trusts and unit trusts – out of our account.

The question for this chapter, therefore, becomes: have the pension funds *and* insurance companies exercised great power? It is a question that concerns the relation between finance and industry and the changes in it that could have resulted from the growth of those investment institutions. Although it is true in an almost tautological sense that the rapid growth of pension funds and insurance companies has made a difference, assessments of their role are often clouded by an automatic assumption that, because they are big, they exercise great power over industry. In fact, the conclusion reached in this chapter is that they have *not* become the masters of industry. This is partly because they have not directed their funds towards industry as they might have done, partly because they have not exercised to the full the power of the paymaster who can call the piper's tune, and partly because the pension funds have in large measure ceded control over their wealth to the banks.

The booming business of old age

Pension funds and those insurance companies that provide (long-term) life insurance are in the business of providing for old age. The savings that they amass are, in the main, being put away to provide a pension, superannuation or lump sum for retirement or for a widowed spouse (although, of course, life insurance companies also handle other endowment policies, such as those through which housebuyers save to pay off their mortgage).

In the provision of income for old age four parties interact: the individual, the state, employers and financial institutions. In the political conflicts that accompanied the construction of the welfare state since the end of the nineteenth century, reformers and propagandists for different interests have sought to assign dominant roles to one or other of these actors, although the debates have polarised around the relative roles to be attributed to the state and the financial institutions (pension funds and insurance companies). The reasons for this concentration on only two of the parties are straightforward. Individuals cannot save for their old age on a mass scale by putting money under the bed; if they were to take the initiative in making prudent provisions, following Samuel Smiles's self-help principles, they would have to invest in financial securities. Under capitalism the individual cannot do as a peasant might – buy a means of production such as a cow as provision for old age – but s/he can, through buying financial assets, accumulate titles to the income ultimately generated by production.

Thus, as soon as we think of the individual taking the initiative in saving for old age, we are face to face with the role of the financial system; and although individual saving decisions have some effect upon the system's operation, the financial institutions' own operations are far more significant for understanding how provision for old age affects the economy. Similarly, the role of employers as independent, self-sufficient providers of pensions or other income for old age has been severely limited in Britain (unlike Germany). British employers provide pensions by investing their and their employees' contributions in financial assets. This 'pension fund' is a part of financial capital, an element in the financial system, in ways that we shall analyse in this chapter.

Thus, the two major types of income provision for old age in Britain have been supplied through the state and through the financial system. Neither the individual workers nor the employing company can arrange effective provision for old age except through one or the other of these.

The core of the state's income provision for old age in the form of retirement pensions has been a flat-rate allowance as part of the National Insurance system. The term 'National Insurance' served to underline the close conceptual connection between pension and life insurance schemes. In the reformed National Insurance system envisaged by Beveridge, the benefits were to be designed to keep pensioners above the subsistence line by paying pensions as a right, without a means test. Today, the scheme provides pensions for a vast number – 8.5 million in 1979/80 – but one-fifth of these are forced into the means-tested supplementary pensions scheme in order to subsist. In addition, the state has made provision for contributory earnings-related pensions (the most significant reform in this direction having been enacted in 1975); but, surrounded in controversy, these have languished, while private occupational pension funds, with which this chapter is concerned, have grown dramatically as a source of earnings-related pensions for the employees of private firms, nationalised industries and local authorities.

As far as pensions are concerned, the welfare state in Britain has been a 'mixed system', and has been so as a matter of design. The tax treatment of contributions to private pension schemes (and the schemes' earnings) has been central to their growth and stems from provisions that were made available to taxpayers as long ago as 1921, while even the Beveridge Report in 1942 envisaged a role for private occupational pensions above the state's basic retirement pension. The 1975 Act allowed employers to contract out of the state earnings-related scheme if their private scheme provided adequate benefits and conditions, and the Minister of State for Social Security made clear that the growth of these schemes was certainly not to be discouraged by the state's scheme: 'Sound pension provision of this kind can play an important role in the future of the nation. It means a better future in retirement and ill-health for all people. . . . Occupational pension provision has therefore a vital part to play in the development of a fair and firmly based prosperity in the future.' And the occupational pension schemes have, indeed, grown to fulfil their role in making up, for their members at least, for the inadequacies of state provision.

The figures for all employers' occupational pension schemes show a remarkable growth whichever way one looks at them. Between 1955 and 1975 the expenditure of all these schemes on pensions to their members increased by 340 per cent in real terms (i.e., excluding the direct effect of inflation); the numbers of employees contributing increased from 7.7 to 11.5 million; and the number receiving pensions has risen dramatically from 1 to 3.4 million. These employed members and pensioners were organised in a large, but unknown, number of pension schemes of varying sizes. As the Wilson Committee reported in 1980, 'The latest survey by the Government Actuary estimated that there were about 85,000 pension schemes (other than arrangements essentially only for individuals) in operation in 1975, of which about 24,000 had 10 or more members.'

For analysing the role of pension schemes in the financial system, however, the number of members and the amounts paid in pensions are not adequate. Instead, we need to know the volume of assets they have and the ways they are deployed, and not all occupational pension schemes do hold assets. Only those schemes that are pension funds hold assets, and although these are the vast majority, they do not include the schemes covering civil servants and some other state employees. A word of explanation is in order.

There are two ways of running a pension scheme. The first is to accept the contributions of members and their employers during the members' working lives, invest the proceeds in bonds, shares and other financial assets, and pay pensioners out of the interest, dividends and capital gains received from these investments. Such a scheme is a pension fund. The alternative is to accept contributions during members' working lives and, instead of investing the proceeds, use them in the year received to pay the pensions due to retired members in that year. The latter method (called a pay-as-you-go scheme) does not involve the accumulation of assets, the building of a pension *fund*. It is the method used by the government to finance the occupational schemes of civil servants, including the armed forces, police, teachers and the employees of the fire service and National Health Service (and it is also supposed to be the principle underlying the ordinary state pensions). Almost all other occupational pension schemes are based on the first method, the building of a pension fund or, simply 'funding'.

Pension funds are not the only institutions in this mushrooming business, for they are now matched by insurance companies. More specifically, income provision for later life (if not always synonymous with old age) is the distinguishing feature of 'long-term' insurance. Deferred income provision by insurance companies takes two forms. One is the group pensions business, in which small employers typically buy into a group pension fund run by an insurance company, instead of establishing their own pension fund for their employees. It is estimated that group pensions account for as much as one-third of total insurance company business.

The other form of deferred income provision is the more traditional one associated with various types of life insurance policies. The latter vary according to the emphasis they place on the life cover component ('whole of life' policies, which pay the full sum issued on death) or the long-term savings component ('endowment' policies, which may have only negligible life cover). Since the end of the eighteenth century, life policies have been the forerunner of modern earnings-related pension schemes, but traditionally they have been the preserve of the middle classes. Eventually, however, they filtered down the class ladder, so that the Wilson Report (1980) was able to record that four out of five UK households had life cover of some sort and that over 100 million life policies were in operation (implying that a proportion of households held several policies).

In the UK long-term insurance business is transacted by specialised life insurance companies or by composite insurance companies. The latter combine long-term insurance with the general insurance business – they cover your house, car and video recorder with as much care and probity as they cover your life. General insurance has no connection with deferred income provision, and it is relatively small as compared with the magnitude of long-term, life, business.

Although over 500 insurance groups are authorised to write insurance business in Britain, the UK insurance industry displays the same unmistakable trend towards concentration as other financial institutions. Partly as a consequence of a wave of amalgamations between 1956 and 1968, the nine largest insurance companies accounted for 45 per cent of the accumulated assets of the insurance companies by the end of 1978. A recent trend has seen foreign insurance companies buying minority stakes in UK insurance companies, the most noteworthy of which has been the West German Allianz Versicherungs' 29 per cent in Eagle Star. However, some of the larger life companies are protected from outside stakes or takeover bids by their mutual corporate status, which means that formally they are owned by their policy-holders rather than shareholders.

Amassing assets

Pension funds and insurance businesses have two faces. From one side, they offer a benevolent prospect of husbanding the small savings of ordinary individuals; from the other they are seen as the possessors of vast financial assets. The total amount of these assets is shown by the growth of their balance sheets set out in table 5.1. In the 1957–81 quarter-century, the total assets of the investment institutions (including investment and unit trusts) grew by a factor of 19 times to attain a total of £154.2 billion, or 62 per cent of GDP at the end of 1981. The growth rates of both trusts and insurance companies fell short of this aggregate growth, which was boosted by the spectacular expansion of pension funds. From a humble base of £2.1 billion in 1957 (which then only just surpassed total trust assets), pension fund assets had swelled by a multiple of 30 by the end of 1981.

A similar phenomenon is seen by looking at the amount of new funds the institutions have available for investment each year. These investment institutions receive money both from savers and from the income yielded by their existing investments. Having met their various expenses, they use their surplus to acquire additional assets. This annual surplus has increased almost twelve-fold between 1957 and 1981, from £1.2 to £14.6 billion, the latter being divided equally as between insurance companies and pension funds with the trusts contributing only 4 per cent of the total.

Table 5.2 demonstrates that the institutions' net acquisition of assets has taken on formidable proportions but it appears to have its first aggregate decline in 1982. The table also demonstrates how the pension funds' cash flow has slowly but consistently been catching up with that of the insurance companies and even surpassed it in 1980 and 1982.

The rate of growth of pension funds is, therefore, remarkable. Disregarding inflation, it has benefited from two main factors: increases in the number of people belonging to a scheme, and improvements in the value of the pensions to which members are entitled. Expansion of the numbers covered was an important source of growth between 1955 and 1965, with contributions to funds growing by 50 per cent. However, since 1965 the number of participants has been relatively constant, representing about half the employees in the economy, and growth has resulted from

TABLE 5.1   THE INVESTMENT INSTITUTIONS' ASSETS, 1957–1981

	1957	1962	1967	1972	1977	1978	1979	1980	1981
				(at end of year: £ billion)					
Insurance companies	4.9	8.5	12.8	22.9	41.6	46.8	52.2	65.3	74.3
Pension funds	2.1	4.0	6.4	12.0	25.0	31.1	41.0	54.7	63.8
Trusts	1.2	2.6	4.8	10.1	10.0	10.6	11.8	14.5	16.1
Total	8.2	15.1	24.2	45.0	76.6	88.5	105.0	134.5	154.2

Sources: Financial Statistics (London: HMSO); the Wilson Report (1980).

TABLE 5.2 INSTITUTIONS' NET ACQUISITION OF ASSETS, 1963–1982

	1963–67	1967–72	1972–77	1978	1979	1980	1981	1982
					(cash value of transactions; annual averages 1963–79: £ million)			
Insurance companies	678	1121	2602	4856	5954	6013	7640	6649*
Pension funds	411	671	2204	4681	5590	6617	6827	6753
Trusts[†,‡]	142	336	147	273	97	227	674	826
Total	1231	2128	4953	9810	11,641	12,857	15,141	14,228

* Excludes changes in agents' balances and other short term assets.
† Property unit trusts date from March 1966.
‡ The net contribution by investment trusts has been negative in several years since the mid-1970s.

Sources: Financial Statistics (London: HMSO); the Wilson Report (1980).

improvements in the benefits offered to members with the increase in value of contributions that this necessitated.

The reasons for this growth in the numbers covered and in the value of the benefits are more complex. The immediate causes have varied from one period to another. In the 1970s they included the impact of inflation, the desire of employers and employees to achieve pension improvements in lieu of wage rises in times of pay restraint, and the interest of high-salary executives in receiving pension rights instead of salary increases which would be taxed at a higher rate. But underlying the postwar growth of pension funds and the other investment institutions has been the interest of the financial system in stimulating its growth; for their strength has greatly contributed both quantitatively and qualitatively to the operations of financial capital as a whole. The following pages examine how.

Where do the institutions put their money?

Commentators on the financial system in the 1970s paid special attention to the growth of investment institutions. Indeed, concern over this issue was one of the factors behind the establishment of the Wilson Committee, for the question of how these institutions were using their money had become a political issue. What was clear, and was confirmed by the Wilson Committee, was that they were becoming increasingly large holders of ordinary shares in companies and of British government stock. In the two decades following 1957 pension funds and life insurance companies came to be the principal owners of ordinary shares in companies quoted on the Stock Exchange, and the main lenders of money to the government. This picture of institutions owning a major block of shares and holding the purse-strings of the government's borrowing suggests that the institutions are in a position of power over industry and government, which, if true, would make a mockery of democracy. That picture is too crude, but it is sufficient reason for examining more closely the institutions' holdings of assets.

In the previous section we examined the institutions' total holdings of assets; we now turn to their composition. Because the nature of the institutions' liabilities is essentially long-term, they will typically concentrate their investments in assets that, in aggregate, are expected to give a sound long-term return without too great a risk of loss. Their estimate of the future performance of different types of assets will change over time, and the institutions will actively buy and sell assets constantly. The net result of these two parallel activities, the investment of new cash flows and the reshuffling of existing investments, manifests itself in the stock of assets they hold at any one time. But the desire for flexibility, to be able to reshuffle the portfolio, means that 'long-term' investment has a special meaning for the institutions. It does not mean putting funds directly into industrial companies with a commitment to support a long-term project: it means buying shares and bonds that are not going to be repaid in the near future but can be sold on the stock market quickly and easily (or buying other easily marketable assets such as property).

The range of the institutions' assets is overwhelmingly narrow, consisting primarily of holdings of company securities, government securities and property. The balance of other assets is typically small, and will include short-term liquid assets as well as smatterings of more exotic investments such as *objets d'art*. Table 5.3 compares the major assets held by investment institutions at the end of 1957 and 1981. In 1981 just under 50 per cent of their aggregate assets were held in the form of company securities (including ordinary shares principally and also preference shares), a majority of these being in UK companies whose shares are traded on the Stock Exchange. As these are ordinary shares, the institutions, as owners, receive dividends that vary with the company's profits; they also have a right to vote, proportional to their shareholding, on the affairs of the company. A further 21 per cent of

TABLE 5.3 INVESTMENT INSTITUTIONS' HOLDINGS OF ASSETS, 1957 and 1981

	1957		1981	
	£ million	%	£ million	%
Company securities	3637	44.9	76,746	49.8
Government securities	2313	28.6	33,607	21.8
Property	520	6.4	28,017	18.2
Other	1617	20.0	15,717	10.2
Total	8082		154,177	

Sources: Financial Statistics (London: HMSO); the Wilson Report (1980).

institutions' assets were held in British government securities. These are bonds of varying types issued by the government to raise money. The financial institutions that buy them when they are first issued are lending money to the government. They receive interest on the loan, but the bond, and hence the title, to interest may be sold on the Stock Exchange's secondary market to other institutions before the government repays the loan. Finally, 18 per cent of institutions' assets took the form of holdings of property or real estate. The property covers the whole spectrum, from agricultural land to city centre commercial sites.

Industry and commerce, government finance and property are three pillars of British capitalism that have held particular architectural importance in the postwar period. Industry and commerce have suffered a long-term decline in profitability, and their core, manufacturing industry in the UK, has shrunk to proportions that the planners of the new order at the end of the Second World War could never have envisaged. Government finance came to dominate economic and political developments in the 1970s and 1980s following the dramatic rise in the amount of money the government needed to borrow in 1975. But this expansion coincided with the growth of its problems: the interest rate on government bonds, which had reached historic heights, was nevertheless in many years lower than the inflation rate. Meanwhile, property, having attracted the money and expertise of a new breed of capitalists in the 1950s and early 1960s, experienced new boom periods in the 1970s and, despite some years of stagnation, acquired a reputation as a form of investment that could not fail to keep or increase its value in inflationary times.

Given the development of this view of property as the strong asset of our age, while industry, commerce and government finance were problematic, it is hardly surprising that the institutions significantly increased their holdings of property; they trebled from 6 to 18 per cent of total assets between 1957 and 1981. Considering the overhang of government debt from the war and the low or even negative real rate of return on bonds – the rate of interest after allowing for the erosion of money's value by inflation – it is equally unsurprising that the institutions should have reduced their relative dependence on government (including local authority) finance as a home for their money: it fell from 29 to 22 per cent of their assets between 1957 and 1981. What *is* surprising, however, is that, given the much proclaimed problems of British industry and commerce, the pension funds have steadily increased their stake in company securities, having built up their holdings over the period 1957–81 from 44 to 50 per cent of their total assets. Why should such an apparently suicidal switch of activity have occurred? We provide an answer later, but in the meantime note that holdings of company securities cannot be simply identified with holdings in industry and commerce.

The concern that was reflected in the Wilson Committee over where the institutions put their money focused on two possible evils. Some claimed that investment institutions were acquiring too great a weight in British industry and the London stock market, while others maintained that they were diverting too many funds into real estate, fine art or overseas assets and were starving industry of funds. Some argued, not necessarily inconsistently, that sins of both commission and omission were occurring. The question of whether the pension funds and insurance companies have diverted savings abroad has, however, become particularly acute since the abolition in 1979 of all controls over foreign exchange.

Investment and unit trusts have long invested overseas. In 1957, for example, 35 per cent of their total assets consisted of overseas company securities. The comparable figure for pension funds is not known although it is believed to have been negligible, while that for insurance companies amounted to only 3.8 per cent in 1957. Since the abolition of exchange controls, however, pension funds have rapidly expanded their overseas company securities holdings. Their purchases of these securities as a proportion of their total transactions increased three-fold between 1979 and 1981(I), accounting for just under a a quarter (24 per cent) of their transactions in 1981. Since the beginning of 1980 their transactions in overseas ordinary shares, for example, have almost matched, and in one quarter surpassed, transactions of UK ordinary shares. The upshot of all this is that by the end of 1981 overseas company securities made up one-tenth (9.6 per cent) of total pension fund assets. Insurance companies' transactions in overseas company securities have responded less vigorously to the freedom to invest overseas: by the end of 1980 their holdings of overseas shares had increased to only 5.3 per cent of their total assets.

Nearly two years after exchange controls were lifted, a *Financial Times* article under the headline, 'The Stream Becomes a River', commented:

Investors – from large pension funds to individuals with only a small portfolio – are falling over themselves to invest overseas. . . . [The] figures underline the fact that the psychological dam built up during 40 years of exchange controls has finally burst. And while it would be an exaggeration to say that the flood gates have now opened, it is clear that the big UK pension funds and insurance companies are significantly increasing their assets held abroad. . . . The most popular stock markets outside the UK for private and institutional funds appear to be in the Far East and North America. [*Financial Times*, 13 June 1981]

The prognosis behind Arthur Scargill's refusal to endorse the coalworkers' pension fund's investment plan and behind the left-wing critique of the funds is that this stream that became a river will starve British industry of funds. Will the first of the three pillars – industry and commerce, government finance, and property – be replaced by overseas speculation? One view is that the high rates of investment in foreign stock markets after 1979 represent a temporary adjustment taking immediate advantage of abolition, of exchange controls (which itself could turn out to be temporary), but another is that it marks the beginning of a new long-term phase in the export of capital that we discussed in chapter 2.

The Stock Market and venture capital

One of the main criticisms of the investment institutions' provision of finance for industry has been that they have failed to finance the economy's new growth points. If the crises of the 1970s and the depression of the 1980s are the economy's way of clearing the decks for a new spurt, for decades of renewed growth, it is widely believed that the future will lie with industries exploiting the new miracles of bio-engineering, micro-electronics, and information technology. And the critics have argued that the pension funds, insurance companies and related institutions have failed to provide long-term finance to such new enterprises. Precisely because they are new they are untried and risky, and that presents several obstacles.

One is that fund managers, believing real estate, foreign investment, and the 'blue chip' shares of long-established giant enterprises to be safe, will direct funds toward them rather than the untried harbingers of the brave new world. Another is that until recently, the small new companies hoping to exploit particular innovations for all they are worth and thereby become giants have found that their very youth and smallness have prevented them from selling their shares on the stock market.

To have its shares traded on the stock market, and hence to be able to raise money by selling new shares on that market, a company has to sign a 'Listing Agreement' which gives full details of its financial structure and, most importantly, of its profit record over the past five years. It would then have to sell at least 25 per cent of its shares, and usually more, to stock market investors with the result that outsiders could obtain great influence over a company and even take it over at a price which its founders could not predict. As a result, not many of the small companies at the forefront of new industries would issue shares on the stock market.

That need not have prevented pension funds and the other institutions from financing them. They could have advanced money by buying shares privately from the existing shareholders, or they could have given loans directly to finance a new plant. Such 'venture capital' may well have made all the difference between great success and hopeless failure for some new developments. But investment institutions are understandably reluctant to become so directly locked in to a risky venture, or any venture. Indeed, the rules of local authority pension funds generally prevent them from investing more than a small proportion of their portfolios in shares which cannot be traded on the stock market.

Partly in order to overcome this problem, and the danger recognised by the Wilson Committee (1980) that small companies may fail to obtain long-term finance, the Stock Exchange developed a new side to its operations in 1980. It instituted a system known as the Unlisted Securities Market under which small new companies could more easily obtain the right to issue shares which could then be traded. They would have to submit their profit record for only the previous three years, and they would have to make available only one tenth of the company's total shares, thereby enabling the founders and original shareholders to retain a larger and more secure stake in their baby.

This new market has been partially successful in its aims; nearly three years after it was opened more than 140 relatively small companies' shares have been placed on it. Nearly half of those companies have been engaged in the high risk areas of electronics, energy and minerals. Others have held out the promise of profits from bio-engineering, although some have been innovators in a more traditional mould – the founders of Superdrug being innovative only in retailing, and then only in the sense that they applied to drugstore products the discounting supermarket techniques their father had used in selling groceries two decades earlier.

The Unlisted Securities Market has been successful, too, in the sense that it has drawn in the pension funds and other investment institutions. When a company issues its shares, the institutional investors invariably take up as much as three quarters of the number on offer. This, however, has its dark side, too, for it has been one factor which has made the Unlisted Securities Market a godsend for some speculators.

The facts that the companies are themselves small, that they issue only a small proportion of their shares for sale on the market, and that only a small number of these are left over after the investment institutions have taken their stake, means that the share prices are highly susceptible to wild fluctuations. If large numbers of private investors try to obtain shares, their prices rise dramatically because of the small number available. When Superdrug issued its shares in 1983, the price went from 93p to 268p each in the first week. But the small volume traded also means that a few investors who become pessimistic and sell their shares can have a disproportionately large influence on the share price – which can then fall dramatically. And investors' moods are particularly susceptible to pessimism and optimism in such a market where the ventures themselves are risky: two of the earliest companies on the market, Hesketh Motorcycles and Euroflame Wood Stoves, brought a mood of severe doubt to the whole market when their production and marketing hopes failed to be realized.

Thus the Unlisted Securities Market has represented one step toward increasing the ease with which the institutions' money can be tapped by venturesome entrepreneurs in new industries. But it also can be tapped by entrepreneurs whose cleverness lies in making money a long way from the frontiers of new industry, and its inherent instability severely limits this market's potential role. Like all market methods of financing, but to a greater degree than some, this new arrangement is in danger of becoming dominated by speculation. It contrasts unfavourably with financial arrangements which would bring the institutions into a careful assessment of and close partnership with the new centres of industrial growth. The real challenge is to develop such new firm links between the pension funds, insurance companies, and trusts on one hand and industry on the other.

The concentration of ownership

One of the outstanding features of the pensions and insurance institutions today is the concentration of share and bond ownership in their hands. It is easy to quantify, but as we pick our way through the data we have to take care to avoid being blinded by figures. In particular, we need to remember that ownership is not the same as control: the figures may show that ownership is highly concentrated, but control may be dispersed or concentrated in a different pattern, as we shall see later.

The problem of general interest in this chapter is whether the ownership of industry is being concentrated in the hands of the investing institutions; and, although it only tells part of the story, the ownership of company shares and bonds quoted on the Stock Exchange is central to it.

The proportions of UK company shares and their bonds held by insurance companies (including those acquired on the basis of non-life insurance), pension funds and trusts are shown in tables 5.4 and 5.5. The data show that the *aggregate* holdings of the investment institutions completely dominate the market for quoted UK company securities. At the end of 1981 they held almost two-thirds of such bonds (with insurance companies being especially important holders) and over half of company shares (equities). The pension funds alone owned well over one quarter of total shares.

The investment institutions have achieved their domination in the ownership of equities by actively purchasing shares in the stock market while individual shareholders sold theirs. Individual ownership of ordinary shares has shrunk from almost two-thirds (65.8 per cent) in 1957 to an estimated 32 per cent of total shares in issue in 1980 (see the Wilson Report, 1980, Appendices, table 3.67). Since then some evidence has suggested a reversal of the decline in share ownership by persons, a trend that is compatible with the stabilising of institutional ownership since 1979. None the less, this still leaves us with an overall picture of the institutions owning well over 50 per cent of total UK equities and individuals owning perhaps over one-third of the total, with the residual owned by other corporate bodies.

But for several reasons, this concentration of share and bond ownership in the hands of the institutions does not represent the ownership of industry. First, not all industrial companies have

TABLE 5.4 INSTITUTIONAL HOLDINGS OF LISTED UK COMPANY BONDS

	1978		1979		1980		1981	
	£m.	Holdings as % of market value	£m.	Holdings as % of market value	£m.	Holdings as % of market value	£m.	Holdings as % of market value
Insurance companies	2079	37.8	1945	36.8	2092	45.5	2015	42.1
Pension funds	890	16.2	824	15.6	865	18.8	859	18.0
Trusts*	234	4.3	150	2.9	126	2.7	177	3.7
Total institutions*	3203	58.3	2919	55.3	3083	67.0	3051	63.8

* Includes unit trusts' holdings of unlisted company securities.
Source: The Stock Exchange Fact Book (London: The Stock Exchange).

TABLE 5.5 INSTITUTIONAL HOLDINGS OF LISTED UK EQUITIES

| | 1978 | | 1979 | | 1980 | | 1981 | |
	£m.	Holdings as % of market value	£m.	Holdings as % of market value	£m.	Holdings as % of market value	£m.	Holdings as % of market value
Insurance companies	11,376	18.0	12,227	18.3	16,248	18.9	18,744	18.9
Pension funds	15,331	24.2	18,305	27.3	22,846	26.6	27,060	27.2
Trusts*	6298	9.9	5761	8.6	6736	7.8	7913	8.0
Total institutions*	33,005	52.1	36,293	54.2	45,830	53.3	53,717	54.1

* Includes unit trusts' holdings of unlisted equities.
Source: The Stock Exchange Fact Book (London: The Stock Exchange).

shares or bonds quoted on the Stock Exchange, and the very large sector of private (unquoted) industrial or commercial companies like Littlewoods is virtually untouched by institutional investors. Recall that the institutions want to hold marketable assets instead of making a long-term commitment to a particular company, and that effectively precludes investment in private companies. (Although the fact of a share being quoted on the Stock Exchange does not guarantee its marketability, for a large holder may be able to sell its shares only by greatly depressing their price.)

Second, not all the companies in which the institutions hold shares are industrial. Minns (1980) has catalogued the fact that pension funds have tended to invest strongly in the shares of financial companies, building a strong strand in the complex web that binds the banks, investment institutions and other operators in the financial sector to each other. If metaphors could be mixed or a web were not so asexual, the connections within the financial sector could be said to be incestuous; but whatever the morality, a proportion of the shares whose institutional ownership we have commented upon are the equities of financial rather than industrial companies.

Third, ownership of bonds and shares is not the same as ownership of the companies themselves. Bonds are issued by companies as a vehicle for borrowing: their owners are entitled to interest and eventual repayment but not to ownership of the firm. Shares are often considered to be a measure of ownership, each share being regarded as a title to a proportion of the firm's assets. But in the normal course of events they are a title only to a proportion of the firm's net profit, a share in the total dividend if profits are distributed.

Nevertheless, ownership itself is of relatively little interest: concern over whether it has become concentrated is part of a more fundamental concern over whether *control* of industry has become concentrated in the hands of pension funds and insurance companies.

The control of shareholdings

Has the control of industry largely fallen into the hands of a small group of men who carry dull attaché cases and wear sober off-the-peg suits and, in one or two cases, a discreet hint of extravagance in their Gucci shoes or a silk tie? Has it fallen into the hands of the professional managers of the pension and life funds?

Even though the ownership of industrial bonds and equities, at least for quoted companies, is relatively concentrated in the institutions' hands, control does not automatically follow. Bonds do not give control to their owners, although they do exert a general constraint on the company that issued them because their terms generally specify certain conditions that the company must observe (similar to the conditions attached to many bank loans and surveyed in the next chapter). Ownership of ordinary shares does carry voting rights, including the right to vote for and hence change the board of directors. But although the institutions' aggregate holdings of shares constitute a formidable block, each individual institution holds a relatively small proportion of any company's share. In order for them to intervene effectively in a company, the institutional shareholders would have to have a desire not only to intervene, but also to cooperate with each other and pool their weight.

We shall examine those aspects of control shortly, but first it is necessary to judge a different aspect of control: are the institutions themselves in control of their own shareholdings? Do the pension funds, in particular, control the disposition of their wealth between different assets? In large measure they do not, and this has led to a great concentration of control over shareholdings. This concentration occurs in the following way. Some pension funds employ their own managers, but others hand over their management to outsiders – merchant and commercial banks, stockbrokers and others. Because the leading external managers of funds' assets control the assets of a number of pension funds, it follows, as Richard Minns (1980) has clearly demonstrated, that the control of pension fund assets is much more concentrated than is their ownership This makes it much easier for the shareholdings in a particular industrial company to be pooled in order to influence it. Much the same conclusion could be drawn about the control of trusts' assets. To anticipate a little, the external management of the assets of some pension funds (and trusts) facilitates a degree of aggregation of institutional interests in specific companies by banks and other external managers.

There are several ways in which external managers exercise control of the pension funds' assets, and the extent of their freedom to make day-to-day decisions over the funds' investment varies from one type of fund and one type of adviser and manager to another. But the evidence that exists reveals that in general the outside adviser and manager have a great deal of influence over investment decisions. At one extreme, they have effective control over the day-to-day decisions on purchase and sales. Minns concludes from his survey of the 1978 position of pension funds that the first type of outsider – the manager, and in a real sense the controller of pension funds' assets – handled two-thirds (67 per cent) of the assets of pension funds.

Two-thirds of pension fund assets may well be owned by the pension funds in a legal sense, but they were controlled by different institutions. Which were these institutions? Minns calculates that two-thirds of the assets managed by outsiders were managed by banks while a quarter were managed by stockbrokers and a tenth by other organizations. Minns's estimates of the breakdown of external management by type of institution and his emphasis on the predominance of banks have been corroborated by a recent survey of over 200 pension funds (see the *Financial Times*, 5 July 1982). Merchant and clearing banks managed the funds of 59 per cent of surveyed pension schemes at the end of 1981; stockbrokers managed 21 per cent, and other financial institutions 20 per cent of surveyed schemes.

The assets of pension funds are not the only external assets controlled by banks and other financial institutions. Minns (1980) estimated that at the beginning of 1977 banks controlled 40 and 18 per cent of unit and investment trust assets respectively, while insurance companies controlled a further 28 per cent of unit trust assets.

Among investment institutions, insurance companies are unique in that they control all the assets that they own. But even in the case of insurance companies ownership and control diverge, for, as hinted above, insurance companies, through portfolio management, control more funds than they own. Indeed, if one is to judge from the largest insurance company (the Prudential), in future, insurance companies are likely to compete more vigorously for the management of other institutions' funds. The Prudential has reorganised its fund management system so that PPM (Prudential Portfolio Management), its investment management company, has taken over responsibility for Prudential Assurance's (the parent company) £8.3 billion funds in addition to the £1.8 billion unit trust funds it had previously managed. With management responsibility for funds in excess of £10 billion, PPM now ranks as the number one investment management concern in the UK. In addition to managing the Prudential's insurance and unit trust funds, PPM is now competing for the management of US pension funds and UK corporate pension funds. It therefore appears likely that in future insurance companies may mount a stiff challenge to the banks' existing hold over the external management of pension funds.

In the preceding paragraphs we have examined the ownership of equities and other assets by the investment institutions – pension funds, insurance companies and trusts. We have established that for each of these institutions control over equities diverges from their ownership. Pension funds and trusts control a much smaller proportion of equities than they own, while insurance companies control rather more than they own. Through management of a large part of the assets of pension funds and trusts, they control a sizeable proportion of UK equities despite their minimal level of ownership of such assets.

In table 5.6 we use Minns's (1980) assumptions to calculate the divergence between ownership and control of UK equities in 1980. Banks and insurance companies (and, to a lesser extent, some larger pension funds) emerge as the unequivocal controllers of UK equities. The remarkable feature is that money derived in large part from the pensions business has been accumulated over the years under the control of banks and insurance companies, and has contributed to the fact that those institutions together controlled some 42 per cent of all equities (by value) on the Stock Exchange in 1980. Together with the 9 per cent of shares that remained under the control of internally managed pension funds, the total stock market stake under the control of the trinity amounted to more than half (51 per cent) of the shares quoted in 1980.

These figures certainly suggest a concentration of the control of quoted companies' shares in the hands of banks, insurance com-

TABLE 5.6 OWNERSHIP AND CONTROL OF LISTED UK EQUITIES, 1980

	Ownership (%)	*Control (%)*
Banks	2	22
Insurance companies	19	20
Pension funds	27	9
Trusts	8	5
Total	56	56

Source: Financial Statistics (London: HMSO); author's calculations.

panies and pension funds; a holy trinity. But is this equivalent to a concentration of *power*? What does the control of shares imply?

The control of companies?

The institutions that we have considered to be in a controlling position control shares in the sense that they have the authority to buy and sell them; but this, by itself, does not confer power over the activities of the companies whose shares are held.

For any group of financial institutions to exercise control over a company, it would have to capture at least one of two levers: either it would have to control the availability and terms of funds to the company, or it would have to be able to control the membership of the board of directors. Control of shares quoted on the stock market does not immediately deliver control of either lever. Regarding the availability of funds, when institutions buy shares on the Stock Exchange they are not, generally, supplying money to the companies that issued the shares. Instead, they are buying them from another shareholder, and the shares themselves represent money that was subscribed to the company in the past – perhaps as long as a century before. Regarding the control of appointments to the board of directors, institutions generally have voting rights in proportion to their holdings of ordinary shares, but this does not necessarily mean that they wield effective power in the boardroom. In most companies, the appointment of the directors is not generally a contentious matter where shareholders' votes count; in addition, the proportion of votes in any one company that any one institution can muster is low, and it may prove difficult to obtain concerted action between institutions holding a large proportion between them. Nevertheless, it would be wrong to leap from saying that the control of shares does not *automatically* and *directly* confer power to saying that it confers no power.

The institutions' control of a high proportion of shares does give them a two-fold influence over the availability and terms of funds for the companies whose shares they own. First, it has an indirect influence through its effect upon the price of a company's shares. If institutions particularly favour some companies or sectors rather than others the pressure of their demand for those shares may push up their price (relative to the companies' profits or dividends); and that makes it easier for those companies to raise money by issuing new shares, since investors as a whole are willing to buy them at a high price reflecting the high price of existing shares. Second, the institutions' control of large holdings of existing shares gives them an even more direct influence over the terms upon which firms may raise money by issuing new shares. The most significant method of issuing new shares is, since the 1960s, by a 'rights issue' or, in other words, the offer of new shares to existing holders; since the institutions have much significance within that group, their view on the price and terms on which the new shares are offered has a determining influence.

Moreover, the institutions' importance in holding and managing shares is a basis for a *potential* control over the direction and management over a company even though it does not automatically imply that control is exercised. The concentration of control over large blocks of shares in the hands of a small number of banks, insurance companies and pension funds simplifies the coordination problems that would exist under a more diffuse system of control. Despite the dispersion of the ownership of UK shares, individual members of the 'holy trinity' (and banks and insurance companies in particular), in their portfolio management function, can mobilise control over blocks of shares far in excess of what they legally own. In other words, their portfolio management is a crucial vehicle for aggregating the equity interests associated with the dispersed ownership of shares. This aggregation occurs as part of their day-to-day operations, but in addition investment institutions consciously aggregate control over various blocks of shares in specific instances through the mechanisms of various institutional committees. Thus insurance companies, pension funds and trusts participate in Investment Protection Committees (IPCs), Institutional Shareholders' Committees (ISCs) and in various *ad hoc* committees formed for the furtherance of their interests in specific enterprises.

Insurance companies, pension funds and unit trusts each have an established IPC made up of senior investment managers and staffed by a permanent secretariat. The Wilson Report (1980, pp. 252–3) provides some information on the oldest IPC – the Insurance IPC. This committee examined an average of about 200 cases a year during the 1970s. Between 5 and 10 per cent were concerned with a management problem and rather more with the voting rights of shareholders and consultation on changes in the structure of a company, while the majority dealt with technical issues of lending contracts and capital rearrangements. In sum, this information hardly suggests that the institutions actively intervene in the affairs of companies despite having at their disposal an established mechanism.

Moreover, the pension funds, insurance companies, trusts and banks that control such large quantities of shares rarely intervene in the 'real' activities of the companies. Except in unusual circumstances, they stand aside from decisions on the production, location, rationalisation and expansion of plant and sales. But they do have a greater interest in companies' financial structure – the dividends they pay, the proportions of shares and bonds they have issued, the terms of a 'rights issue' of new shares and, particularly, the terms of a takeover bid. These financial matters directly affect the institutions' investments, and although their interventions in such company affairs are relatively rare (probably because companies frame their decisions to satisfy the institutions' needs), almost all of them do concern such financial matters.

The institutions may organise or become involved in a boardroom coup if their financial interests are sufficiently jeopardised, but their intervention in financial affairs has been particularly prominent when companies in which they hold shares have been taken over. Richard Minns (1982b) notes their involvement in 'dawn raid' takeovers, suggests that this demonstrates the pension funds' concern with short-term profits rather than long-term commitment to investing in growth (despite their claim to invest for the long-term provision of pensions), and concludes that the dawn raids were facilitated by the fact that, as we have seen, control of shareholdings is more highly concentrated than their ownership:

> in 1980–81 there were over 40 'dawn raids' and 'sudden death' takeovers. In a dawn raid a stockbroker will ring up a few pension funds and insurance companies and ask if they want to sell their shares in a certain company at 'a premium': this means the stockbroker has a buyer willing to pay, say, £1.50 for a share worth £1. The raids are over in a matter of minutes because the stockbroker has only got to ring a handful of institutions to get a large number of shares. . . . If only institutions did not sell out so quickly they could get a lot more for their shares, and they could also take a more reflective view about the future of the company affected. . . .
>
> It could reasonably be argued that these activities were facilitated by the concentration of fund management. . . . A stockbroker would find it almost impossible to contact thousands of individual holders to offer to buy their shares at an attractive price. But with far fewer institutional holders, and with investment managers, such as banks, effectively coordinating the decisions of many pension

funds and unit trusts, the whole process is much more straightforward. In the dawn raid on Eagle Star Insurance, stockbrokers
Rowe and Pitman instructed 30 staff to make three phone calls each
to a total of 90 institutions. As a result, 14.9 per cent of the shares
were bought in minutes at a cost of £59.2 million. [Minns, 1982b,
pp. 18–19]

Dawn raids epitomise the divergence between the control of
shares and the control of companies. The former facilitates rapid
changes in the ownership of companies' shares, for example
through dawn raids. The institutions' participation in dawn raids
also highlights their lack of concern with or abrogation of the
responsibility for the control of companies even if by early 1983 the
institutions appeared less disposed towards selling in dawn raids.

Conclusion: a sleeping giant?

The institutional investors, together with the banks that control
much of their asset portfolios, dominate the Stock Exchange holding of shares and bonds in UK companies, but the explicit use of the
power that this could confer has been limited to relatively few
instances of direct intervention in financial decisions and of
activities facilitating takeovers. However, this does not mean that
the giant is completely asleep.

First, if it is sleeping it has one eye open. We would not expect to
find evidence of much explicit intervention in companies' financial
decisions, for intervention would occur only if control were slip-
ping. The most effective influence occurs through companies
knowing they always have to satisfy these investors and thus formu-
late their policies appropriately to ensure that the watching sleeper
stays asleep.

Second, the industrial crisis has led to the giant being forced out
of bed. About ten of the larger institutions (such as the Prudential,
M and G, and the pension funds of the Post Office and National
Coal Board) have become more directly involved in the restructuring of industry under the lead, or prodding, of the Bank of
England. In some ways they have little option, for their shareholdings in the major companies are so large, and (apart from foreign
investment) there are so few alternative homes for their money,
that they have to be concerned to assist in rebuilding the profitability of major companies rocked by the slump.

The extent to which the institutional investors have become

'locked in' to their shareholdings, combined with the prodding given by the Bank of England-led 'industrial Lifeboat', has caused the pension funds, trusts and insurance companies to intervene more frequently, or at least more publicly, in the management of firms and not merely on purely financial matters. They still rely on the old claim of British bankers and financiers – 'we leave the solution of industrial problems to the industrialists themselves' – to ensure that they are very rarely involved in forcing through decisions about the firms' physical operations, but to a greater extent than before they now take a hand in choosing the firms' management itself. Two cases exemplify the trend.

When the sales and profits of the asbestos manufacturers, Turner and Newall, were hit by public exposure of the health hazards of asbestos and by a potential liability to pay damages to workers who had suffered the consequences of asbestos dust, the investment institutions could not recoup their money by selling their shares. The Prudential and the others took the problem in hand by installing a new man with a singularly inappropriate name, Sir Francis Tombs, to revamp the firm and attempt to raise profits. Similarly, when the sprawling Rank Organisation, whose recent strength had been built on profits from Xerox machines, lost its dynamism and glamour, the Prudential stepped in to bring in a management that could turn the company round. After profits had fallen sharply and the dividend was cut in 1982, several of the institutional shareholders got down to 'doing some work on the [Rank] group', as Mr Jim Findlay of the Prudential subsequently put it (*Financial Times*, 18 March 1983). Under the leadership of the Prudential, institutions that between them controlled 25 per cent of Rank's shares had talks with Rank from February 1983. The result of this external pressure was that, by the annual general meeting in March the powerful group president, Sir John Davies, had agreed to resign and the mandatory retirement age for directors was lowered (from 73 to 70!), thereby clearing the decks of the old guard. The institutions had forced the board to seek a new vice-chairman 'with the specific responsibility of reassessing the company's objectives and strategy', a person who would come to assume overall responsibility. The Prudential's prudence had achieved a result in the boardroom. Having decided that attack was the best form of defence, the intervention in Rank may signal a new phase in the use of institutional investors' power over industry. But it has yet to be seen whether boardroom changes are enough to produce changes in management decisions at the workface.

Whether the investment institutions use their power or not, a fundamental problem is their responsibility and accountability. Insurance companies and trusts are as accountable as any firm is under company law. That may not be adequate considering the power they have to affect the economy and people's lives, but pension funds are even less accountable. Both the terms on which they provide pensions (including the fact that most members lose pension rights when they change jobs) and the way in which they dispose of their assets and can influence the economy are matters of public concern. Yet they have grown up under archaic trust laws so that they are neither accountable to their members or the public, nor even have to publish or disclose full details of their operations.

The secrecy and autocratic power of pension funds has become a scandal to the extent that the *Financial Times* argued: 'it is essential that pension fund accounts and actuarial reports should be available not just to the members but to the public. Given the size and importance of the pension funds in the economy, wider accountability is justified on more fundamental grounds' (*Financial Times*, 28 February 1983).

No doubt Arthur Scargill would agree. But his action in vetoing the National Coal Board fund's investment plan suggests he thinks that accountability alone is not enough; there has to be stronger control over what the funds do.

6

Banking on the City

In February 1983 Midland Bank led a syndicate of 13 prestigious international banks in advancing a $12.6 million loan. In normal circumstances such a loan would have passed unnoticed, for the sum of $12.6 million is hardly conspicuous by the standards of the Euromarkets. What was unusual about this loan is not that it was to finance the purchase by Air Jamaica of two A-300 Airbuses, but rather that this was the second occasion on which the Midland had helped to finance the purchase of these same aircraft. Only three years earlier the Midland was the leading bank in the syndicate that financed the original purchases of these A-300 Airbuses by Laker Airways. When in December 1982 Laker became the most celebrated casualty of the current recession, Midland, which had put in the receiver, was left holding the three Airbuses.

The fate of Laker Airways seems genuinely to have captured the imagination not only of those inclined towards *wanderlust* and those who supported Laker's own buccaneering *laissez-faire* attitude, but of the public in general. The bankruptcy had been a spectacular media event. It could not fail to be, for Freddie Laker had built the company's image on his own personality and on his claim to be the people's champion against the system, so bankruptcy had all the necessary ingredients of human interest and big money. But it also highlighted the peculiar nature of the relations between banks and industry and commerce, the peculiarities that are at the heart of the question of whether banks exert power over industry.

Two elements stand out. On the one hand, banks' power to close firms overnight by calling in the receiver, a power they have used on a growing scale, was exhibited when Laker was closed and airliners turned back in mid-flight. On the other hand, banks' frequent failure to use their power to affect the operation of a firm while it is still alive was exhibited in an extreme form. The banks financed Laker, putting in much more money than the owners (Laker and his former wife) and allowing the firm to expand even though competition for passengers, fluctuations in exchange rates and interest rates and the variability of oil prices made the business extremely risky; and they did so while leaving the business of management to Sir Freddie instead of taking a hand themselves. Each of these elements has characterised banks' relations with industry in general, and each has increasingly become controversial. In the case of Laker, the controversy was heightened by the fact that the banks appeared to land on all fours, while their action and inaction seemed to have contributed to holidaymakers and employees alike shedding tears on television.

Laker was a trading company rather than a representative of Britain's manufacturing heartland. It is manufacturing industry that has borne the brunt of the recession, although the insolvencies of medium-sized industrial companies have not fired the public imagination in a similar fashion to Laker even when they are steeped in controversy. When in April 1982 Stone-Platt Industries was placed in receivership the news did not seem to filter past the financial pages of the quality daily and Sunday newspapers. This was despite the fact that it was a highly contentious affair, with two major institutional shareholders breaking rank and being seen publicly to criticise the banks for being overly hasty. Moreover, the chairman of Stone-Platt made a public statement that was openly critical of City banks and institutions and of the existing arrangements for enabling companies to extricate themselves from financial difficulties.

Other manufacturing victims of the crisis included all the major British toy firms (Airfix, Berwick Timpo, Dumbee-Combex-Marx and Lesney) and the Sheffield cutlery firm, Viners. In all of these instances the banks' status as creditors with security has enabled them to pull the plug on companies experiencing financial difficulties. In this chapter we look at the power banks have over industry and whether it is always exercised. This question will be raised in a general form in chapter 8 through a discussion of the critics of a money trust and the theorists of finance capital, who mainly were concerned with the power that banks had through owning industrial shares (as in Germany) or through controlling the disposition of pension funds' stock market investments. Here we look at a different aspect, the power that banks exercise over companies through lending to them.

The questions have been made acute by the difficulties firms found themselves in as the world economy went into crisis, and the two problems highlighted by the Laker collapse are the central ones. What is the basis of banks' increasingly used power to call in the receiver and determine a company's life or death? And to what extent do banks' exercise their potential power to influence the running of firms, to steer them towards increased profitability? In order to answer the questions we first have to describe the nature of banking in Britain.

Balancing the books

Banks in the UK are very varied and they share the distinguishing mark of banks everywhere: their business is financial. Whereas an industrial or commercial firm's balance sheet shows real assets – plant and machinery, inventories and work in progress – banks' assets, apart from the branch and headquarters buildings they own, are almost entirely monetary. They consist of cash and short-term loans (including one-day and overnight loans) that are almost as liquid; loans to governments, firms, people and other financial institutions in the form of bonds and bills; and other loans to such borrowers through overdrafts and medium-term credits. On the other side of the balance sheet, banks' liabilities are very largely deposits held by their customers in current accounts, deposit accounts or large (wholesale) deposits made when the customer buys a certificate of deposit (CD) or borrows from other banks in the interbank market.

It is this wholly financial nature of banks that makes the question of their potential control of industry interesting and sometimes emotional. A reaction often felt very sincerely by long-term employees of a company shut by the bank's action is that there is some injustice, some asymmetry, about a bank, which has 'only put money in', being able to determine the life or death of a company into which 'we have put our labour'.

The balance sheet of UK banks given in table 6.1 does more than indicate that their business is money and finance: it also shows quite forcefully that they, like the City of London as a whole, play a major international role, for if we distinguish sterling from (foreign) currency deposits and loans we find the latter are surprisingly high. This balance sheet may look rather complex, but we should not allow that to discourage us from noting some of its

TABLE 6.1 UK BANKS' BALANCE SHEET, DECEMBER 1982

Liabilities	%	Assets	%
Currency deposits*	43.3	Currency loans and advances	51.6
Interbank currency deposits and CDs[†]	26.3	Sterling loans and advances	17.6
Sterling deposits	17.0	Interbank currency loans and CDs	16.1
Interbank sterling deposits and CDs	8.0	Interbank sterling loans and CDs	7.4
Other sterling liabilities	4.4	Sterling notes and coins	0.3
Other currency liabilities	1.0	Other sterling assets	4.3
		Other currency assets	2.7

* The adjective 'currency' means 'foreign currency'.
† Certificates of deposit.
Source: Bank of England Quarterly Bulletin.

salient features. Perhaps the most striking is that foreign currency items make up about 70 per cent of both the liabilities and assets of banks in the UK. This sets banks apart from other sectors of the UK economy in terms of degree of internationalisation, which is remarkable even by the standards of other financial institutions such as pension funds, insurance companies or building societies. A second feature is that interbank transactions and certificates of deposit form an important component of total foreign currency assets; on the liabilities side, foreign currency deposits far exceed total sterling deposits. This feature is related to the manner in which we have chosen to present the balance sheet. Frequently, interbank transactions are consolidated or netted out instead of being presented on both sides of the balance sheet. The size of interbank transactions and CDs illustrates the high degree of inter-dependence within the banking sector, a topic we discussed in chapter 3. In this connection banks' other liabilities consist mainly of their shareholders' funds. These are continuously being built up both by raising new share capital on the Stock Exchange and by adding retained profits to reserves and they form the banks' last line of defence in the event of large losses.

The balance sheet of banks in the UK has highlighted two obvious features about banks' assets and liabilities by presenting the balance sheet in a particular way. Other methods of presentation highlight different features. Given the predominance of foreign currency assets and liabilities, one may have guessed that this implies an important role for overseas transactions, which is indeed the case. Excluding the inter-bank assets and liabilities, overseas firms', individuals' and governments' currency deposits and lending comprised 75 and 74 per cent respectively of UK banks' liabilities and assets at the end of 1982. This is yet another index of the City's *entrepôt* role in international banking; its position as an enclave within Britain, acting as a stopover on international credit's flight around the world.

The large volume of deposits denominated in dollars, yen, marks and so on does not quite square with our usual image of British banks. Surely all those people queuing on a Friday afternoon with their cheque cards to draw money to tide them over the weekend don't hold dollar deposits? No, indeed; but banks in Britain conduct many types of business, the distinction between wholesale and retail banking being the sharpest dividing line.

The High Street versus Lombard Street

The range of banks operating in the UK is enormous. They cover a spectrum from a single office of an overseas bank to a bank like National Girobank, which operates through some 21,000 post offices. This immediately raises the question of the definition of a bank in the UK. Until the 1979 Banking Act no proper legal definition of a bank existed in Britain. Under the new Act the Bank of England divides deposit taking institutions into:

(a) those that, according to the Bank's criteria, supply the full range of banking services;
(b) those that do not supply the full range of banking services.

Only the former are legally allowed to call themselves 'banks', the latter being rather cumbersomly designated 'licensed deposit-takers' (LDTs). Despite the Bank's arguments to the contrary, a two-tiered banking sector has emerged in which LDTs are treated as second-class banks. Nevertheless, we do not distinguish between legally defined 'banks' and licensed deposit-takers, and we employ the term 'bank' to cover both types of institutions.

For data purposes the Bank of England lists the following institutions as contributing to banking statistics, or those of the monetary sector, to give it its full title. They include only those banks that have agreed to maintain common cash reserve ratios, plus the Bank of England Banking Department and the discount houses and brokers. For this reason some 200 offices of the overseas banks are excluded from the officially defined monetary sector. Table 6.2 shows the number and total assets of the major types of recognised banks as at February 1983. This system of classification is based partly on function and partly on ownership, though there is a degree of overlap between the major categories.

Retail banking

An important functional distinction, irrespective of who owns the banks, is that between retail and wholesale banking. The former corresponds with the popular notion of holding an account at your local High Street branch, obtaining the occasional overdraft from your friendly manager and receiving and writing out cheques for the settlement of bills. It is that banking business that is concerned

TABLE 6.2   BANKING INSTITUTIONS IN THE UNITED
KINGDOM MONETARY SECTOR, FEBRUARY 1983

	Number of banks	Liabilities or total assets (£ billion)
Clearing banks		
London	6	96.4
Scottish	3	11.3
Northern Ireland	4	2.2
Total clearing banks	13	109.9
Other British banks		
Accepting houses	36	20.8
Discount houses and brokers	11	5.6
Other British	246	84.4
Total other British banks	293	110.8
Overseas banks		
American	65	97.8
Japanese	25	108.5
Consortium	25	17.2
Other overseas banks	236	125.9
Total overseas banks	351	349.4
Total in the UK	657*	570.1

* Some 54 banks are Channel Islands or Isle of Man subsidiaries of City-based banks.
Source: Bank of England Quarterly Bulletin; own calculations.

with money withdrawal and transmission services for both individuals and companies, and which is dominated by the Big Four
clearing banks (Barclays, Lloyds, Midland and Nat West), other
clearing banks and a handful of other banking groups including the
Co-op, National Girobank and the Trustee Savings Banks (TSBs).
    Although 40 per cent of adults do not have bank accounts (the
Great British Unbanked, according to bankers, who would like
them to be banked, as, say, Americans), the Big Four clearing
banks are recognised by everyone, for their branches are everywhere, but even banks with different names are owned by them.

Nat West own Coutts (the smallest member of the London clearing banks) and Ulster Bank, and also 40 per cent of Yorkshire Bank ('other British banks') and 4.7 per cent of the large insurance company, Commercial Union. Barclays holds 35 per cent of the equity of the Bank of Scotland and 32 per cent of Yorkshire Bank. Midland owns the Clydesdale Bank and Northern Bank (Northern Ireland clearer) and 15.9 per cent of Standard Chartered Bank ('other British banks'). Lloyds owns 16.4 per cent of Royal Bank of Scotland Group (which in turn owns the other London clearing bank, Williams and Glyn's), 21 per cent of Grindlays Bank ('other British banks') and 20 per cent of Yorkshire Bank. To sum up, the Big Four either wholly own or have a stake in all the other clearing banks with the exception of the two smaller Northern Ireland clearers registered in the Republic of Ireland (Allied Irish Banks and Bank of Ireland). This is not to deny the innovative contribution of the Scottish clearers. Branch banking was a Scottish innovation; the Royal Bank pioneered the now-famous overdraft; and more recently Scottish banks have been to the forefront in the development of automatic telling services (plastic and banking).

Retail deposits account for between half to three-quarters of the clearers' sterling liabilities. In turn, current accounts on which the holder earns no interest comprise about one half of their retail deposits. Much of this is the deposits of persons rather than firms, whereas personal lending does not dominate the banks' assets – although one of the clearers' responses to overseas bank competition in the UK during the 1970s has been to increase the share of retail loans or consumer credit in their portfolios by, for example, their attack on the mortgage market. In addition to their retail business with the personal sector, the clearers play an important role for UK firms. Because the clearers operate much of the country's system of payments – settling cheques and bills – virtually all companies in the UK have a bank account with at least one of the clearers. Traditionally, the clearing banks have lent to companies by giving them overdrafts, but in recent years they have shifted towards other ways of lending money to companies.

The distinction between lending to firms by overdraft as opposed to other means has considerable significance for the issues we shall look at in chapter 8, for it can affect the degree of influence that banks have over industry and commerce. We shall return to this again soon to look at it from that perspective, but for the present the thing to note is that overdraft lending is very much retail in character. Although the sums can mount up (a football club's overdraft of a million pounds or so is not large by corporate standards), overdrafts are small-scale compared with the size of other types of loans, and they depend on a customer–banker relationship not unlike that between a family and the local retail shop. The amount borrowed fluctuates according to need (up to a prearranged limit) and interest is charged only on the amount used. They may or may not be secured by a collateral of some sort. Recently, however, the clearing banks have attempted to increase their wholesale lending to companies. This involves lending (possibly in foreign currencies) very large sums, for fixed terms and often in a definite, rather than variable, amount.

The clearing bankers, then, are becoming less like giant retailers, and that is true, too, for the way in which they raise their money. Up to a half of their funds come not from retail deposits – current accounts, deposit accounts and so on – but from large tranches of loans made to the bank by firms and other banks. The clearers' involvement in the big, wholesale, end of banking is also marked by the fact that they own subsidiaries for which this is the main type of business: each of the Big Four has a fully owned international subsidiary while three are the sole owners of merchant banks and have stakes in consortium banks. The latter are banks that are owned by a consortium of other banks and operate in the wholesale international (Eurodollar) markets.

Wholesale banking

But now we have introduced the other world of wholesale banking, the banking business that is associated more with Lombard Street and other City locations than with the local High Street. Wholesale banking is genuinely a world of big business, where the only membership requirement is the size of the deal countenanced. In today's wholesale markets this will range from the £100,000 minimum deposit accepted in these markets to jumbo loans of up to $4 billion (the size of a loan that France raised in the Euromarkets in 1982). Whereas High Street retail deposits are accepted by the clearing banks, wholesale banks bid competitively to purchase wholesale deposits in the specialised money markets. They bid for money as certificates of deposit or as inter-bank loans by offering competitive interest rates in fast-moving telex and telephone deals. When the youngsters in the money market rooms of the banks buy and sell these large chunks of short-term credit they talk telephone numbers in more senses than one.

The result of this bidding process has on occasions driven up the interest rates on very short-term (overnight) wholesale deposits to well in excess of an annualised rate of 100 per cent while intervention by the Bank of France pushed interest rates on Eurofranc deposits to the astonishing annualised rate of 5000 per cent in March 1983. Given the size of the deals involved, it is not surprising to find that companies (including other banks) and institutions rather than individuals are the usual suppliers of funds in these wholesale markets, and that these markets are also the major source of medium-term loan facilities to companies. In the case of both deposits and term loan facilities, the companies involved are likely to be among those included in *The Times* '1000' list of top British industrial and commercial companies.

We have already mentioned that the clearing banks own a range of wholesale subsidiaries. Barclays has two, Barclays Merchant Bank and Barclays Bank International; Lloyds has LABCO (a wholesale subsidiary which is now destined to be assimilated into the parent company) and Lloyds Bank International; Midland owns Samuel Montague (an accepting house) and Midland Bank International; while Nat West can boast of County Bank (a merchant bank) and International Westminster Bank. While the image of sleepy giants may apply to the Big Four's retail business, it can hardly be said to ring true for their wholesale subsidiaries, most of which are highly competititve within their specialised fields. These subsidiaries are included in the 'other British banks' category presented in table 6.2. This category additionally includes a dozen discount houses and brokers (which engage in wholesale trading in short-term bills and bonds), approximately 40 offshore subsidiaries of British banks in tax havens such as the Isle of Man or Channel Islands, 33 accepting houses or merchant banks, 2 ex-colonial banks (Hongkong and Shanghai and Standard Chartered) and a handful of retail deposit banks such as the Yorkshire Bank, which is jointly owned by the clearing banks.

Of all of these types of banks one of the most interesting and powerful is the group of 33 *merchant banks*. As in most walks of City life hierarchy is the order of the day, for these 33 merchant banks divide into 17 ordinary merchant banks and the 16 *accepting houses*, which are privileged with membership of the Accepting Houses Committee (AHC), described by some as the City of London's smartest club.

The accepting houses' main business is acceptance credits (accepting bills of exchange), corporate finance and investment or fund management. Until August 1981 the accepting houses comprised more than half of the 32 names on what has been described as one of the 'City of London's most arcane lists', namely the small circle of acceptors of commercial bills eligible for rediscount at the finest rates of interest at the Bank of England. The others were comprised of mainly the clearers and British overseas and Commonwealth banks but included one 'Bank of England customer of long standing', Ogilvy, Gillanders & Co., which is not even a bank but a merchanting business. As well as the inevitable prestige associated with it, eligibility gave the accepting houses and others on the list a price advantage over banks not on the list. In August 1981 the Bank of England finally recognised the anomaly of this situation and extended the privileged circle by adding selected overseas banks to its new list of 96 eligible banks.

Most larger UK companies employ a merchant bank adviser, though this lucrative and powerful role, 'the corporate finance function', is dominated by just four accepting houses – Hill Samuel, S. G. Warburg, Morgan Grenfell and Schroder Wagg. They advise companies especially with respect to changes in their financial structure such as takeovers, new share issues and, more recently, financial restructuring. The final important function of merchant banks is investment management on behalf of clients, in particular pension funds. The most recent entrant into the AHC (Robert Fleming) is reputed to have the largest investment portfolio of all the accepting houses. Both of these functions mean that accepting houses have a significance in influencing the affairs of companies far beyond that suggested by the size of their balance sheets since the largest accepting house, Schroder Wagg, had deposits of only $4.8 billion at the end of 1982 (*Banker*, June 1983).

The ownership structure of merchant banks and accepting houses is quite interesting, and probably has provided the basis of claims that it is no longer valid to see banking, commercial and industrial companies as separate entities. Three accepting houses are at present owned by industrial holding companies: Charterhouse Japhet, Guinness Mahon, and Lazards. The latter is part of the S. Pearson Group which publishes Penguin Books and the *Financial Times*. Recently, Arbuthnot Latham has been excluded from the AHC following its takeover by the US chemicals group, Dow. The insurance broker Willis Faber has a 21 per cent stake in Morgan Grenfell, and Eagle Star has a 16 per cent holding in Hill Samuel through its associate, the Philip Hill Investment Trust. Singer and Friedlander used to be part of the insurance broker (T. Bowring) but was sold to the shipping group European Ferries in 1980 following the US takeover of Bowring. The Midland is the only clearer that owns an accepting house (Samuel Montague), although Bank of Scotland, Barclays and Nat West each has a wholly owned merchant bank subsidiary. Thus we see that accepting houses have ownership links with banks, other financial companies and industrial and commercial companies. One reason for this is their specialist nature (investment banking), which potentially could be of strategic use to any sector of capital. But such ownership links do not validate claims that the interests of banks and other companies are coalescing, as implied by the idea of finance capital which we examine in chapter 8.

The other major group of wholesale banks are those categorised as '*overseas banks*' in table 6.2, even if a few of them like Citibank have limited retail outlets. Numerically and in terms of total assets, the 247 overseas banks recognised by the Bank of England are the dominant group among UK-based banks, and their banking business is almost entirely wholesale in nature. Historically, large banks established branches in London to service the international financing needs of their indigenous company clients. Since London was the world's leading financial centre until the outbreak of the First World War its choice as an international centre by overseas banks was relatively straightforward. However, London lost its financial pre-eminence in the interwar period, so that even by 1959 the Radcliffe Report could identify the presence of only 45 overseas banks in London. The dramatic increase since then in the numbers of overseas banks with London branches has paralleled the equally dramatic growth in the Euromarkets and the re-establishment of London's position as a leading world financial centre.

The presence of overseas banks in London has contributed to the internationalisation of production and trade in two directions. On the one hand, the presence of a sizeable group of Japanese banks in London can promote the establishment of other Japanese companies in the UK and Ireland or, through trade finance, imports of Japanese-produced goods to the UK. Conversely, the aggregate presence of so many overseas banks in London increases the potential of UK companies to develop their international business both through the acquisition or establishment of overseas units and through exports.

Numerically and in terms of total assets, US banks were by far the most significant group of overseas banks in London but since

1982 the total assets of Japanese banks have exceeded those of American banks. Other important groups are consortium banks, while Arab banks have expanded rapidly in recent years.

The *consortium banks* mushroomed in the 1960s and 1970s as a particular form of the international banks. They were formed by a limited number of existing banks cooperating to establish a new jointly owned banking company. Their operations are totally wholesale in nature, and in many cases they were geared towards a specialised market; for example, the Nordic Bank specialises in the Scandinavian market. Although we have classified consortium banks as part of the overseas banks, it should be noted that British banks participate in many consortia. Until the late 1970s Midland relied largely on consortium banks in its internationalisation strategy. The fact that it has since acquired overseas banks abroad directly indicates some dissatisfaction with the consortium concept. Further evidence of this is provided by the acquisition in 1981 of Orion Bank (one of the more successful consortia) by one of its participating banks, the Royal Bank of Canada.

American banks in London are the current largest single group of overseas banks in the UK, representing 59 separate banking groups. They have enjoyed a long tradition in the City. In 1887 the Jarvis Conklin Trust Company (a predecessor of Chase Manhattan) established in the City what proved to be the first foreign branch of an American commercial bank. Between 1887 and 1931 a further five large US banks opened offices in London. The objective of all these banks was to service US subsidiaries located in the UK, Europe, the Middle East and Africa and to finance international trade. A second wave of large and medium-sized banks flocked to London during the decade following the commencement of the Euromarkets in 1958. In that decade US banks expanded the range of their services to medium-term finance for multinational companies and syndicated (group) loans for governments and large-scale investment projects. A final group of smaller regional US banks began arriving in London from 1968 onwards.

Since the late 1960s US banks have continued to play an active role in the Eurodollar markets, and an active role in sterling business, particularly following the introduction of a more liberal banking environment through 'Competition and Credit Control' in 1971.

American banks in London are wholesale banks *par excellence*, since the costs of building of an extensive retail branch network in the UK would be prohibitive. The alternative to constructing a new branch network from scratch would be to acquire a British bank with its existing branch network. Indeed, this was what both Standard Chartered and the Hongkong and Shanghai attempted to accomplish with their contested bids for the Royal Bank of Scotland in 1981. In the event, the Monopolies Commission's rejection of both bids scuppered the UK retail banking ambitions not only of the two ex-colonial banks but also of some of the larger US banks. The latter had been hoping to emulate in the UK what the British clearing banks had achieved in the United States through their acquisition of large banks with retail networks. The outstanding example is Midland, which in 1982 acquired a majority stake in Crocker National, the fourteenth largest US commercial bank.

Even if the UK retail banking ambition of US banks has been thwarted for the moment, this has not impeded their progress in capturing several profitable areas of bank lending. By carefully selecting and targeting their customers, the invasion of American banks into the business of lending to British business has meant they have become major lenders to commodity dealing firms, finance houses, leasing companies, shipping, North Sea Oil, electronics and aerospace industries. Most of these sectors are either financial or related to modern technologically based industry. In these areas the US banks have provided stiff competition to the clearing banks even if this stems principally from the half dozen largest US commercial banks – BankAmerica, Citibank, Chase, Morgan Guaranty, Manufacturers Hanover and Bankers Trust.

The American banks' invasion is significant not only because of the Ivy League suits and button-down collars it has brought to the City's restaurants; bankers' familiarity with airport lounges means that they tend to dress alike nowadays. Nor does it really matter to an industrial firm whether the bank's loan officer they deal with has an English accent or a board in New York. The invasion is important to industry because it has influenced the terms on which firms can obtain credit. It has influenced the way business is done, and it has implications for the degree to which banks exercise power over industry. At the start of this chapter we signalled the power that banks in Britain have exercised to call in the receiver when times are hard; but the question of bankers' power over industry is both broader and more intricate than that.

The power of the purse

In Britain, the role of the banker *vis-à-vis* industry is popularly misconceived at two levels. Bankers have typically been portrayed as modern-day Scrooges failing or refusing to advance the funds necessary for the development of worthy investment projects. In fact, events since the mid-1960s have increasingly made such a picture misleading. Related to that image of the bankers is the view that, even where they do finance industry, they don't bother about how the industry is run as long as their bank gets its money back. This has some truth in it, but it runs directly against the grain of the old adage on the privileges of paying the piper, especially at times of recession, when the bankers' task of getting their money back may become more circuitous. The reasons for the power of the purse being underestimated are complex, but perhaps the most plausible rationale is that the muscle of bankers is rarely transparent.

The power of large shareholders, even when masked behind webs of nominee company accounts, can be documented, and major changes in company structure normally require the approval of public shareholders' meetings to be formalised. The power of bankers is an altogether more elusive concept in general, even if it can manifest itself very concretely in the case of specific companies. For all that, the bankers' privileges for paying industrial and commercial pipers are crucially important, frequently amounting to the power of life and death over companies. How has this come about? And how is it that the power of bankers has come more into public focus in recent years? How were banks in a position to call in the receiver when companies like Stone-Platt Industries and others became enmeshed in financial difficulties? The answer to such questions lies in the way that banks have emerged since the late 1960s as the principal external financiers of industry, and in the way their position as creditors (lenders of money rather than shareholders) confers potentially far-reaching powers upon them, powers that depend on the exact nature of their credit relationships.

Companies generally can choose to obtain credit (or, what is the same thing, to sell debt) in one of two ways. On one hand they can issue long-term corporate bonds, generally at a fixed rate of interest, which typically will be purchased by insurance companies, pension funds or other investment institutions. By buying bonds the investment institutions are supplying long-term (15–30 years') credit to companies. These corporate bond issues may be secured, by a charge on the company's assets (known as debentures), or unsecured (loan stock), but in both cases they will be subject to detailed loan agreements. Typically, an insurance company on behalf of all bondholders acts as trustee to a bond issue in which capacity it monitors the performance of the company against the conditions the lenders have imposed, and it negotiates with the company on behalf of bondholders should the need arise. The snag with corporate bonds is that they generally carry a fixed rate of interest, although some corporate Eurobonds (bonds where the loan is in Eurodollars or other Eurocurrencies) have a floating or varying rate of interest. The fixed-interest nature of corporate bonds discourages companies from issuing them when interest rates are high (12 per cent has frequently been mentioned as a ceiling for industrial companies' bonds) because they are loathe to commit themselves to paying high interest rates for periods of 20 years of more.

For this very reason, since the mid-1960s short- and especially medium-term bank finance at floating interest rates has increasingly been used as an alternative to issuing bonds by industrial and commercial companies. Indeed, the UK corporate bond market completely dried up between 1975 and 1981 as the high levels of nominal interest rates discouraged finance directors from tapping this source of funds. Although some companies like BOC took the plunge in the corporate bond market in 1982, the net result has been that banks have firmly established themselves as the major suppliers of external finance to industry. Since 1965 this share has never dropped below 50 per cent and on occasions it has been as high as 80 per cent.

This in itself does not tell us a great deal about the power of bankers, just as investment institutions' predominant holdings of ordinary shares is not very revealing about their particular powers. What it does tell us is that the image of the banker as a Scrooge has become somewhat *passé*. To understand the power of the banker it will be helpful to look at the two major types of banking business, retail and wholesale banking.

Retail banking has been the traditional *metier* of the clearing banks even if, during the 1970s, they became increasingly involved in wholesale banking. It has focused on a company's current account for the recording of receipts and payments and on a particular approach to the supply of credit by means of secured overdraft facilities, which simply involved banks' crediting a company's current account up to an agreed maximum limit.

Before we look at the supply of credit or bank finance, let us first look at the relationship between current accounts and the operation of the payments system by the clearing banks. At the simplest level, the operation of the domestic payments system or money transmission system in modern economies is concerned with minimising the use of cash for settling transactions (especially large commercial transactions) within a country. What is the alternative to the use of cash? One obvious one is a current account at a clearing bank, but it would not make much sense to write out a cheque or use an Access or American Express card each time you wanted to buy a bag of peanuts. Indeed, the *Financial Times* has estimated that some 95 per cent of transactions in the UK involve small amounts and are invariably settled in cash. None the less, what is striking is that non-cash payments are estimated to account a staggering 99 per cent of the value of all transactions, the major part of which will be commercial transactions. Cheques alone account for two-thirds of non-cash transactions, and the clearing banks operate a clearing system for settling mutual indebtedness. The major reason why the clearing mechanism is operated by the clearing banks is because of their extensive retail branch network. The London and Scottish clearing banks operated through no less than 13,050 outlets in 1982.

As well as ordinary cheque-clearing, the clearers also operate what is known as the town-clearing. This applies to cheques of £10,000 or more drawn on and paid into about 100 City bank branches and so is especially geared to the needs of companies. Town-clearing cheques are exchanged and settled on the day they are paid in.

Now, given the clearing banks' central role in operating the money transmission system (including the town-clearing system), it is not surprising that in the *Stock Exchange Yearbook* virtually all publicly quoted companies in the UK list at least one clearing bank as one of their principal banks. But why should this have any significance? The reason is that all companies require the services of the money transmission system, and the clearing banks hold a virtual monopoly of these services in the UK. This need not be a bad thing in itself; however, when the money transmission services are combined with the supply of credit facilities, the clearing banks have a very powerful mechanism for monitoring loans by watching the fluctuations in the borrower's current account. The monitoring mechanism is rendered all the more powerful by the historical tendency of all but the largest companies to rely on a single clearing bank for money transmission and other bank services. And despite the fact that the largest multinational enterprises may have credit facilities with several hundred banks, it remains the case in the UK that they generally consolidate their money transmission activities through a current account with one or two of the clearing banks. In short, the banks that operate the clearing system have at their disposal a very powerful mechanism for monitoring the liquidity of all companies (indigeneous and foreign-owned) operating within Britain.

Even if companies' current accounts do provide the clearing banks with a powerful monitoring mechanism unmatched elsewhere, its existence *per se* provides no direct evidence that the clearing banks give company directors sleepless nights. The implications of the supply of credit by the clearers is quite another matter, for here the strings attached to bank finance offer a felicitous reminder of the truth in the saying, 'there ain't no such thing as a free lunch.' The difficulty in unravelling such strings is that they form part of a private contractual agreement between a company and its bankers. A company's annual report may disaggregate its total credit facilities by term or maturity, by whether it is secured, guaranteed or unsecured, and perhaps by a range of relevant interest rate margins; however the restrictions contained in bank loan agreements, the conditions that banks impose on the borrower's action, are rarely if ever expressly disclosed.

The liquidation approach

In the case of retail banking this need not bother us unduly, for the restrictions generally applied when short-term overdraft facilities are provided are two types of security over a company's assets: the fixed charge or mortgage, and the floating charge. The essential purpose of security is to enable creditors like banks to ensure that their loans will be repaid on the due date. Since this seems a perfectly straightforward matter, the question is why creditors frequently insist on intricate security arrangements.

Let us take the simplest case of a company operating with credit facilities not subject to security arrangements. The proprietors or directors of the company can operate it as they please subject to normal commercial requirements so long as the company remains solvent. Should the company become insolvent, however, the proprietors or directors cease to be masters of their own house and have to cede control to a receiver or liquidator. In such circumstances, where the value of the insolvent company's debts exceeds that of its assets, the unsecured creditors are treated *pari passu* or on an equal footing, receiving a share from the proceeds of the sale of the company's assets proportionate to the amounts owed to them.

It is precisely to get ahead of the pack of unsecured creditors that the clearing banks developed a tradition of supplying overdraft credit subject to various forms of security, for by definition secured creditors in principle have their claims repaid in full before the unsecured creditors get even their first bite at the cherry. Moreover, since calculations in respect of security requirements have to be based on estimates of the proceeds of the forced sale of a company's assets in the event of liquidation, the clearers' approach to the supply of secured overdraft facilities has been characterised as the liquidation or 'gone concern' approach. Despite the clearing banks' protests to the contrary, the liquidation approach remains an apt characteristic of any approach to lending based on security calculations, since receivership or liquidation is the normal circumstance under which security claims are enforced. Competition from overseas banks, who offered softer terms to attract the large lucrative borrowers, has forced the clearing banks to limit their insistence on secured credit facilities to the cases of smaller companies, where overseas bank competition is negligible, and to the cases of some larger companies in financial difficulties. Despite this, we estimate that up to 50 per cent of the clearing banks' outstanding facilities are secured in various ways.

It is now common for the clearing and other banks to combine the two major forms of security (fixed and floating charges) and codify them in a written loan agreement referred to as a 'bank debenture'. Despite being included in the same document, fixed and floating charges are quite distinct forms of security, conferring in each case very specific powers on banks. A fixed charge has certain parallels with the mortgage over owner-occupied properties that building societies take when they lend for house purchase. Historically, banks' fixed changes have attached to the fixed assets of a company such as land, buildings, or plant and machinery; but since 1978 the scope of a fixed charge has been dramatically extended so that it can also attach to a company's book debts or debtors. In other words, the clearing banks can now secure a loan by way of a fixed charge over both a company's fixed assets and the item that frequently comprises the major part of its current assets, debts owing to the company. The great merit of the fixed charge is that it confers on banks virtually absolute property rights over the secured assets should any problems arise with regard to the repayment of their loan facilities. This is how the Midland Bank came to be the proud owner of three jetliners shinily waiting at Gatwick for buyers when its customer, Laker Airways, went broke.

The rights conferred on banks by the floating charge element of a bank debenture are at once less and more powerful than those associated with the fixed charge. They are less powerful to the extent that the claims of banks under a floating charge in the event of a liquidation generally rank behind their claims under a fixed charge but ahead of the claims of unsecured creditors. But they are more powerful in the sense that they grant banks the power of life and death over companies in the event of a breach of any of the conditions of the bank debenture. Floating charges, whose history dates back to 1870, are a peculiarity of the English legal system (they were introduced in Scotland only in the 1960s). They have been described by a banking textbook as 'a charge which floats or hovers like a hawk over all the assets of the company as they change in the ordinary course of business' (Mather, 1966). This hawk swoops on the assets when the company goes into liquidation or if it defaults on any of the relevant conditions of the debenture. As a result, banks' reliance on it is controversial.

The controversy stems from the ease with which the bank with a floating charge can place the company in receivership in the event of an apparent default. The Bank of England (1980) estimates that the London clearers appointed receivers in an average of 150 companies a year in the 1970–74 period, in a slightly higher annual number of enterprises in the 1975–79 period, and in some 400 enterprises in the first ten months alone of 1980. This recent sharp increase in the number of receivers appointed is a clear indication of how the power of banks is at its sharpest during recessions. Banks counter that only unprofitable companies are placed in receivership and point to the absence till now of the insolvency of any large company, but the point is that the banks have become the leading whistle-blowers. The cause of industrial and commercial companies' difficulties is the economic crisis, but the banks possess exceptional power to call in the receiver; they have an incentive to do so, for their charges mean they are more likely to get their money back by selling off assets than by hoping the company will turn round; and they do wield that power. The banks, unlike ordinary, unsecured creditors, have acquired the position of judge, jury and executioner. They administer and set the rules, they assess the evidence by monitoring the borrower's accounts, and they pull the awful lever by calling in the receiver.

The powers that banks have over companies become tighter the more formal and documented are the agreements between bank and borrower. In Britain, there used to be a tradition of relatively informal agreements. The bank manager, or even its local director, knew the family that owned and managed the factory or warehouse, and knew that a short-term overdraft could be provided (even though it was likely to be renewed and effectively was a long-term commitment) with an informal understanding between them. However, retail banking is changing, albeit slowly, and more formal agreements are increasingly the order of the day.

The 'going concern' approach

In wholesale banking, loan agreements can be formal in the extreme; they are good business for the lawyers. In Britain they have been pioneered by American banks and to a lesser extent by accepting houses. Within this formal framework US banks have fostered a new approach towards evaluating the creditworthiness of individual companies to whom they offer medium-term unsecured loan facilities. It has been called the 'going concern' approach, since it focuses on the ability of companies as going concerns to repay their loans from their future cash flow or net trading profits. So the profitability of companies, rather than the resale value of their assets, is crucial to the going concern approach, and this has two implications. On the one hand it leads US banks to focus their efforts on selling loans to those companies and sectors of industry and commerce with a proven track record in terms of profitability. They have lent only to leading UK companies, typically within the upper quartile of *The Times* '1000'. An additional factor in their choice of companies tends to be international links either in the form of direct exports or overseas subsidiaries. The tendency of US banks to concentrate on leading companies is paralleled by other overseas banks, which effectively leaves the clearing banks with a virtual monopoly of the banking business of medium to small companies.

Partly because of competition between different banks and partly because of companies' own bargaining power, loan agreements involving larger companies tend to have fewer and less onerous restrictions than those involving smaller companies. By the same token, the interest rate margins paid by larger and smaller companies (of similar profitability) on equivalent loans show a large divergence in favour of larger companies. For example, a small company hovering around the fringes of *The Times* '1000' may pay on interest rate margin of up to 5 per cent (over base rate) on its secured overdraft facilities while a blue chip company may pay a margin of only $\frac{1}{2} - \frac{3}{4}$ per cent on its unsecured medium-term loan.

One puzzle is how US and other wholesale banks can protect themselves against default on their unsecured medium-term loan facilities. Can the 'going concern' approach, in the absence of security, somehow ensure that companies remain profitable so that their loans will be repaid? The brief answer is that they cannot. None the less, US banks have developed the concept of elaborate loan agreements (in place of the clearers' banks debentures) to provide them with an early warning system on financial problems within companies. How is this achieved? Loan agreements contain various types of conditions called 'covenants' which, if not complied with, enable the bank to demand immediate repayment of its loan.

Various types of restrictive covenants are in common usage. One class is designed to protect the bank's interests even though it is an unsecured creditor. Typical among these are covenants that prohibit a company from disposing of any of its major assets (called the 'alienation of assets' clause) without the prior permission of the bank (this has an effect similar to one of the effects of a fixed charge). Another is the 'negative pledge', which prevents a company from granting security to any other creditor without the consent of the bank.

More controversial are those financial covenants designed to monitor the financial performance of companies, such as their capital gearing (net borrowings/shareholders funds) and liquidity restrictions. These financial or ratio covenants are typically those that companies in financial difficulties fail to keep, so they provide the bank with a warning that something is going wrong. A capital gearing limit of 1.25:1 may appear quite comfortable for the typical industrial company, for it means only that the company must not borrow (net) more than 1.25 times its equity and reserves; but it has to be borne in mind that gearing ratios are often subject to pincers type of deterioration. A company in trouble not only finds itself borrowing more, but, even more seriously, it suffers a decline in shareholders' funds owing to the incidence of extraordinary and exceptional cost items in the profit and loss account (such as the costs involves in closing a plant) or to the swallowing up of reserves by losses. To drive this point home many industrial companies on banks' 'intensive care' lists today have capital gearing ratios in excess of 2:1.

Another contentious covenant is the cross-default clause. This provides that, if one bank declares or is in a position to decare a company to be in default of its loan agreements, all that company's other banks can automatically declare a default on their respective loan agreements. The purpose of this clause is to prevent a bank from breaking ranks, from taking its money and running, should the company get into financial difficulties, while other banks are left holding the baby. Such is the significance of these clauses that they have become a standard element in the documentation of all but short-term loan agreements; while larger companies will normally be able to get rid of some financial covenants from their loan agreements, their ability to negotiate on cross-default clauses is strictly circumscribed. The same can usually be said of the negative pledge or other covenant to protect unsecured creditors. In the absence of such covenants banks would probably insist on some catch-all covenant such as the 'no material adverse change' clause to protect their interests. Finally, in the case of companies in financial difficulties banks will normally insist on a clause restricting the payment of dividends.

In contrast to the clearing banks' facility in monitoring their corporate client's current account US banks' monitoring ability is clearly restricted. Typically, they will have to rely on companies' published interim and annual reports to monitor compliance with their covenants. This certainly places them and other wholesale banks at a disadvantage *vis-à-vis* the clearing banks, which they attempt to counter by insisting on detailed loan agreements to provide them with an early warning system for detecting a possible deterioration in companies' finances. The other manner in which US banks minimise their risks is by concentrating their lending on the largest firms, even if this is not proving to be a fool-proof strategy in the current recession. The clearing banks have responded to the US bank challenge by setting up central corporate finance units to cater to varying degrees to the needs of their large multinational clients.

Receivership versus re-structuring

We are now in a position to appreciate the bankers' ability and traditional propensity to call the tune should a small- to medium-sized company default on any of the conditions of its loan agreement. Both Stone-Platt Industries and Laker Airways defaulted on capital gearing covenants, which in both cases enabled the Midland to call in the receiver because the bank syndicates it represented had floating charges over the companies' assets. Because Laker was a private company (90 per cent owned by Laker and his former wife holding the residual 10 per cent of equity), banks were the major supplier of external finance in the form of bank credit facilities. Further, because Laker was a trading company able to use its assets (aircraft) as security, its capital gearing was approximately 6:1 before its collapse. This contrasts with a normal operating upper limit of 1:1 for manufacturing companies and the actual level of Stone-Platt's gearing before receivership. Because the Lakers were the only shareholders in Laker Airways, the receivership proved relatively straightforward; but although the dismemberment of the cadaver was easy, the scandal was that the bankers had ever allowed the company to expand with such a high amount of debt compared with the Lakers' own funds. A ratio of 6 to 1 may have reflected Freddie Laker's self-confidence, but it also reflected bankers' willingness to lend and lend again without looking at what was happening to passenger traffic and the industry's costs – until, that is, the crisis became inescapable. Then they called in the receiver to recover their debts, while the unsecured creditors (many of them families that had paid for flights and holidays in advance) had to wait and hope in vain.

The case of Stone-Platt is better known for a different scandal, the public conflict between Stone-Platt's institutional shareholders and its banks. Stone-Platt had two major institutional shareholders, Equity Capital for Industry (a wholly owned subsidiary of the clearing banks), which held 20 per cent of the Stone-Platt's preference shares, and the M & G unit trust group, which held a £1.9 million equity stake. Both of these denounced Stone-Platt's bankers (Midland, Barclays, Nat West and Williams and Glyn's) for acting too rashly in calling in the receiver. The institutions' view was that disposal of a loss-making division and some property would have enabled the group successfully to re-structure. The view of the institutions received public support from the former

Stone-Platt chairman. So the Stone-Platt case illustrates the power of banks' floating charge in enabling them to appoint a receiver even in the face of institutional opposition.

In recent years the power of the banks *vis-à-vis* large multi-national companies has come to the fore in numerous countries, as the plight of AEG in Germany, Dome Petroleum in Canada and Grupo Industrial Alfa in Mexico (to name but a few) attests. The issues in these instances are not as straightforward as in the case of small- to medium-sized companies, so that receivership is no longer perceived by the banks as being in their long-term interests. Instead of placing these companies in receivership or declaring them insolvent, banks have abandoned their hitherto arm's-length approach to industry and become actively involved in re-structuring the operations and finances of companies in financial difficulties. The banks' more interventionist stance can hardly be said to have been enthusiastically adopted by the banks, for it was more in the nature of a Hobson's choice for them. In Britain the banks' current response in favour of re-structuring has been prompted in no small measure by discreet pressure from the Old Lady of Threadneedle Street, the Bank of England, under whose aegis the industrial Lifeboat has been launched. The aim of the Lifeboat is to provide a private sector response to the resolutions of industry's current difficulties, and indeed, it resembles the interventionist role of the then private Bank of England in the 1930s to help re-structure parts of industry.

The Lifeboat is now estimated to include some four dozen companies including names like BPC, BSR, Duport, ICL, International Harvester, Massey Ferguson, Newman Industries, Norvic and the Weir Group. If the Lifeboat includes some of the better-known names of British industry, its list of 36 companies is not fully indicative of the extent of UK banks' interventionist efforts at re-structuring. For example, at the beginning of 1983 the Midland Group had some 80 companies on its 'intensive care' list involving loan facilities of £350 million, and the other clearers have similar lists. The question that arises is what exactly the role of the re-structuring by these intensive care units is, and whether the banks' new role as industrial surgeons is likely to succeed. At a general level, the clearing banks' unprecedented willingness to subscribe for various types of convertible preference shares or quasi-equity does appear to be indicative of a new attitude on the part of the clearing banks. Let us look at some trends in their efforts at re-structuring.

For banks, one of the main objectives of re-structuring must be for companies to make some reduction in the aggregate level of their indebtedness. This can normally be achieved only by the disposal of assets and/or subsidiaries. The dilemma facing companies in this situation is that loss-making subsidiaries and plants are not very saleable as going concerns. The harsh option is closure of and redundancies in unprofitable concerns and the sale of at least some profitable concerns. For example, Duport was forced during 1981 to sell its steel-processing interests to British Steel Corporation. This in turn made Duport's newly constructed smelting plant in Llanelli redundant, and its closure alone involved the loss of 1500 jobs in South Wales. The estimated cost to Duport of closing this modern plant some 12 months after its opening is some £34 million. A second aspect of the re-structuring of companies is a reduction in their working capital requirements through cuts in the labour force. To an extent this follows from the closure of disposal of plants and subsidiaries. However it can, as in the case of Duport, be supplemented by the merging of existing subsidiaries, as part of a general effort to increase worker productivity.

A final aspect of re-structuring is the re-scheduling of the company's loan facilities. This can take a number of forms. One form involved reducing the overall maturity of bank borrowing to a short-term or overdraft basis. The inherent difficulty in such an arrangement is that short-term facilities have to be renewed or rolled over periodically at the discretion of the banks. And if the case of Stone-Platt is typical, insolvency may be the eventual outcome. A more complex financial re-structuring is involved in cases such as Duport or Massey Ferguson, where, in addition to maintaining or increasing credit facilities, banks subscribe for quasi-equity (usually convertible preference shares or loan stock) to improve companies' beleaguered capital gearing ratios. If Midland were to convert its preference shares and loan stock in Duport to ordinary shares, it is estimated that it would end up with a 29.7 per cent stake in the company. The subscription by the clearers for quasi-equity that on conversion would result in equity stakes by banks of 25–30 per cent in large manufacturing companies is unprecedented in the recent history of the clearers. Johnson (1981) estimates that the clearers could eventually end up with equity holdings amounting to about 1 per cent of their assets. An additional complexity of the Massey-Ferguson case is that banks are to receive ordinary shares in lieu of outstanding interest payments under a C$257 million 'interest forgiveness' programme.

We have stressed the role of banks in re-structuring companies, but they are not the only financial institutions involved in re-structuring. A limited number of institutional investors such as the Prudential, M & G Unit Trust Group and Equity Capital for Industry has also played an active role in company re-structuring and have often ended up with large equity stakes in the companies involved. Nevertheless, the banks remain the primary agents in most cases of re-structuring. And in nursing ailing companies back to profitability they have intensified their monitoring activities. In cases of re-structuring banks will insist on monitoring not only the company's current account and its compliance with detailed loan agreement covenants, but also the company's monthly management accounts, and it may additionally appoint a non-executive director to the company's board.

Such a degree of intervention by banks in UK industry is unprecedented, and to date it has chalked up a number of successes such as in the case of the Weir Group and ICL. However it remains to be seen whether this will become a permanent feature of banks' new relationship with industry or whether the old arm's-length type of relationship will reassert itself when (and if) the current crisis has run its course.

Thus far we have focused exclusively on the power of the clearing and other commercial banks over the operations of companies, powers that derive in the main from the banks' lending function but may be supplemented by their operation of the payments mechanism and by banks' new role as holders of (quasi-) equity in industry. The power of the lending function of banks becomes more apparent at times of crisis when companies become engulfed in financial difficulties. Quite distinct from this power are those exercised by the accepting houses in their corporate finance function. These powers have received little attention, yet they crucially affect many aspects of a company's normal operations. Critical among these is the ability of a company to increase its shareholders' funds by making a rights issue (offering shares to existing shareholders) or to issue a corporate bond. In both instances the advice of the accepting house on the details of the issues (such as timing and pricing) and its ability to get investment institutions to underwrite the issue are crucial to the overall success of the venture. Equity rights issues are normally required at periodic intervals to maintain capital gearing ratios at acceptable levels. The other critical role that accepting houses normally play is with respect to disputed takeover bids, for here the future independence of the victim of the bid depends on the success of the accepting house advisor in protecting its client.

While securities issues and takeover bids have no necessary connection with the effects of crisis on companies, accepting houses also play an active role in re-structuring. Morgan Grenfell advised one of the Lifeboat companies, British Sound Reproducers (BSR), in its recent successful rights issue, which at one fell swoop cut BSR's capital gearing ratio from 200 to 40 per cent. More generally, the accepting house advisors on behalf of their Lifeboat corporate clients have negotiated refinancing packages with the banks and investment institutions. Finally, Lazards has developed a plan for rationalising the castings sector of the steel industry, which was characterised by over-capacity. The plan, codenamed 'Phoenix', has just come to fruition and has changed the face of the castings sector. These examples illustrate the very wide brief that the role of accepting houses as corporate advisors gives them in influencing the fortunes of British industry.

Conclusions

We have seen that banking covers a diversity of bank firms and financial markets. While not in any way wishing to deny that diversity, we have sought to look at some of the common features of the whole of banking but have found that particular institutions specialise in specific banking functions. Thus, for example, the clearing banks operate a major part of the payments mechanism. This confers a very important monopoly upon the clearers, which in turn gives them an ability to monitor the liquidity of companies unmatched not just by other banks but also by other financial institutions.

Advancing credit to industry is another *potential* source of influence exercised by banks over companies. We strongly emphasise that this influence is potential, since the issue does not normally arise in the case of relations between banks and profitable companies. Indeed, some writers go so far as to posit an alliance between banks and other sections of industry such as multinational corporations. However, as soon as companies or, indeed, sectors of industry become unprofitable, banks exercise their influence in two directions. First, further credit to the company or sector is generally curtailed or is supplied only subject to very stringent conditions. Second, and perhaps more significantly, existing credit facilities may be withdrawn; even worse, banks may exercise their power to call in the receiver. In cases such as these banks have the power of life and death over companies. The life option will normally involve re-scheduling of existing loan facilities but invariably will be accompanied by more rigorous loan agreement conditions involving the re-structuring of the company involved. The present UK crisis has given rise to many manifestations of this type of power by banks.

The two types of bank power we have looked at are ambivalent. On one hand, banks have taken either a liquidation or a 'going concern' approach to the firms to which they lend. They have sought to protect their assets without getting involved in the way that firms are run, and their power has been exhibited principally through their lead in closing firm's doors. This has particularly characterised the retail business of British banks lending to medium and small firms. On the other hand, particularly in the wholesale business of lending to multinational corporations (and to a lesser degree in the case of smaller companies) banks have increasingly become involved in changing the very structure of the operation. That involvement, however, has not been willingly chosen; banks have been drawn into it by the imperatives of the economic crisis and by the suasion of their central banks.

Banking, like the City as a whole, is at a crossroads, and the future relations between banks and industry are far from settled. They are the most urgent problem for policy toward the City.

7

The Building Society Habit

In November 1982 the Earl of Selkirk was succeeded by a more illustrious member of the aristocracy as the President of the Building Societies' Association, the societies' trade association. The new incumbent was the seventeenth Duke of Norfolk or, more elaborately, Miles Francis Stapleton Fitzalan-Howard, whose existing battery of titles included Baron Beaumont, Earl, Earl Marshall, Earl of Arundel and of course Premier Duke. A trade journal stressed the Duke's knowledge of housing in the following manner:

> The Duke can certainly claim to have considerable knowledge of housing from the consumer's viewpoint: during a long period of army service he lived in 19 different homes. . . . The Duke's connection with housebuilding dates back to 1964 when . . . he formed a building firm, Ladybridge Developments, with the idea of putting up homes on land owned by the family. . . . The Duke's housing experience goes even further. . . . As he puts it wryly, 'I have inherited one or two extraordinary houses.' These include Arundel Castle . . . and Carlton Towers in Yorkshire, the present Duke's own family home. In addition he has a home at Henley-on-Thames and a *pied à tierre* in London. [*Building Societies Gazette*, February 1983]

However impressive the level of the Duke's housing experience, it can hardly be said to touch even tangentially on the major problem confronting growing numbers of the customers of his association's member societies. We refer to the dilemma of failed and failing mortgagors whose plight Karn highlighted thus:

> Under 2 in every 2000 building society loans (0.16 per cent) were 6–12 months in arrears at the end of 1979. . . . By June 1982 . . . [a]rrears had more than doubled . . . to nearly 4 in every 2000 (0.37

per cent). The figures . . . are aggregated – for some building societies the increase has been much more dramatic. From 1979–82, one West Midlands society had a ten-fold increase in arrears of six months and over. [Karn, 1983]

Karn argues effectively that increasing unemployment is the root cause of the problems experienced by owner-occupiers, which explains why mortgagors' problems are all the more severe in areas like the West Midlands. More generally, the growing evidence of such failures serves to remind the societies that their financial activities ultimately cannot be divorced from the bricks and mortar of the real economy, just as the international banks' dependence is on the performance of the world economy. The incipient problems of owner-occupiers have to be placed in perspective. On the one hand, it can arguably be said that owner-occupiers constitute the most privileged section of the population in a property-owning democracy, so that their problems are but the tip of the iceberg of a much wider housing problem. On the other hand, as owner-occupation, largely through the efforts of the societies, has steadily established its legitimacy as the majority tenure in Britain today (some 55 per cent of all householders were owner-occupiers at the end of 1981), the societies have opened their doors to borrowers lower down on the income scale that hitherto. This has exposed them to the types of problem Karn has documented.

We shall return to Britain's housing problem later in the chapter, but meanwhile we briefly sketch the history of societies' friendly society status, their financing of property transfers through savings, and the growing battle between the societies and banks for the custom of the personal sector.

Growing out of their friendly society boots

At the beginning of the 1980s it would not be inappropriate to portray the building society movement as a contemporary Janus, but not because Janus was, *inter alia*, the Roman god of doorways. Rather, the image reflects the rather schizophrenic fission that has opened up within the movement over the years. On one side, a handful of nationally based societies project a forward-looking image of the movement as the mimesis of 'other financial' monoliths: thus, the largest two societies are second only to banking houses in terms of the assets at their disposal. On the other side, a large number of societies still hark back to the original ideal of the movement as a collection of local and caring friendly societies: in mid-1982, 56 of the 179 members of the Building Societies' Association (BSA) (which is responsible for 99.9 per cent of societies' total assets) could be classified as local societies in so far as they did not possess a branch structure. In this section we are concerned to explain how this fission or dichotomy within the movement has emerged, while in a later section we will argue that the giant societies are increasingly going to stamp their image on the movement.

To understand the movement's present dichotomy it is necessary briefly to sketch the origins of building societies. As the name suggests, the original societies, formed in the last quarter of the eighteenth century (Ketley's, the earliest recorded society, dates from 1775), comprised up to 30 members, who paid a regular contribution to a fund that was used to buy land and build houses. When all their members had been housed these societies ceased to operate: hence the description, 'terminating' societies. By the beginning of the nineteenth century the epithet 'building' had become redundant, for the societies no longer engaged in the building of houses. Instead, they developed their *métier* in the direction of financing the mortgages for existing private dwellings as well as for the construction of new dwellings, increasingly by collecting savings from those people with surplus funds. And after 1845 many societies ceased to wind up their operations, to establish the *soi-disant* 'permanent' societies, some of which survive till today but many of which have been swallowed up through mergers.

One of the principal reasons for the dichotomy within the building society movement is that the special corporate status of the societies is largely founded as a piece of Victorian legislation (Building Societies Act 1874), modified to a degree and consolidated under the Building Societies Act 1962. The 1874 Act emerged following the report of a Royal Commission on friendly societies established in 1870, for it was the tradition of friendly and related cooperative societies that had spawned building societies in the first instance. The 1874 Act established the societies as a distinct legal form with specific objectives that apply even today. In other words, the societies remain outside the remit of the Companies Acts, and, by comparison with most registered companies, their operations are circumscribed fairly tightly by legislation. To appreciate this we quote how section 1(1) of the 1962 Act (following the 1874 Act) prescribes the activities of the societies:

> The purpose for which a society may be established under this Act is
> that of raising, by the subscriptions of the members, a stock or fund
> for making advances to members out of the funds of the society
> upon security by way of mortgage of freehold or leasehold estate.

This section restricts the societies to lending only on the security of
a mortgage on leasehold or freehold property, which incidentally is
why building societies hitherto have not been able to expand
outside the British Isles. Not only that, but the legislation stipulates
that societies can lend on first mortgages only: that is, on propety
on which there are no existing secured loans. In addition, the
legislation lays down that not more than 10 per cent of societies'
lending can be above £60,000 (currently) or be advanced to corporate bodies. Finally, the societies are confined to investing their
liquid assets only in bank deposits and public sector bills and bonds.
These restrictions were designed to ensure the financial viability of
societies; but, as the memory of the 1978 débâcle of Grays Society
serves to illustrate, they have not always succeeded.

Apart from restrictions on their lending activities, the legal
structure of societies has a number of other peculiar characteristics.
Perhaps the most significant of these is that the societies are owned
by their customers rather than by equity shareholders, as in the
case of registered companies, which is why the societies are sometimes described as mutual organisations. How have customers
come to own societies? Part of the answer lies in the peculiar
meaning of 'ownership', which in the case of societies is based on
'share' investments through which they raise most of their funds.
Now 'share' investments in societies are essentially no different
from deposits in other financial institutions, except that 'share'
(account) holders automatically become members of the societies,
and it is in this limited sense that they may be said to 'own' societies.
Moreover, voting power in a building society is not related to the
value of 'share' holdings but rather is on the basis of one vote per
member. Finally, a building society 'share' holder does not receive
dividends, for retained earnings are ploughed back into reserves.
Instead, s/he receives regular interest payments just like depositors
in other financial institutions. And like other depositors, 'share'
investments' capital value does not fluctuate and the investments
are more or less readily withdrawable.

The dichotomy within the movement is well illustrated by the
societies' attitudes to profits. On the one hand, the societies' positive ideals proclaim them to be non-profit-making friendly

societies, and this leads to much coyness in describing the difference between societies' total revenue and total costs: instead of
describing this as retained profits, societies employ the bowdlerised
terms of 'surplus' or 'balance'. Indeed, Gough (1982) could
identify only one society (the Wishaw) with the temerity to call a
spade a spade and use the term 'profit' in its directors' report.
Despite their past prudery about the term, profits matter for
societies (as the recent BSA (1983) report acknowledges), for two
reasons. First, societies normally need to show positive retained
profits ('surplus') to sustain customers' confidence since, *in
extremis*, losses could trigger off a liquidity crisis through a run on
'shares' and deposits. Second, the addition of retained profits to
their reserves is societies' only vehicle of growth in the absence of
amalgamations (societies' reserves are the equivalent of shareholders' funds in registered companies). These reserves are
accumulated *exclusively* from retained profits, for the societies are
not allowed to raise long-term funds on the Stock Exchange and
their own 'share' investments do not count as long-term capital.
The growth of reserves is critical, for societies have to maintain a
minimal prudential ratio between their general reserves and total
assets.

To circumvent this brake on growth through the build-up of
internal reserves, some of the more ambitious societies have taken
advantage of amalgamations to accelerate their rate of expansion.
It is now inconceivable to imagine that in 1895 the total number of
building societies reached the peak of 3642. By 1976, 81 years on,
this total had shrunk to a mere tenth of its nineteenth-century
apogee. And the process of the disappearance of smaller societies,
and its mirror image of concentration of assets among the larger
societies, has not stopped there: during 1982, for example, a
further 24 societies were engulfed by amalgamations and mergers
to reduce the ranks of societies to a new low of 227. Table 7.1
documents the history of the almost continuous demise in the
numbers of societies: the two exceptions are 1930, when the
number of societies remained constant, and 1932, when a net
increase of 1 was recorded. Up till the 1920s a substantial part of the
decline in numbers was due to the normal winding up of terminating societies, but since then amalgamations have become the
principal vehicle responsible for the dwindling total. In particular,
the pace of the amalgamation movement has intensified sice 1955,
and we shall argue that this trend is likely not only to continue but
to become exacerbated over the course of the next few years.

Before we do this it should be noted that the secular trend of both total members (shareholders) and borrowers has consistently been upwards, although an increasing divergence between the two is becoming apparent. Until 1955 shareholders outnumbered borrowers by a factor of 3:2. Since then the building society habit has become so popularised that, even allowing for an element of double-counting, societies can now boast of four shareholders for every one borrower. The diffusion of the building society habit can be partly explained by the ten fold increase in the building society branch network between 1940 and 1982.

TABLE 7.1   NUMBERS OF SOCIETIES, 1895–1982

	Number of Societies	Number of shareholders (million)	Number of borrowers (million)
1895	3642	0.6	n.a.
1905	1950	0.6	n.a.
1915	1451	0.6	n.a.
1925	1092	1.1	n.a.
1935	999	1.9	1.2
1945	890	2.1	1.3
1955	783	3.0	2.0
1965	605	5.9	2.9
1975	382	17.9	4.4
1981	251	33.4	5.5
1982	227	n.a.	n.a.

Source: Building Societies Association.

In a number of respects, the societies' amalgamation experience since the 1950s is a replay of the amalgamation movement that decimated the ranks of the smaller banks in the two decades preceding the First World War. The puzzle is why amalgamation has not proceeded even further and sooner than it has within the building society sector. Two explanations can be adduced for this. The first is that the societies' aggregate monopoly over mortgage finance has not been subjected to a serious challenge from other financial institutions until quite recently, as we shall see in the next section. Largely owing to this lack of external competition, the societies since 1939 have been enabled to operate an interest rate cartel, the recommended rate system, in which interest rates are determined by the Building Societies Association. The parallels between the recommended rate system and the clearing banks' interest rate cartel before 1971 might suggest that the life expectancy of the former system is limited, especially given the Wilson Committee's unequivocal recommendation that it be abolished. That it still survives is no doubt due to the concern of some within the building society movement about the ineluctability of further amalgamations should the recommended rate system be scrapped. It is interesting that the advocates of cartel abolition such as Gough and Taylor (1979) fail to grasp the nettle of resultant amalgamations.

The corollary of amalgamations in which large numbers of smaller societies are swallowed up is the growing concentration of societies' assets in the hands of relatively small numbers of nationally organised societies. The extent of concentration as at the end of 1981 is set out in table 7.2. It will be seen that the five largest societies (Halifax, Abbey National, Nationwide, Leeds and Woolwich), which operate throughout the UK, owned and controlled 55 per cent of all societies' assets, compared with an equivalent figure of 39 per cent in 1930. The next 12 largest societies have branches throughout a large part of the UK and account for a further 28 per cent of total assets. The top 17 societies' proportion of total shareholders is even more concentrated than their share of total assets, although their share of total branches is rather less concentrated.

TABLE 7.2 CONCENTRATION OF BUILDING SOCIETIES, END 1981

Size (£m)	Number of societies	Total assets (£m)	(%)	Number of branches	Number of shareholders
3000	5	34,078	55	2407	19,831,788
700–3000	12	17,056	28	2154	8,316,812
160–700	21	5,575	9	1005	2,962,453
40–160	46	3,721	6	562	1,670,798
2–40	105	1,351	2	206	589,425
2	62	27	–	5	20,000
Total	251	61,808	100	6203	33,391,276

Source: Building Societies Association.

The question arising from the merger mania within the movement is not the ineluctability of further amalgamations, which
seems fairly clear-cut, but how rapidly the ranks of the smaller
societies will be decimated. Certainly, all the indications are that
amalgamations are set to continue unabated or even to accelerate
owing to the continued competition from the clearing banks and
the proposed widening of societies' powers and functions, which
we discuss in a later section. The only unknown is the possibility of
state intervention designed to restrict further amalgamations, just
as the state effectively halted the amalgamation movement within
banking after the First World War. State intervention or not, the
big five societies are so firmly ensconced at the head of the movement that the other societies have little choice but to 'follow the
leaders'.

Nest eggs and mortgages

By the end of 1982, building societies had accumulated total assets
and liabilities to the (book) value of £73.8 billion. This impressive
achievement meant that, in terms of size, the societies ranked only
just behind the much vaunted pension funds, although their total
assets are still dwarfed by those of the banking sector. A general
impression of the societies' operations and growth can be gleaned
from their balance sheet over time. In table 7.3 we set out such a
balance sheet for 1955–82. The outstanding feature of the table is
the pace of expansion of building societies: total assets multiplied
by a factor of more than 35 in the 27 years between 1955 and 1982,
with the most rapid growth occurring since 1970, when the societies
doubled their asset base in the course of the two subsequent
five-year periods. This balance sheet expansion reflects the success
of the societies in furthering their role as repositories of people's
'nest eggs' and as providers of finance for home ownership.

Let us now examine the societies' liabilities in more detail.
Societies' reserves can be regarded as equivalent to shareholders'
funds in other enterprises, while in recent years accrued interest
(interest not credited or paid out) has come to be the main item in
other liabilities. This leaves the major component of the societies'
liabilities – shares and deposits – which since 1960 have consistently
accounted for approximately 92 per cent of total liabilities. The
bulk of this 92 per cent comprises shares: ordinary and term shares
account for 81 and 12 per cent respectively of total shares and

TABLE 7.3   BUILDING SOCIETIES' BALANCE SHEET, 1955–1982

Year	Total assets/ liabilities (£m)	Liabilities			Assets		
		Shares/ deposits (%)	Reserves (%)	Other liabilities* (%)	Mortgages (%)	Cash/ investments (%)	Other assets† (%)
1955	2,076	94.2	4.6	1.2	84.7	14.6	0.7
1960	3,183	92.5	4.5	3.0	83.5	15.5	1.0
1965	5,577	92.6	4.2	3.2	82.2	16.7	1.1
1970	10,940	92.7	3.7	3.6	80.5	18.3	1.2
1975	24,364	93.2	3.3	3.5	77.5	21.2	1.3
1980	54,306	92.0	3.5	4.5	78.6	19.4	2.0
1981	62,292	91.8	3.7	4.5	78.6	19.3	2.1
1982	73,846	91.3	8.5 (combined)		77.0	20.6	2.4

* Other liabilities include provision for taxation, government loans and interest not credited or paid out.
† Other assets include land, buildings and equipment.
Source: Building Societies Association; Financial Statistics (London: HMSO).

deposits (BSA (1979), the Stow Report). Term shares have increased particularly rapidly since 1974, when interest rate differentials between ordinary and term shares were widened. At the end of 1982 the societies were able to boast of some 33.4 million shareholders (accounts), allowing for an element of double-counting (individuals holding more than one building society account), approximately 21 million British residents (53 per cent of the 1981 adult population) were members of building societies. Such a high membership rate is impressive, particularly when one considers that membership tends to be the prerogative of mainly white-collar workers or, in the words of the *Financial Times*, the lower middle classes.

To understand that building society shares can properly be regarded as deposits, it is necessary briefly to examine the market within which shares are collected. This is the market for retail deposits where building societies compete against the clearers and other banks (including the savings banks) and the Department of National Savings to protect the deposits of the persons and charities that comprise the personal sector. These nest eggs of the private sector are often described as liquid assets, for they can be withdrawn and converted into cash at relatively short or no notice. Table 7.4 shows how building societies have fared in competing for such liquid assets in the 1963(I)–82(IV) period. It shows that they have achieved a remarkable success in expanding their market share from a mere 20.8 per cent in 1963(I) to a peak of 47.7 per cent

TABLE 7.4   SELECTED LIQUID ASSETS OF THE PERSONAL SECTOR, 1963–1982

	Total (£m)	Building society shares/deposits (%)	Bank deposits (%)	National Savings (%)	Other (%)
1963(I)	17,221	20.8	33.6	44.1	1.5
1968(I)	24,258	29.2	29.7	28.8	2.3
1973(I)	38,558	37.9	41.1	19.6	1.4
1978(I)	69,171	47.7	37.3	14.6	0.4
1981(IV)	123,147	46.0	38.7	14.7	0.6
1982(IV)	140,527	47.5	36.8	15.4	0.3

Note: Owing to some re-definitions, this series is not entirely consistent but can be taken as indicative of broad trends.
Source: Financial Statistics (London: HMSO).

in 1978(I) and in maintaining an equivalent market share thereafter. Since 1976 they have displaced the banking (monetary) sector as the market leader – remember that the banking sector's share had overtaken National Savings only in the mid-1960s.

Just as the personal sector is the principal source of the societies' main liability – shares and deposits – so also it is the ultimate destination of the societies' major asset, mortgages, which comprise about 80 per cent of their total assets. This again serves to highlight the preponderantly retail nature of societies and their current unique role among the largely financial institutionas as intermediaries predominantly between persons. We emphasise this as the *current* position of the societies, for at the tail end of the last century many societies were indistinguishable from banks, and the possibility of a repeat of this situation is considered in a later section. In addition to their huge and illiquid stock of outstanding mortgages, the societies hold almost one-sixth of their assets in investments (government and local authority securities and certificates of deposits), the bulk of which have an initial maturity of five years or less. The societies' remaining assets occupy both poles of the liquidity spectrum: these comprise their cash holdings and bank balances on the one hand and their fixed assets, such as land, buildings and equipment, on the other.

Thus far we have utilised the societies' balance sheet as one vantage point on their operations, and this perspective has focused attention on their role in amassing the savings of (mainly) the middle classes on one hand and in doling out mortgages to aspiring members of a property-owning democracy on the other. To obtain a more detailed insight into societies' role, we need to document the nature of the changes in their sources of mortgage funds, which can be classified as follows:

(a) net receipts of new savings;
(b) interest credited to (but not withdrawn from) existing accounts;
(c) repayments of principal by existing borrowers.

Net receipts include both savings from current income and the investment of larger capital sums. The contribution of interest credited to investors' accounts has risen sharply to surpass that of net receipts in 1981. Mortgage principal repayments include both regular repayments and redemptions (the complete paying off of mortgages); given that the average life of a mortgage is now only

5½ years,[1] it is not surprising that redemptions exceed regular payments by a factor of 3:1. In the 1970–78 period, net receipts accounted for 45 per cent of societies' funds, interest credited 17 per cent and principal repayments 38 per cent (see the Stow Report – BSA, 1979), though as we have pointed out interest credited has increased in importance in more recent years.

From the nature of the societies' operations, it is evident that they do not conduct their affairs in a financial vacuum. They are compelled to compete against other financial institutions for their two major activities, savings and mortgages, and it is not coincidental that their major competitors in both instances are the clearing banks, since the strategy of both is to cater to the needs of the personal sector. It is to this question that we now turn.

The Tweedledum and Tweedledee of the credit markets

In early 1983 the Building Societies Association shook off its fuddy-duddy image by publishing a set of proposals that, if implemented, would have far-reaching repercussions for the future of the movement. On one hand, the Association proposed that the societies be enabled to offer a complete package of services to house buyers, including, for example, conveyancing and structural surveys. More fundamentally, the Association recommended that societies' power be extended to permit them to employ risk capital through establishing or taking a stake in recognised banks, insurance companies, companies to acquire and hold land, and companies to advance personsl loans and hire purchase finance. Despite the novelty of these proposals, the Association recommended that the societies retain their mutual status for the conduct of their main housing business while the activities involving the use of risk capital should be transacted through the establishment of corporate subsidiaries.

It may appear from these proposals that the societies are on the verge of embarking on a relatively radical course of expansion, and this is partly the case. Nevertheless, the proposals need to be placed in perspective, for the financial supermarket model for which the societies have opted represents (with the exception of land acquisition and house-building) a catching-up by the societies

---

1 Although the repayment life of a mortgage is normally 20 or 25 years, most people move house well before the end of the repayment period, pay off their old mortgage and take on a new one.

in matching the 'own brand' financial services range of the clearing bank groups. Moreover, the proposals may be regarded as the societies' latest riposte in their current battle against the clearers, which was prompted by the latter's vigorous assault on the societies' mortgage territory, including Lloyds Bank's pathbreaking venture into estate agency business and Barclay's Saturday morning opening. Indeed, such is the degree of convergence between the banks and building societies that they can now be dubbed the Tweedledum and Tweedledee of the credit markets. To appreciate this recent development, it is necessary to examine the nature and causes of the battle for personal sector business in the credit markets.

During the 1970s the building societies enjoyed a relatively cosy monopoly of the housing finance market. Their market share of outstanding loans for house purchase never dropped below 75 per cent, while in 1976–78 their share of net advances for house purchase exceeded 94 per cent each year. This is not to deny the fact that other institutions, such as the public sector, insurance companies and banks, between them held a market share of around one-fifth throughout the 1970s, and that at specific periods banks and local authorities temporarily captured a larger slice of the net advances market. But the undeniable trend in the 1970s was one of the societies' securing and consolidating their market dominance.

Since 1980 this picture has altered dramatically. The swiftness of the charge has taken many, not least the building societies themselves, by surprise. In a book published in 1980 M. Boddy could quite justifiably devote a mere one page to competition from the banks, such was the security of societies' hold on the house finance market. Since then the inroads that banks have made on the mortgage market is most dramatically illustrated in terms of their share of net advances shown in table 7.5. In the space of just 12 months (1980(IV)–1981(IV)), banks have almost quintupled their share of net advances to capture a peak market share of some 41 per cent by the end of 1981. The corollary of this was the slashing of societies' market share from some 80 per cent in 1980(IV) to only 48 per cent in 1981(IV). Since then the societies have succeeded in clawing back a portion of the banks' market share, which may now stabilise at less than a quarter of net advances.

The banks' impact on the housing finance market appears dramatic in table 7.5, since this shows *marginal* changes only. However, only if such changes could be sustained over a period of time would the market share of the stock of outstanding mortgages

TABLE 7.5 NET ADVANCES FOR HOUSE PURCHASE, 1978–1982

	Building societies ($£m$)	(%)	Banks* ($£m$)	(%)	Insurance companies ($£m$)	(%)	Public sector[†] ($£m$)	(%)
1978(IV)	9225	86.7	83	5.9	72	5.1	29	2.1
1979(IV)	7239	74.5	182	11.0	106	6.4	136	8.2
1980(IV)	1712	80.3	172	8.2	79	3.7	169	7.9
1981(I)	1562	78.7	241	12.1	62	3.1	119	6.0
1981(II)	1810	74.4	446	18.3	61	2.5	117	4.8
1981(III)	1562	60.8	797	40.9	61	2.5	147	5.7
1981(IV)	1299	47.9	1139	38.6	54	2.0	220	8.1
1982(I)	1225	49.1	960	36.2	38	1.5	270	10.8
1982(II)	1946	55.4	1270	36.2	41	1.2	253	7.2
1982(III)	2066	55.3	1430	38.3	47	1.2	192	5.2
1982(IV)	2618	67.6	1052	27.2	37	0.9	165	4.3

* Monetary sector and Trustee Savings Banks.
[†] Local authorities and other public sector.
Source: Financial Statistics (London: HMSO).

alter accordingly. Table 7.6 shows that, despite banks' marked gains in net advances their share of outstanding loans for house purchase was still only 14 per cent by the end of 1982. This share was none the less sufficient to enable banks to overtake the public sector as the second source of mortgages for the first time in the postwar period. Even so, it left the societies with the predominant share of 75 per cent.

The question that follows is the wider significance of the increasing involvement of banks in the housing finance market. To understand this we need to explain why banks had been endeavouring to expand their market share since 1979. One reason already hinted at has been the operation of the various state controls over banks' balance sheet expansion. It is not coincidental that bank lending for house purchase enjoyed a brief rally in 1972–73 prior to the initial implementation of the so-called 'corset' in December 1973, and that the recent expansion of bank lending has followed the final dismantlement of the corset controls by the Tories in June 1980. Essentially, the corset penalised the excessive growth of banks' (interest-bearing) sterling deposits on three separate occasions during the 1970s (see the Bank of England, 1982 for details); and because it was confined to banks' sterling business, it hit lending to the personal sector more directly than lending to companies, which possessed the ability to circumvent these controls.

However, the abolition of the corset is only a necessary condition for the expansion of bank lending for house purchase: it does not explain why banks should choose to expand in this direction. In this context one has to take into account banks' two domestic outlets for potential expansion in a context of increasing competition between financial institutions during the 1970s. In one of their major outlets, the corporate market, UK banks were facing severe competition from overseas banks at least in the upper segment of that market. By contrast, overseas banks had given the UK banks a relatively free rein so far as the personal sector was concerned. Allied to this was the perceived low risk factor associated with house purchase finance as compared with the growing riskiness of a large portion of corporate finance. In other words, a concerted assault by the banks on the mortgage market not only appeared as the softest option for expansion during a period of high interest rates, but also presented lucrative possibilities for the marketing of the clearer's array of financial services.

Now that, by early 1983, banks have begun to draw back their horns somewhat, the question that follows is whether the banks'

TABLE 7.6 LOANS OUTSTANDING FOR HOUSE PURCHASE, 1978–1982

31 Dec.	Building societies (£m)	(%)	Banks (£m)	(%)	Insurance companies (£m)	(%)	Public sector (£m)	(%)
1978	31,715	82.4	1795	4.7	1623	4.2	3377	8.8
1979	36,986	82.2	2392	5.3	1847	4.1	3744	8.3
1980	42,708	81.8	2975	5.7	2117	4.0	4446	8.5
1981	49,039	79.1	5640	9.1	2204	3.6	5075	8.2
1982	56,894	75.1	10,600	14.0	2300*	3.1	5941	7.8

* Authors' estimate.
Source: Financial Statistics (London: HMSO).

assault on the mortgage market was merely a flash in the pan. In our judgement the answer has to be no. Admittedly, in the periods of relatively low interest rates the clearing banks find themselves at a disadvantage, though in the long run this has to be set against the endownment element of profits accruing to them through the fact that they do not pay interest on current accounts while they do receive interest on their loans (so that the endowment profits rise during periods of high interest rates). Moreover, they can claw back profits by bringing the costs of their money transmission services more in line with their economic cost, and this is the current trend. However, there is a more powerful factor in compelling banks to remain in the mortgage market, and this is that the societies have begun to encroach on traditional banking functions.

The societies have not stood idly by watching the banks build up their stock of outstanding mortgages. As early as November 1979 the Anglia Hastings and Thanet Society (not one of the household names) briefly hit the headlines by becoming the first society to borrow funds on the wholesale money market. That the trickle of societies following on the heels of the Anglia did not develop into a flood as societies tried to build up their resources to finance increased mortgage lending (a total of 10 of the top 30 societies formally borrowed from the markets) is explained by the intervention of the Financial Secretary to the Treasury in 1980. He warned that if societies continued to bid for money market funds he would reconsider their exemption from the prudential requirements of the Banking Act, and in the short term societies have judged that the costs of prudential regulation outweigh the benefits of tapping the money markets. Despite this and the Stow Report's (BSA, 1979) rejection of the money markets as an appropriate source of funds, the societies' current proposals to operate banks must inexorably lead them in the direction of the money markets.

Besides their money market activities, the societies have begun to make inroads into the clearers' monopoly over money transmission services, in which the societies' big selling point is their long opening hours (even though Barclays now match them on Saturday morning opening). In this sphere the societies have flinched from open competition with the banks and have opted instead for what the *Financial Times* (14 January 1983) has described as 'marriages of convenience' with various banks.

It will be evident from table 7.7 that the partners in such marriages are almost exclusively the large societies: indeed, only the Woolwich and the Anglia out of the top eight societies have not yet announced plans to provide some money transmission services. In addition to the listed links with banks, some of the larger societies like the Halifax are planning to introduce their own cash dispensers; but because this is an expensive option we may expect to see further instances of links with banks in this field.

Finally, as the societies themselves are keen to emphasise, an increasing proportion of their lending falls under the category 'other lending', which covers mainly home improvements. 'Other lending' as a proportion of societies' total lending increased from 7.8 per cent in January 1981 to 11.3 per cent in November 1981 (BSA *Bulletin*, no. 29, January 1982). Indeed, such was the concern that this 'other lending' and bank house purchase advances were being partly used for purposes other than house purchase/ improvement that it led to the Bank of England taking the unprecedented step of issuing joint credit guidelines to both banks and building societies. The BSA proposals for the extension of the societies' role into banking, HP credit and other personal lending are clearly designed to give an added impetus to the provision of wider credit facilities by the societies to the personal sector. However, as the Bank of England has warned them, being a bank is different from being a building society. Banks have a different capital structure, are subject to different legal requirements and are supervised in a different way. It is doubtful whether even the largest building societies would wish, or be able, to make the complete transition.

The new absentee landlords

The history of housing in Britain this century is one of the inexorable squeezing of the private landlord and the privately rented sector between a burgeoning owner-occupied sector on one side and a sizeable municipal housing sector on the other. The days of the traditional absentee landlords and their rack rents certainly are numbered; but, as we saw at the beginning of the chapter, the cherished dream of one's home being one's castle is crumbling around the ears of the growing number of owner-occupiers. Arrears of mortgage repayments are one symptom of the rot: more startling is the increasing incidence of what are euphemistically described as 'possessions'. This is the taking over and subsequent sale of homes by the societies where borrowers are considered to be in serious (six months' upwards) arrears, and it is in this that the

TABLE 7.7 BUILDING SOCIETY AND BANKING LINKS, MAY 1983

Society	Size (£b)	Customers (million)	Bank	Service
Halifax	11.9	6.1	Barclays	Cheque books
Abbey National	10.0	6.8	Co-op	Cheque books
Nationwide	5.4	2.9	Midland	Access credit cards
Leeds Permanent	3.5	1.8	Lloyds	American Express traveller's cheques
National and Provincial	2.9	1.5	Nat West	Access credit cards
Leicester	1.8	0.9	Citibank	Credit card
Bristol and West	1.3	0.55	Standard Chartered	Cheque books
Nottinghamshire	0.17	0.15	Bank of Scotland/British Telecom	Home banking

Source: Financial Times; own research.

societies' new role as landlords is most apparent. Let us examine the question of possessions in more detail.

Like other lenders, building societies like to contain the problem of arrears in payments of their mortgages before they get out of hand. And instead of the re-scheduling arrangements that banks offer to corporate borrowers, the societies proffer their willingness to negotiate 'forbearance arrangements', which essentially postpone or defer capital repayments while interest payments continue. Karn (1983) was unable to garner much evidence of actual forbearance arrangements from either the societies or local authorities. In the absence of such arrangements, the only option for the societies often is either possession or forced sale. In the first half of 1982 building societies possessed about 9 in every 10,000 properties (5,320 in all) mortgaged by them – rather more than the total for 1979 as a whole.

But surely this affects only a tiny minority of the societies' mortgage holders, and one cannot impugn them with the title of absentee landlords for this? It is true that possessions affect only a small section of property owners, but there is a more fundamental sense in which the societies have acted not unlike absentee landlords. Just as the classical image of the latter portrays them as ruthless individuals, failing to improve the land and buildings they own, so the building societies have ultimately failed to secure a well-housed population. Britain's housing strategy has consistently envisaged a major role for the owner-occupier with a property-owning democracy being the dream of policy-makers, and building societies' growth has been the policy's financial foundation. But the strategy has failed to solve the housing problem. Homelessness is no nearer to eradication, and the nation's housing standards are comparatively low.

The continuing housing problem is not the fault of the building societies, nor are its causes located only in the private sector; rather, private owner-occupation backed by building society finance has failed to deliver a housing system with satisfactory housing standards. Moreover, some building society practices have undoubtedly contributed to specific problems: the societies have been accused of contributing to inner-city decay by 'red-lining' areas in which they will not lend (although they deny the accusation).

Just as some of the investment institutions are beginning to realise that their role as the financiers of industry may push them into a deeper involvement with industry, so some of the more enlightened societies are prepared to admit that they may have housing duties outside of and beyond their purely financial role, even if their present efforts in carrying out this new role tend to be fairly cosmetic. If the societies are to be in a position to repudiate the charge of being new absentee landlords, they will have to play a much more positive role in Britain's housing market in future. In the meantime, they continue to face two ways: on the one hand they remain the friendly local friendly society, looking after nest eggs and the hopes of young couples for a modest home; on the other, they are competing with the banks for growth and aiming to secure their position at the retail end of the City.

PART III

THE CITY, POWER
AND POLICY

The City's position in the economy has changed and developed over its history. Since the early 1960s it has undergone rapid and dramatic changes which have been analysed in previous chapters. Partly as a result, the City's problems and its future role are quite unsettled. These are issues for policy; governments have to take a perspective and either attempt to shape the financial system or leave its future to autonomous forces. But the position of the state with respect to the City is conditioned by the power that is concentrated within the financial system.

The concept of a 'money trust' has, at times, been used to describe one aspect of financial power, its potential hold over industry and commerce, and we consider it in chapter 8.

As a distinct focus of power, the City has at times held sway over government economic policy; in recent years it has often been argued that monetarism was a City policy which it succeeded in foisting on the state during both Mr Callaghan's and Mrs Thatcher's administrations. In chapter 9 we examine the connection between monetarism and the City as one possible instance of the City's influence on policy.

The final chapter examines the possibility of nationalisation as a radical proposal for the future of the financial system; it would involve constructing a role for finance rather different from its present and past roles.

8

The City as a Money Trust?

The year 1918 marked the publication of an influential report whose principal theme was the desirability and possible consequences of the impending emergence of a money trust or banking combine in the City of London. This report was not one of the periodic left-wing diatribes against City banking houses that had characterised British politics since Marx's exposure of City speculation in the financial crises of the mid-nineteenth century. Instead, the document boasted impeccable establishment credentials. It was the report of a committee of top-rank bankers, industrialists and merchants, chaired by Lord Colwyn (hence referred to as the Colwyn Report) and charged with investigating the consequences of the contemporary wave of amalgamations, the merging of banks on a large scale.

The Colwyn Report concluded by opposing these amalgamations, for they brought the potential threat of a banking monopoly or money trust which the Committee felt carried two unsavoury implications for the City. One was the fear, publicly articulated by the Establishment for the first time, that the emergence of a money trust might transform the City's bugbear about nationalisation from a nightmare into reality or, at least, into public demands for such a course of action. The other was the fear that a money trust could undermine the position of the Bank of England as the watchdog of the City and might go so far as to abrogate some of the influence of government.

It is worth emphasising that worries about the menace of a money trust were not confined to the City of London, for similar fears had been manifested even earlier in the other leading financial centre of the day – New York. As early as 1912, the Pujo Committee had cross-examined the then ageing Pierpoint Morgan and other leading New York bankers concerning allegations that they headed a money trust of great power (see Sinclair, 1981).

The spectre of a money trust more or less simultaneously haunting the corridors of both the British and American Establishments at the beginning of the twentieth century raises two important questions with which we shall engage in this chapter. The first concerns the reasons why the threat of a money trust should have arisen at this juncture and why it should have manifested itself as the power of banks rather than of other financial institutions – or indeed as the combined power of all financial institutions. One possible answer is to be found in the Marxist theories of finance capital that flourished at that time, and below we explore the seminal exposition of this theory by Hilferding.

The second question that arises from the historical threat of a money trust is why public concern about the power – overweening or otherwise – of banks appears to have subsequently disappeared from the political agenda to be confined only to some left-wing circles. Admittedly, charges of a 'banker's ramp' have occasionally re-surfaced in the UK since 1918, but these have typically been confined to one-off policy questions such as the City's opposition to devaluation in the mid-1960s. (On this see Stewart, 1977, and Coakley and Harris, 1983). Two responses to this question are possible and we examine them both in the following sections. Some might argue that the boundaries of the relationship between the City and the rest of the economy have ben transformed beyond recognition – as we argued in the earlier chapters, this has happened with regard to the City's international role. A different response might be that the growth of multinational enterprises, with their own great strength, has prevented the City's financial institutions from exerting power over industry and commerce. Indeed, to the extent that power relations are recognised at all, some would say that the boot is on the other foot: the multinationals have replaced the money trust as the behemoth of the 1980s.

In the first three chapters of the book we looked at the City's international roles, but its relations with the rest of the world are only one side of the City's work. The other is its relation to the industrial and commercial sector in Britain. The two sides are, of course, linked, because industry and commerce also have an international dimension, and, as we saw in chapter 4, they combine to produce the risk of a crash. In the subsequent chapters we examined the connections between specific City institutions – the banks, pension funds, life insurance and building societies – and the British economy; the present chapter takes a more general overview of the issues at stake and links them with the international business of finance. The question of whether the City institutions did, do, will or could form a money trust with enormous power to control industry and commerce is central, and we start by examining the classic idea that they do from such a trust, the idea encapsulated in the term 'finance capital'.

The concept of finance capital

In 1910, two and eight years respectively before the Pujo and Colwyn Committees were established, a 28-year-old Austrian economist, Rudolf Hilferding, published *Das Finanzkapital*, thereby promulgating the concept of 'finance capital' which has subsequently been much misunderstood. Hilferding employed the concept to depict the *economic* characteristics of the (then) latest phase or stage of capitalist development. He defined these economic characteristics as those processes of centralisation and concentration that (a) lead to the formation of cartels and trusts in industry, and (b) involve the integration of finance in the hands of banks with production in the hands of industrial companies.

Such was the attraction of Hilferding's economic analysis to Marxists that political adversaries like Lenin and Bukharin were able to take on board many of Hilferding's ideas and apply them to their subsequent analysis of imperialism. What were the attractions of Hilferding's analysis?

At the most basic level; it could be claimed that Hilferding's achievement lay in his perception of the overwhelming power at the disposal of giant banks from the labyrinth of inter- and intra-capitalist relations. But banks and their power were only one (if the most significant) of the features of modern capitalism that he described, for banks do not operate in a vacuum. Instead, Hilferding envisaged the monopoly tendencies prevalent in the economy as operating to reinforce the growth of both banks and industry, while simultaneously eliminating or subsuming other forms of capital. For industry, the primary vehicle of growth was the joint stock company or corporation, whose facility in mobilising equity capital and raising bank credit ensured it a dominant position *vis-à-vis* other sections of industry. But whereas the joint stock companies became monopolies in their own line of industry, Hilferding thought the aggrandisement of banks came by annexing institutions with rather different functions and activities. Bearing in mind that banks themselves typically collect short-term savings deposits, he believed that they attempted to secure a monopoly of both long- and short-term savings of all society by taking over the operations of commodity and stock exchanges and of non-bank financial houses.

According to Hilferding, the integration of banks and industry in the advanced capitalist countries provided the springboard for the division of the world into imperialist spheres of influence. In one sense, the counterpart of the annexationist policies of banks at the national level was the colonial policies embarked upon by the advanced capitalist countries at the international level. Colonial policies facilitated the export of capital by the giant banks and industrial trusts, and the latter process was furthered by the use of tariffs as part of domestic policy.

One of the criticisms levelled against Hilferding is the particularity of his analysis. By refining the complex of inter-capitalist relations into an all-embracing monopoly banks–monopoly industry axis, in which economic power is vested predominantly in the hands of the banks, he precludes other forms of capital and, by extension, other inter-capitalist relations. What some have questioned, then, is Hilferding's portrayal of modern capitalism as an inexorable process whereby the banker – the latter-day *rentier* – presides over the demise of the industrial entrepreneur and the extinction of merchants and traders. Critics may concede that this picture of capitalism found a greater resonance in continental Europe where the Hanseatic banking tradition of universal banks prevailed than in the Anglo-Saxon world. But if that is the case, how do we reconcile it with the subsequent concern about the emergence of a money trust precisely in those countries (the UK and the USA) where the concept of finance capital was deemed to be least appropriate? And is it just a coincidence that the concepts of finance capital and a money trust should pinpoint the economic power of banks rather than other or even all financial institutions?

To answer those questions it is necessary to draw a distinction betwen the nature of the money trust threat in the United States and the UK, to outline the events affecting each banking system and the measures adopted in each country following the recommendations of the Pujo and Colwyn Committees. In the United States the Pujo Committee Report was followed by the adoption in 1914 of the Federal Reserve Act, which established America's unique form of central bank and, more interestingly for our present purposes, an Antitrust Act. The latter placed a two-pronged restriction on banks: it prohibited interlocking directorships between national and locally based private banks. Two years later interlocking directorships were permitted, but restrictions were reimposed in the aftermath of the 1929 Wall Street Crash.

If banks in the United States did wield some measure of economic power, it is difficult to imagine how prohibitions on interlocking directorships might have curtailed it. Instead, it was the 1929–33 Depression that was responsible for trimming the sails of US banks. For not only did the Great Depression decimate the US banking industry by causing the suspension of 9,735 smaller banks, but in its aftermath the leading banking houses were dissected by the 1933 Glass Steagall Act. This legislation ordained the separation of investment and commercial banking, which hitherto had been combined by the large banking houses in a manner not dissimilar from the Hanseatic banking tradition.

In Britain, by contrast with the United States, the preoccupations of the Colwyn Committee were narrow in that they focused largely on the banking system alone. Their recommendations, which were against further large-scale bank amalgamations and interlocking directorships between large banks, did not formally enter the statute book, but their substance, in Sayer's (1957b) phrase, 'passed into the unwritten law of the land'. The menace of a money trust in the UK was perceived in terms of a banking monopoly emerging from centralisation and concentration within the banking system rather than in terms of banks exercising excessive power or control over industry. The Colwyn Committee did not ignore the implications for industry of the trend towards a banking monopoly, but it tended to view the problem as a diminution of the number of banks between which firms could choose: the Committee was concerned about a decline in competition rather than an increase in power.

The Colwyn Committee's notion of a money trust in the UK and Hilferding's concept of finance capital, therefore, did not coincide, even if they shared a common emphasis on the trend towards a banking monopoly. However, the concern of the Pujo Committee – that is, the allegation of a money trust in the USA – more closely approximated Hilferding's view. What is unclear is why the different concepts of finance capital and a money trust should share a common concern with the existing or potential economic power of banks *vis-à-vis* industry instead of with the power of all financial institutions. The most plausible explanation would seem to centre on the dynamic growth potential of credit through the banking system. Moreover, the prominent role of other financial institutions (insurance companies and pension funds) in the financing of industry is a recent postwar phenomena, since prior to that individual investors tended to place their savings directly (in shares or bonds, for example) rather than in investment institution funds. Apart from private individuals and the sum of small savings, the banks were the principal suppliers of finance to industry in the first three decades of the century, so establishment and left-wing commentators alike chose to focus on the economic power they concentrated in their hands.

Since the finance capital and money trust controversies of the early twentieth century and the interwar years, the concept of a money trust has been banished to limbo, but that of finance capital has been both resuscitated and denounced in various guises. Its controversial character stems from the fact that several crucial aspects of the concept of finance capital are problematic. In particular, the notions of the integration of banks and industry and of the power and control exercised by banks in relation to industry are far from straightforward.

One of the problems with Hilferding's and Lenin's classical theories of finance capital is the dual notion of the integration of banks and industry within the imperialist blocs centred on their capital cities. On one hand, such theories postulated the integration of monopolistic banks and industrial trusts, a consequence of the forces that, in the words of Hilferding, 'bring bank and industrial capital into an ever more intimate relationship . . .'. This is accomplished by banks' annexing as their *métier* the financial and trading activities associated with modern capitalism. We return to this aspect of integration later in this section. On the other hand, the classical theories put forward the idea of an international integration of finance capital *within* the various imperialist blocs, so that it was possible to allude to, for example, British finance capital as embracing the capitals of Britain, her overseas colonies and her other spheres of influence.

Because the classical theories conceived of a world divided into relatively hermetic imperialist blocs, integration at the international level was constricted by the respective territorial limits of each bloc. We may contrast this thesis of limited international integration with that of unmitigated integration between the two types of large enterprises, banks and industrial trusts. Despite these clear-cut differences with respect to their limits, these theses on integration shared one crucial characteristic: they both embodied the notion of an asymmetric or unequal integration – integration achieved through the dominance of one of the constituent elements of the integrated bloc. Thus, for example, banks were seen as the predominant partner in the integration between banks and industry, while international integration within imperialist blocs was orchestrated from and by the finance capitals of the metropolitan countries.

Multinational corporations

'Finance capital' is a concept that focuses attention on the connection between finance and other economic activities – industry, commerce and international expansion. But many claim that the concept has long been made redundant by international developments. First, the trend towards decolonisation has undermined the basis of the old imperialist blocs, even if some maintain that the post-colonial economic relationships have remained largely unaltered. Second, and perhaps more significantly, the postwar period has been characterised by the inter-penetration of capitals *between* the erstwhile imperialist powers; and this cross-investment between the advanced capitalist economies has been achieved chiefly through investment directly in production facilities on the part of the multinational corporations.

This direct investment by multinationals is seen by some as a formidable challenge to the classical theories, which emphasised the export of financial capital through the purchase of bonds and shares (see, for example, Olle and Shoeller, 1982). Because multinationals are not now constrained by the old boundaries of Empire, they dismantle that limit to international integration. Typical of proponents of the view that modern capitalism has transcended all such barriers is Nigel Harris, who envisages a world capital as the result of the contemporary trends:

> There appears to be, in essentials, only one economy, a world system, and one world capital operating in many different countries. Furthermore, some of world capital's most important activities operate outside the supervision of any official [state] agency – for example the Eurocurrency market. . . . In the 1970s, the national 'managed economy' in the industrialized countries had steadily declined, each national part being increasingly incorporated in integrated global production and financial system. [Harris, 1982, p. 358]

Harris's concept of world capital operating on the stage of a global market may appear attractive but it is difficult to reconcile it with the role of multinational corporations. Certainly it cannot be denied that multinational corporations and banks do operate subsidiaries, branches and offices across the globe, and in a number of respects they do cooperate and share similar interests; but this is not equivalent to saying that they operate as or are integrated into world capital. For the fact remains that they remain nationally based in the main.

First, multinationals are predominantly owned and controlled by various national capitals, and in this sense it is valid to speak of US, British, German or Japanese multinationals. The only obvious exceptions to this are the various consortium multinationals and the handful of dual-nationality multinationals such as Unilever and Dunlop–Pirelli. Second, one of the implications of nationally based ownership is that, to raise capital on their national stock exchanges, multinationals have to file their accounts with the relevant supervisory authorities, which in practice entails translating their world-wide transactions into a national currency with its attendant foreign exchange risks. Thus, British multinationals file their annual reports and accounts at Companies House as one of the conditions for being incorporated in Britain, for raising capital and being quoted on the London Stock Exchange. Investors on the Stock Exchange will wish to be kept informed of not just a multinational's net profits but of the *sterling value* of its net profits.

Third, the trend for multinationals has been to centralise strategic decision-making (as opposed to day-to-day management decisions) at their domestic head offices. Among the strategic decisions centralized by multinationals are those concerned with the pace and direction of their internationalisation, the mobilisation of finance, and the monitoring of the profitability of both domestic and overseas subsidiaries. Decisions concerning the mobilisation of finance for overseas subsidiaries are quite critical for multinationals, for they involve foreign exchange, interest rate and tax considerations as well as the maze of transfer pricing. *Ceteris paribus*, head offices will want their overseas subsidiaries to raise finance locally, assuming that the local financial markets can accommodate the scale of funds required; but in practice this means that a hard distinction can be drawn between multinational subsidiaries located in advanced economies and those located in many developing economies. The former will tend to raise a considerable proportion of their finance requirements locally, while local financing in the latter case is likely to be negligible or non-existent. This difference increases the ties that multinational subsidiaries in poor countries have with their headquarters.

Finally, although controversial, a multinational's head office is, *in principle*, ultimately responsible for the debts on which any of its ④ overseas subsidiaries or branches may from time to time default. That this responsibility is controversial is reflected in the uncertain legal status of the instruments employed to guarantee the debts of overseas subsidiaries or branches. Typically, multinational head offices will issue 'letters of comfort' to banks as a minimal form of security for their subsidiaries' borrowings. While the nature of such support may be moral rather than legal, the fact remains that multinationals will be loath to repudiate their subsidiaries' debts, for such a course of action would irrevocably damage their credit rating within the international financial markets.

Those nationally based dimensions of multinationals highlight the constraints on the international integration of capital and the barriers to the emergence of a global or world capital. (For a different critique of the idea of a global capital see Aglietta, 1982.) This is not for one moment to deny that today's multinationals operate on a global scale; but rivalry and competition between nationally based multinationals is the order of the day. (See the parallels with Rowthorn's (1971) argument.) What is more, this rivalry has spilled beyond the hermetic boundaries of the pre-first World War imperial blocs into the very front gardens of the former imperial powers. In brief, the development of multinational corporations since the Second World War has dissolved the limit to integration that existed at the time *Finance Capital* was written, the limit imposed by the boundaries of the great powers' respective empires. But it has strengthened the international integration of firms in a way similar to that which was envisaged by Hilferding: production and finance around the globe are in the hands of giant trusts or multinational corporations, with nationally based head-quarters and with rivalries for supremacy.

Central to the idea of finance capital was the view that such trusts integrate both financial and industrial activities with the former dominant, but is that a characteristic of today's multinational corporations?

Banker industrialists or industrialist bankers?

The central idea of finance capital was that banks had come to dominate industry and that they had done so in such a tight embrace that bankers had, in essence, become the new industrialists. However, one of the most remarkable developments of the last decade in the relation between industry and finance is that multinational corporations whose principal business was industrial and commercial have developed purely financial operations which challenge the banks: the industrialists have become bankers and financiers. This appears to turn on its head the money trust idea of finance capital; moreover, whereas the theory of finance capital explained the export of capital as the result of a money trust, the process by which industrialists have apparently become bankers and financiers is the result rather than the effect of internationalisation, for it is a development within multinational corporations. But how significant are these developments?

Why should internationalisation have induced multinationals to annex some financial functions? This has occurred since the advent of a regime of floating exchange rates in the early 1970s, for that made multinationals more vulnerable to foreign exchange risks both on their long-term investments and on their short-term trading activities. As a result, a number of large multinationals have made a foray into the foreign exchange markets by establishing overseas foreign exchange subsidiaries (see the *Financial Times*, 16 September 1982). It is estimated, for example, that BP's currency trading turnover surpassed that of the Bank of England in March 1982, which offers one insight into the enormity of the task a central bank may face today in defending the exchange rate. Some estimate that 20–30 giant multinationals in the car, oil and chemical industries are sufficiently powerful to alter exchange rates through their individual dealings. Moreover, the multinationals' own treasurer's departments are influential powers affecting interest rates in the markets for bonds, bills and credits.

None of this, however, is enough to imply that banks have had their foundations appropriated by industry. At most it is a trend. The giant banks, after all, are responsible for organising the markets or are the market-makers in major currencies, even if multinationals like BP, Renault or Volkswagen (VAG) are important dealers. Finally, while these foreign exchange subsidiaries also engage in international banking activities – borrowing and lending on the Euromarkets as well as dealing in foreign exchange – they are rather dwarfed in this respect by the giant international banks.

If multinationals are not yet banks on the same scale as banks themselves, are they competitors with investment institutions such as pension funds in financing overseas investment? One way in which multinationals invest abroad is by taking over or taking an equity stake in overseas companies, while another is to employ the retained profits of overseas' subsidiaries. During seven of the 11 years between 1970 and 1980, multinationals' direct investment via the former method (acquisition of overseas shares and bonds) exceeded the scale of City institutions' overseas portfolio investment. Since the abolition of exchange controls, the latter has increased dramatically, but the acquisition of overseas financial assets by multinationals has also increased, if not quite so spectacularly. Can we deduce from this that multinationals are competing with the investment institutions for the acquisition of overseas shares and bonds?

The answer is not completely clear-cut, but in general one can distinguish between multinationals' desire to control the productive and trading acticities of overseas companies by means of takeovers or majority stakes, and the investment institutions' propensity to hold minority stakes solely for income purposes. And unlike foreign currency subsidiaries, the acquisition of overseas subsidiaries is a long established activity of multinationals. Notwithstanding this, and the fact that multinationals and the investment institutions do not compete directly for overseas financial assets, the deployment of multinationals' retained profits and their funds does have a financial as well as a productive dimension. For this reason, it is insufficient to equate multinationals' activities with just the domain of production, to the extent that this overlooks their financial investment and foreign exchange activities.

The fact that the functions of multinationals extend beyond the sphere of production should serve to remind us that Hilferding's picture of their relatively passive and static role in their integration with banks is not entirely accurate. It is to this question that we now turn.

The coordinates of the City's power

The existing literature is remarkable in that, with a few exceptions, most commentators would deny that the City exercises any power over the companies that go to make up industry in Britain today. Even left-wing critics of the City emphasise only the *negative* powers of the City, in the sense of its denying some companies sufficient means of finance. Two explanations can be adduced for this state of affairs: either the power of the City as a money trust is in reality a complete non-starter in the 1980s, or the theory of finance capital has been superseded by other theories.

There are five possible channels through which the City might be able to exercise a degree of power over companies:

(a) ownership of shares;
(b) advancement of credit;
(c) monitoring current accounts;
(d) interlocking directorships;
(e) alliances with sectors of industry.

The first four channels are those identified in Hilferding's theory of finance capital, while the latter is found in more recent writings on the City. We shall examine each of these channels in turn, and we end by considering possible limitations on the City's power such as the threat of financial crisis.

Ownership of shares

Since the evolution of the joint stock company, the ownership of shares and its attendant powers has been a topic of controversy within economics in particular, where it has fostered what has become known as the ownership and control debate. Within that debate the *managerialist theory of the firm* has achieved such a prominence that, if any one theory can be held responsible for the demise of the concept of a money trust, then it has to be the managerialist theory. For the latter's idea of the aggrandisement of top management within, and their associated internal control of, companies spread like wildfire and deal a death blow to notions that external bodies like the banks any longer exercised any power over enterprises.

Significantly, the modern ownership and control debate can be traced back to Berle and Means's (1932) managerialist critique of the neoclassical theory of the firm. In other words, it post-dated the earlier debates on finance capital and money trust and emerged at the tail end of the decimation of US banks by the Great Depression and a year before the 1933 Glass Steagall Act.

At its most basic level, the neoclassical theory of the firm presents a stylised picture of capitalism under which capitalists or entrepreneurs own and control enterprises and seek to maximise profit. Large capitalists and enterprises may be able to acquire above-normal profits through a temporary monopoly of new technology, process or product.

By contrast, the managerialist theory argues that both profit, as the motive force of capitalism, and the power of large capitalists, as owners and controllers of companies, have been superseded. Its basic proposition is that the joint stock company has engendered a fundamental transformation of modern capitalism, and that the neoclassical theory of the firm was valid only for the early stages of capitalism. The fundamental change, according to managerialists, is the emergence of a new oligarchy composed of the directors or top management of the joint stock companies. The aggrandisement of management has been facilitated by the diffuse ownership of shares while the day-to-day control rests with salaried management. In short, the managerialists envisage the demise of the traditional capitalist or capitalist dynasties and their replacement by a management oligarchy whose power derives not from the ownership of large equity stakes in companies but rather from the *absence* of such stakes. This disjuncture between ownership and control is made possible by management's manipulation of the proxy votes of diffuse shareholders.

The spread of a management oligarchy throughout the economy is only one of the distinctive characteristics of modern capitalism identified by the managerialists. Another is that the new management oligarchy behaves differently from the traditional capitalists by pursuing growth (instead of profit) as their prime objective, typically subject to some financial constraint such as a minimum stock market valuation of their companies or minimum level of dividends paid out. It is in management's self-interest to comply with such constraints, since failure to comply might leave the company vulnerable to a takeover threat and the possible replacement of existing management. The potential role that financial institutions may play in such takeover bids or threats is the only concession that managerialists make to the influence of the financial system.

The managerialist thesis has achieved a considerable degree of orthodoxy within economics, and its attractions cannot be lightly dismissed. On the one hand, it expressed one aspect of the effective disenfranchisement of the thousands of diffuse small shareholders in the typical modern company. On the other, its focus on the pursuit of growth by the management oligarchy can claim to be one rationale for one of the most imposing features of today's multi-national enterprises, namely their sheer size. Indeed, much of the research associated with the ownership and control debate has focused on these two questions: can a dominant shareholder be identified within companies, and do management-controlled companies pursue growth rather than profit? We do not pursue the results of such research here, but rather look at some ideas underlying the debate since in chapter 5 we empirically examined the concentration of shareholdings.

First, a (group of) large shareholder(s) is normally disposed to exercise a degree of control over the management of a company and its strategic decision-making, especially in relation to its financial structure. A group of shareholders can vote out the existing management should that group be in a position to muster a majority vote at a shareholders' meeting. Second, it is incorrect to infer from this that shareholders own the company's assets, for a share constitutes an entitlement to income, not a slice of physical property. The only agents with a real claim over a company's assets are its secured creditors. Thus, in principle, a bank lending to a company has a better claim to ownership of the firm's assets when the company fails than do its shareholders. The managerialists claim, however, that modern companies are essentially self-financing, and therefore that the influence of financial institutions and markets is confined to takeover bids.

Advancement of credit

The second channel through which the City may exercise power over industry is related to the supply of credit by banks. The power of lenders has been a topic of controversy predating the modern banking system, as the character of Shylock in *The Merchant of Venice* illustrated; but Hilferding was one of the first economists to discuss the implications of bank credit for the relationship between banks and companies. He envisaged the supply of credit as one of the levers of banks' dominance over industry. He distinguished between short-term circulation credit to finance stocks of goods and raw materials and long-term capital credit to finance new plant and machinery, arguing that the latter formed one basis for a long-term relationship between banks and industry as a result of which banks took a long-term interest in its performance.

It is not clear exactly what Hilferding had in mind when he referred to 'capital credit', though it would not seem unreasonable to suppose that the nearest contemporary equivalent is the long-term fixed-interest debt – bonds – issued by companies and purchased by investment institutions such as pension funds rather than banks. The fact that bonds are referred to as debt from the company's view point should not cloud the fact that they share all the essential attributes of credit, as well as having a secondary market like shares or certificates of deposit. Indeed, during the 1970s in the UK, medium-term bank credit has come to replace corporate bonds as the major form of credit to companies, and when nominal interest rates fall sufficiently we are likely to see banks and the investment institutions competing for the supply of credit.

A number of reasons could be advanced to explain why the power implications of credit have been largely ignored. The most plausible is that, until the 1970s, UK companies' use of external finance was relatively low, and within their low levels of borrowings most bank credit was of a short-term nature, corresponding in principle if not in fact to Hilferding's circulation credit. The fact that a proportion of bank lending has changed to a medium-term nature (that is, is committed typically for periods of one to seven years) has served to highlight the conditions that banks attach to their credit, a topic we discussed in chapter 6. The other reason is that the powers conferred on banks by attaching strings to loans become manifest only when companies are in default of their loan agreements, a phenomenon that generally occurs only at times of crisis such as the current slump.

The monitoring of current accounts

One aspect of a recent trend towards centralisation within companies is that their finances, including cash management, are centralised in head office bank accounts. The ability to monitor a company's current account and therefore its liquidity position gives some banks yet another channel of influence over that company. The great advantage that this monitoring confers on banks is that the information thereby acquired on the state of the borrower's solvency is more up to date than any other source of financial information on the company. However, this monitoring facility is availably only to those banks that provide current account facilities, which effectively limits it to the High Street banks.

Moreover, the potential monitoring benefits may be somewhat dissipated in the case of large multinationals, which may hold current accounts with more than one bank.

Interlocking directorships

The channels of influence discussed thus far have tended to involve arms'-length relationships between the City and enterprises, but interlocking directorships involve a closer relationship which, because of its transparency, has received a great deal of attention.

Concern about interlocks focused on their anti-competitive nature in the money trust debates, while more recently commentators have emphasised the concentration of power in the hands of a limited number of corporate directors. Direct interlocks are frequently distinguished from indirect interlocks. In the former case two companies directly share one or more common directors on their respective boards, while in the latter case they have common directors via the board of a third enterprise. Writers further distinguish officer (executive director) interlocks from those involving outside directors (see Herman, 1981), where the former are believed to involve closer links and the exercise of a potentially greater degree of power.

It is generally accepted that interlocks between leading companies have been declining since the beginning of the century and that their economic significance is not as great as it was in the years before the First World War. It is also accepted that interlocks, of themselves, convey only the idea of a community of interest rather than power relations between companies, *except* when under-written by other financial relations.

City–industry alliances

For the classical writers on finance capital like Hilferding and Lenin, it was the *combination* of these four channels of influence, concentrated in the hands of the monopoly banks, that formed the basis of their theory of banks' domination over industrial companies. Modern writers on the topic tend to eschew the concept of finance capital and replace it with the notion of interest groups based on interlocks, ownership and, sometimes, credit relations (see Kotz, 1978; Herman, 1981; Overbeek, 1980).

A different conception of the relationship between the City and enterprises is that it is constituted by alliances. Two types are commonly identified. These involve the division of industry and commerce into two classes of companies, namely monopoly and international enterprises, with which the City, it is argued, forms an alliance. The nature of these alliances' power is not always explicitly spelled out, though the usual assumption is that the alliance partners participate on a more or less equal footing. Moreover, the basis on the alliance remains the rather fuzzy one of a coincidence of mutual interests. However, the presumption is that these two classes of company enjoy privileged access to the City's financial markets and other facilities as compared with non-monopoly and domestic (non-international) companies. If any power relations are involved they can be identified as the power of the alliance partners *vis-à-vis* the non-alliance companies.

Coakley and Harris (1983) have suggested a third approach to the relationship between the City and industry, which is that they may have conflicting interests at a conjunctural level while sharing a common interest in the expansion of profitable accumulation. *Ceteris paribus*, the City will at any point in time favour expansion of companies in the growth sectors of industry while simultaneously engaging in various forms of financial rationing *vis-à-vis* those in old or stagnant industries. In this way, the City acts as agent of competition via the credit and capital markets, disciplining or even liquidating unprofitable companies and facilitating the growth of profitable ones.

The merit of this approach is that neither monopoly characteristics nor international links shield companies from this competition and its disciplinary effects; this appears to be borne out by actual cases of the financial restructuring of multinational corporations. In such cases the power of the City is fairly unequivocal, but they are hardly typical of the normal relationship between the City and profitable companies where the basis for conflict is absent.

The material basis of the City's role to act as an agent of competition lies in its ability to influence the two key variables in financial markets, interest rates and exchange rates. The City's banking houses and investment institutions can influence these variables directly through their intervention in the credit, capital and foreign exchange markets. And historically, the Bank of England has represented the interests of the City, bringing its concerns to bear on government economic policy and, especially, monetary policy. In brief, the City has access to both direct and indirect means of influencing interest and exchange rates.

Constraints on the City's power

Thus far we have emphasised the levers of power that the City may exercise over the companies that comprise industry in Britain, but there are constraints on the City's power. One is that the City ultimately is dependent on profits generated by productive industry. Thus, it could be argued that the City would not support a monetarist deflation, which harms the industrial profits on which it depends. That dependency may be the case, but it does not follow that the City expropriates these profits *directly* via its lending to productive industry, for the City generates profits from lending to all types of private and state enterprises including sovereign states themselves. Indeed lending to states is one source of the City's profits the longevity of which exceeds most others, dating from the days when the wealthy City merchant Dick Whittington financed the purse of Henry IV and Henry V. More recently, lending to sovereign states had been one of the most rapidly expanding sources of City profits, until the spate of Third World and socialist states debt problems threw this into disarray.

Ignoring for a moment the intractable problem of possible defaults on some sovereign states' debt, one type of sovereign state lending must be regarded as *primus inter pares* within this category of lending: the City's loans to the British state. Why should this lending be special? The first reason is that sovereign states under-write their respective domestic *credit* systems through their central banks' lender-of-last-resort facility. It needs stressing that only the banking system, and not the whole financial system, is under-written, which goes to underline the centrality of banks (as the principal suppliers of credit), a centrality that the theorists of finance capital and a money trust recognised. What this means in effect is that banking lame ducks are guaranteed a level of state protection unique among modern corporations, financial and otherwise.

The second reason is the safety of domestic government debt. It would be unthinkable for the British state, which has supported the City's aims of retaining its world lead as an international financial centre, to repudiate any of its debts. In other words, British government lending is the most secure source of income for City institutions, as is emphasised by the epithet 'gilt-edged', which designates British government securities. The automatic nature of state support for the City as embodied in the lender-of-last-resort facility and non-repudiation of government debt may be contrasted with the *contingent* nature of state support for other enterprises. In the latter instance, state support depends upon a sufficient degree of political mobilisation, as the cases of the German and Canadian multinationals – AEG and Massey Ferguson – illustrate.

Even if the City can expropriate profits via sovereign states as well as from industry, it is not completely independent of or indifferent to the fortunes of industry, both world-wide and in particular national economies, as the repercussions of the current world crisis serve to highlight. This dependence underlies the danger of financial crisis that we discussed in chapter 4.

Conclusions

From the preceding discussion it is not possible to decide whether the City today constitutes a money trust. The difficulty lies in judging not whether the City has power at its disposal – it clearly has as we saw in chapters 5 and 6 – but in judging to what extent it actively wields this power. The fact that the money trust threat has ceased to be a major topic of discussion may be explained partly by the reluctance of the City to exercise its power and partly by the prevalence of the managerialist and neoclassical theories of the firm; the two theories deny that the City has access to levers of control over companies apart from the takeover threat. A further difficulty is the fact that the modern mechanisms of control are less transparent and obvious than they were when the concepts of money trusts and finance capital were first promulgated at the beginning of the twentieth century.

We think that the power of the City, the essential issue raised by the concepts of finance capital and a money trust, should be on the agenda for public discussion.

9

Monetarism and the City

For many, 1967 is remembered as the year when the devaluation of the pound was finally forced on Harold Wilson's somewhat reluctant government (and an equally reluctant City). But it is also significant for another reason: the Labour government agreed, with the International Monetary Fund, on a target for controlling one definition of the money supply (called 'domestic credit expansion') as part of the strings attached to the loan provided by the IMF to support sterling. Thus, 1967 was a watershed marking the beginning of the decline both of sterling's exchange rate (from $2.80 to below $1.60 in 1982) and of orthodox Keynesianism, which had considered the money supply to be unimportant for a macroeconomic policy designed to stabilize the economy near to full employment. Keynesianism gave way piece by piece until by 1980 the government had appeared to subordinate all its policies to one macroeconomic policy alone: control of the money supply.

The new orthodoxy, monetarism, reached its apogee with Mrs Thatcher's 1979 government. Its effects have been to worsen the depression, increase unemployment and the lead to the collapse of industrial output, but its causes are more obscure. Why should a British government have adopted such a radical policy when it had already been tried and failed in General Pinochet's Chile and other countries? One explanation that has achieved some support is that monetarism is the policy of the City; it was adopted by the government because financial capital required it.

Was the City in favour of monetarism? The conclusion reached in this chapter is that monetarism did conform to the City's interests, but that this conformity was not without its contradictions. Moreover, monetarism and its contradictory relation with financial capital have a history reaching back to the beginning of the nineteenth century. Let us begin by examining the main elements of modern monetarism in the UK, while acknowledging that monetarism during the 1970s has become an international phenomenon.

Monetarism in one country

Since 1980 Britain has been experiencing a crisis or depression that ranks with the Great Depression of the 1930s. Since the May 1979 election, unemployment increased two and a half times over, to reach an official total of some 3.2 million in the spring of 1983 – 13.8 per cent of the registered workforce and the highest total recorded in Britain's history. The national average conceals some of the disparities between regions and localities. For example, the official unemployment rate in Northern Ireland (20.6 per cent) was one-and-a-half times the national average. At the same time, real output (GDP) has been falling or stagnating since the end of 1979, or shortly after the Conservative victory. It fell by some 3.8 and 1.0 per cent, respectively, in the year ending 1980(IV) and 1981(IV).

The crisis has sharpened the pace of de-industrialisation in Britain through a combination of high interest and exchange rates (both in real and nominal terms) and declining production in the initial three years of Conservative rule. The high exchange rate alone implied a 50 per cent drop in international competitiveness during 1979 and 1980 as measured by an IMF index of competitiveness. This has further speeded up de-industrialisation by inducing industrial enterprises to invest and transfer production overseas; for a high pound makes the purchase of overseas assets priced in their local currencies cheaper than otherwise. A further index of de-industrialisation is the trail of liquidations and financial re-structurings left in the wake of the current crisis. The British toy industry is just one sector that has been decimated. Traditional sectors like mechanical engineering have fared only a little better. In chapter 6 we saw that the engineering firm Stone-Platt became the largest victim of the crisis in early 1982. The number of firms required to undertake financial re-structuring with the Bank of England acting as broker (the so-called 'Industrial Lifeboat') is estimated to number about four dozen and includes a number of large multinational corporations.

In the midst of this crisis the City has thrived. Bank profits for the 1980 and 1981 financial years were so high that the Chancellor felt it prudent to tax their windfall element, although by mid-1982 banks were having to set aside high bad debt provisions out of profits. Similarly, since the abolition of exchange controls the financial institutions embarked on a spree of overseas investment unprecedented since the First World War, as we saw in earlier chapters. The only cloud that hangs over the City is the risk of a financial crash as the effects of the crisis in industry, the Third World and Soviet bloc countries spill over on to the financial system.

The fact that under monetarist policies the country has suffered while the City has prospered does not prove that the City has supported monetarism. We have to examine each element of the monetarist package to judge its connection with the City.

Monetarism has three basic elements: (a) the promotion of *laissez-faire*, unhindered competition throughout the economy; (b) deflationary fiscal policy based on high taxes and restriction of government spending; and (c) control of the money supply.

The promotion of laissez-faire

Conservatism has not, historically, always embraced the ideology of *laissez-faire*. The postwar Macmillan–Butler era, although inaugurated by the slogan of making 'a bonfire of controls', was marked by a commitment to state intervention in industry and to the public provision of welfare services more or less removed from the market-place. And nineteenth-century conservatism was based upon protecting British industry and agriculture from foreign competition. But the ideology of free competition and the survival of the fittest has been a consistent organising theme for conservative politics, however much it contradicted the actual practice. The avowed aim of Mrs Thatcher's government was to eliminate that contradiction: monetarism was designed to make competition a reality, to mobilize public opinion against state intervention in the operation of markets, and ultimately to eliminate or reduce that intervention.

Two of the crucial markets from which state intervention was withdrawn by Mrs Thatcher's government were financial markets at the heart of the City: the foreign exchange markets and the credit markets. Previous governments had attempted to control or determine exchange rates and interest rates to varying degrees. Attlee's postwar Labour government had attempted to determine the interest rates on credit very rigidly, forcing them down to low levels and holding them there, while it also attempted to fix the exchange rate between sterling and the dollars: indeed, fixed exchange rates were an internationally agreed regime, part of the Bretton Woods system agreed in 1944. The Labour government that preceded Mrs Thatcher's also intervened in these markets, but instead of attempting to determine exchange rates and interest rates rigidly, it attempted to influence them within a flexible regime. The government installed in 1979, however, claimed to leave these rates entirely to virtually unhampered market forces by abolishing existing controls. We examine these controls in more detail in later sections.

This *laissez-faire* practice in the financial markets means two things. First, banks and other private agents would have no controls imposed over what they could or could not buy or sell on those markets. Most significantly, the removal of all remaining exchange controls in 1979 meant that they could buy foreign assets – invest abroad – without restriction. Second, the government would not throw its weight on the opposite side of the balance, to offset private sector movements in order to try to preserve the exchange rate or interest rates at a particular, announced level. If the pound was being sold for dollars, the government would not buy pounds to offset the downward pressure on sterling and support the exchange rate. Similarly, if the demand for bills were to fall, the government would not buy bills to keep interest rates down (or, the same thing, to keep bill and bond prices up).

Under Mrs Thatcher the government has gone further along the road towards freedom for the financial markets than has any other in Britain's modern history, but it has not been able to withdraw from them completely. At the end of November 1982 a spate of selling hit the pound as a result of which its exchange rate against the dollar fell by 5.6 per cent over a fortnight. The speed of the fall caused alarm in the Treasury and Bank of England and steps were taken to stabilize the exchange rate by buying pounds. Interestingly, though, the government's proclaimed ideology prevented it from announcing a rise in interest rates, a classic measure for attracting buyers back into sterling in such circumstances; since the authorities had renounced their claim to influence interest rates, they could not, as in the old days, announce that rates would be raised. Instead, therefore, two private bodies – Barclays Bank and Midland Bank – were prevailed upon by the authorities to announce increases in their own interest rates, and they complied.

N B

Freedom in the financial markets is not the only aspect of *laissez-faire*: the other – the 'rolling back of the state' – is that which employers and workers in 'the real economy' see as directly affecting them. They relate their closures and redundancies in many cases to the government's *laissez-faire* policy of allowing the full force of competition in industry and commerce to operate unimpeded. Unlike Mr Heath's Conservative government Mrs Thatcher's has stood out against hand-outs to firms that suffer from that competition, and has attempted to ensure that even nationalized industries bow to the force of competition. Those that are profitable or potentially so were sold back to private ownership, while those that suffered chronic losses were forced to react to them in the manner of a private firm: by closures, rationalizations and redundancies linked to productivity improvements.

As in the financial markets, *laissez-faire* in industry has had its contradictions under monetarism. One is that firms in some sectors have benefitted from government support in relation to the expansion of military spending. Another is that firms in difficulties have received aid from their banks and investment institutions with the encouragement of the Bank of England. Indeed, the Bank has taken the lead in organising the City's attempts to rescue enterprises that would otherwise have been pushed over the brink by competitition for shrinking markets. This is a paradox of the government's policies, since the Bank of England is part of the machinery of the state while the government is disclaiming any attempts to prop up lame ducks. Just as the Bank of England could not take its own action to raise interest rates at the end of November 1982 and urged the private banks to do so for it, so the government's own ideology prevented it from aiding industry itself and, through the Bank of England, the private banks and investment institutions were encouraged to do the state's work for it. The situation is similar to the period between the wars in which a government had rejected Keynesian-type intervention encouraged the Bank of England, then a private institution, to give financial support to (even to the extent of buying shares in) major firms in engineering and armaments, steel and shipping. Richard Sayers, the Bank's official historian, described the background to the industrial support of the 1930s as one in which 'nobody else wanted the hot potato but all – including ministers of the Crown – were anxious that it should not be dropped.' And the *Financial Times* of 13 December 1982 commented: 'Plus ça change'.

At the same time, the *laissez-faire* policies of monetarist theory singled out the putative 'monopoly' power of trade unions in the labour markets for special attention. Wages were to be determined by the demand and supply for labour, without any incomes policy 'artificially' holding them down and with measures taken to weaken trades unions' ability to push them up 'artificially'. Despite the vigour of the attack on the trade union movement, this is the element of monetarist theory that has been furthest removed from its practice under Mrs Thatcher, for her government imposed very strict (cash) limits on the pay increases attainable by the state's own employees, whether they were employed directly (civil servants), less directly (health workers) or indirectly (university teachers). Since the number of wage packets and salary cheques that depend upon the state's budget comprises a very high proportion of total wages and salaries, the ceiling imposed on those incomes is, *de facto*, an effective incomes policy.

Thus there were contradictions in and qualifications to the Conservatives' efforts to promote freedom in financial markets, industry and commerce, and the labour market. Nevertheless, *laissez-faire* was the order of the day under Mrs Thatcher's monetarism, and, even if competition was not quite given free rein, its impact was considerable.

Deflationary fiscal policy

Bankruptcy and redundancies in 'the real economy' have been increased not only by a monetarist government opening the door to the winds of competition, and doing so at a time when the economies of all Britain's major competitors were in recession, but also by its pursuit of a deflationary fiscal policy. In other words, the government has attempted to hold down the deficit that exists between what the state receives (in taxes, rates and other revenue) and what is pays out (in salaries and wages, purchases of current goods, construction projects, pensions, social security and other disbursements). In the early days of Mrs Thatcher's government the public sector borrowing requirement (PSBR), one measure of that deficit, became as much a headline indicator of Britain's virility as the national football team's goal-scoring ability. In an attempt to cut the proportion of national income the deficit represents, the government raised indirect taxes (like value added tax), cut some spending programmes, and attempted to induce cuts in the spending of local authorities and other semi-autonomous parts of the state machine.

The government's intention to cut its spending, increase its receipts and reduce the PSBR as a percentage of gross domestic product (GDP) was spelled out in the targets of the medium-term financial strategy (MTFS) it adopted in 1980. Table 9.1 reveals that, while planned tax receipts were to increase consistently over the plan period, real government expenditure was planned to be cut to 95 per cent of its 1979–80 level by 1983–84 and the ratio of the PSBR to GDP was to decline to only 31 per cent of its initial level over the five years that Mrs Thatcher planned for her first term of office.

Such a fiscal policy was bound to have a deflationary effect upon the whole economy, reducing the market for firms' products and increasing redundancies. High taxes meant that consumers and firms had less to spend, while low government spending implied that the state's own demand, and the purchase of the services of teachers, nurses and those whose salaries come from the state, were reduced.

In fact, the government did not manage to hold back state spending to the planned extent. Several unanticipated factors affected the outcome, the most notable being the economic crisis itself; pushing unemployment far beyond anything the government had predicted, it forced an increase in total outgoings on social security, unemployment and related payments. This, combined with the government's planned increase in military spending (planned increases of a steady 3 per cent each year plus full allowance to offset inflation), meant that spending in other areas had to be cut back dramatically. Municipal housing programmes came to a standstill, for example, adding to the woes of the building industry.

To have a deflationary fiscal policy in the midst of a major economic recession could only exacerbate unemployment, and the policy flies in the face of the conventional wisdom of the postwar years (or, at least, the wisdom that was conventional until Mr Callaghan pronounced in 1976 that governments cannot spend their way out of recession). The policy was adopted largely in order to control the money supply (to which we turn in the next section). Indeed, the medium-term financial strategy published its fiscal targets as one element in its targets for the money supply. At the same time, cutting the deficit was part of the monetarist aim of encouraging *laissez-faire*.

The fiscal stance fits with the aim of liberating free market forces, in the general sense that a reduction in state spending would have been the visible monetary effect of 'rolling back the state'. But that does not explain why the policy was to reduce the deficit, for a cut in state spending matched or surpassed by a cut in taxation would have accomplished more for that roll-back without reducing the

TABLE 9.1 MTFS FISCAL POLICY TARGETS

	Actual 1979–80	1980–81	1981–82	1982–83	1983–84
Total government expenditure (£b)	88.7	88.7	86.9	84.5	83.9
Total government receipts (£b)	78.5	80.3	80.3	82.7	84.5
PSBR/GDP (%)	4.8	3.8	3.0	2.3	1.5

Source: Financial Statement and Budget Report, 1980–81 (London: HMSO).

deficit: spending on, say, the 'stifling' welfare state would be cut
and so would the taxation that is supposed to restrict initiative, but
the amount the state borrowed would be higher than if taxes were
not cut. However, reduction of the deficit was seen as essential for
rolling back the state in a specific area – the City and its financial
markets.

High deficits have to be financed: if this were achieved by bank
lending it would jeopardise the aim of controlling the money
supply, but if it were accomplished by government bonds and other
borrowing in a way that did not increase the money supply it would,
it was argued, deprive private industry of finance. This 'crowding
out' would occur because banks, pension funds, insurance companies, investment and unit-trusts and the host of other investors
would have to choose between lending to the government (buying
the newly issued bonds) *or* lending to private industry (buying
newly issued industrial shares). This competition between the
government and private borrowers would push up interest rates
and drive the private borrowers from the financial markets.

The validity of the 'crowding out' rationale for cutting the state's
deficit is tenuous, and even some monetarists have criticised this
use of fiscal policy as an instrument of monetary policy. But crowding out did provide a reason for monetarism's deflationary fiscal
policy which related it to the aim of *laissez-faire* – the aim of
increasing the weight of the private sector in the forces of supply
and demand within the City's financial markets.

Control of the money supply

The most prominent part of the Conservatives' monetarist strategy
was control of the money supply, a brake on the rate at which the
amount of money in the hands of British people and enterprises
could grow. The idea is confusing, since people often have no clear
idea what is meant by 'the money supply' or 'the amount of money
in the hands of' – and, indeed, the government itself found it
difficult to pin down the slippery nature of the beast. At first the
idea was to restrict 'sterling M3' (£M3), which included such items
as notes and coin in people's pockets but predominantly sterling
current (cheque) accounts, deposit accounts and other deposits at
banks. But by 1982 the government had come to consider a broader
money supply (or 'liquidity' measure), which also included
deposits at building societies as part of the total that had to be
restrained. Roughly speaking, then, control of the money supply

meant controlling the domestic stock of spendable resources available to the private sector.

The logic of the policy was as surprising as the rationale for a deflationary fiscal stance: Keynesian conventional wisdom would require discretionary powers of intervention to secure an increase in (or absence of constraints on) money or spendable resources in order to encourage the private sector to spend its way out of the prevailing recession, demanding the goods that the idle factories could produce. The monetarists' argument for the opposite policy stressed the importance of reducing the rate of inflation of prices and wages and the belief that price increases are caused directly by increases in the money supply. Cutting inflation rather than cutting unemployment was to be the aim (although it is doubtful whether the electorate had expressed such a clear choice); and holding back the money supply was to be the instrument, although economists were deeply divided over whether the theory linking the two (the Quantity Theory of Money) was valid.

The medium-term financial strategy, which set targets for the state's spending and revenue, also set targets for the rate of growth of the money supply – defined, then, as sterling M3 (see table 9.2).

TABLE 9.2 MONEY CONTROL TARGETS: MEDIUM-TERM FINANCIAL STRATEGY

	1980–81	*1981–82*	*1982–83*	*1983–84*
Annual growth of £M3 (%)	7–11	6–10	5–9	4–8

Source: Financial Statement and Budget Report, 1980–81 (London: HMSO).

The aim was to decrease the growth range of the money supply by one percentage point per year. In the event, the outcome was that the money supply (£M3) could not be tightly controlled; but, nevertheless, inflation fell dramatically. The reduction in inflation resulted from several factors – unemployment and the weakness of world demand for primary commodities such as oil among them – but, although it was the main purpose behind control of the money supply, that policy can hardly claim the winner's medal.

Within the three elements of monetarist strategy, control of the money supply has an ambiguous status. On the one hand, it appeared to be the principal policy to which *laissez-faire* and deflationary fiscal policy was subordinated; but on the other hand the aim of creating a free-enterprise economy by reducing the role of the state was a more far-reaching aim, a political programme with much deeper roots than control of the money supply. Which element of policy was dominant and which subordinate was not important as long as each complemented the other, but some contradictions became apparent between the elements, particularly in so far as they affected the City.

The greatest difficulty for monetarism is the reconciliation of *laissez-faire* with control of the money supply, of which bank deposits are the predominant component. Control of the money supply requires the government either to impose direct controls on the banks', and possibly other deposit institutions' operations, or to bring its weight to bear on demand and supply in the markets (for credit and foreign exchange) which influence the position of banks. The pursuit of control over the money supply always, therefore, carries the danger that the first of monetarism's three rules could change from 'the promotion of *laissez-faire*' to '*laissez-faire* for all (except banks)'. In consequence, even if the City were to support monetarism, the support of the banks for control of the money supply was always conditional on its being achieved without any direct restrictions on their freedom: it had to be achieved without direct controls on the banks and with the government operating as indirectly and unobtrusively as possible in the markets that affect them. This distinction between direct and market controls is crucial for monetarists, for they find government influence through market operations more acceptable and more commensurate with *laissez-faire* principles.

One type of direct control that had previously been applied to banks was a ceiling on their lending; another was a series of penalties ('the corset') on expanding their deposits. But in July 1980 the Committee of London Clearing Banks made clear that, if the money supply could normally be controlled only by such means, they would not be in favour of that element of monetarism: 'The banks do not believe that reliance should be placed on direct lending controls other than in the most exceptional circumstances [for] such measures inhibit competition in financial markets and lead to a panoply of distortions. . . .'

Similarly, they felt that it would be undesirable for the government to impose controls or penalties to restrict the growth of the money supply generated by inflows of money from abroad, for 'it would be liable to inhibit the operation of international financial transactions, for which the UK is a major centre.'

The City, and in particular the banks, indicated with actions as well as words that they were committed to monetarism only as long as control of the money supply did not directly interfere with their freedom to generate profits. While bankers over a period of years had been pressing Labour and Conservative governments to control inflation by controlling the amount of money in the economy, their banks actively went out of their way to subvert the one major direct monetary control that interfered with their freedom to make profits, 'the corset'.

This control, which applied over three periods, 1973–75, 1976–77 and 1978–80, imposed, in effect, a tax on banks whose deposits had grown too rapidly. But the banks took three steps to circumvent it. One was to build up a surplus of the relevant deposits in anticipation of the corset being imposed (as they did in 1978). Another was to make it easier (at a profit) for depositors with surplus funds officially to bypass the banking system by lending money directly, on 'bills of exchange', to the borrowers to whom the banks would otherwise have lent depositors' money. The latter process is known as 'disintermediation'. A third loophole was the switching of sterling business from the UK to overseas or offshore centres whose sterling business with the UK need not affect the money supply. In 1979 and 1980 the latter two made nonsense of the government's attempts to control the money supply. Since the banks undertook these steps specifically to avoid the restrictions that the corset placed upon their freedom to make profits, some may think the Committee of London Clearing Banks disingenuous for rejecting such direct controls on the grounds of their effectiveness rather than self-interest: 'the disintermediation which [direct controls] generate (such as the 'bill leak' under the corset) reduces their efficacy considerably. . . .;

Market methods of control

Mrs Thatcher's government, sharing the bankers' dislike of direct controls (or, at least, of controls that affect them), attempted to use indirect or market methods of control to achieve its money supply objectives. This may appear surprising to some, for after all, did not the introduction of the Competition and Credit Control (CCC) reforms of 1971 herald a movement away from the direct controls of the 1960s towards a reliance on interest rates as a market control over the money supply? That was certainly the spirit of these reforms until the dramatic growth of the money supply in 1972 and 1973 forced Mr Heath's administration to swallow the pill of additional direct controls in the form of the corset.

The inadequacy of interest rates alone as an instrument of money supply control forced a rethink on the nature of controls which in the late 1970s led to what Artis and Lewis (1981) describe as a supply-side approach to control. In contrast to the usual definitions of money supply in terms of various bank deposits and notes and coin, the supply-side approach focuses on the credit counterparts of the money supply. By manipulating balance sheet identities, one can identify the following counterparts to a change in £M3:

> change in £M3 = PSBR − gilt sales + change in bank lending
> + net external flows − change in banks' capital base.

The attraction of this approach is that the PSBR, gilt sales and net external flows can be identified with fiscal policy, debt management and exchange rate policies, respectively. Now, part of the shortfall between the PSBR and gilt sales to insurance companies, pension funds and other non-banks has to be financed by bank loans to the government (another is financed by people buying National Savings Certificates). Because these bank loans to the government increase the money supply and have achieved notoriety as Mrs Thatcher's 'suitcase money', her government and its City supporters have determined to control the money supply almost exclusively by means of this counterpart by systematically reducing the PSBR (in principle through state expenditure cuts, but in practice through tax increases). This tactic neatly dovetailed in with the other components of monetarism, namely *laissez-faire* and a deflationary fiscal policy. Accordingly, where state expenditure cuts have been made they have been justified on the grounds that a reduction in the PSBR was a prerequisite for the control of the money supply.

But the logic is faulty: econometric evidence is able to demonstrate only a weak relationship, if any, between movements in PSBR and in £M3, and Savage (1980) in fact established an inverse relationship between the two variables. In any event, the combined effects of supporting benefits payments in the current crisis and of increased military spending have led to an overrun of the PSBR targets contained in the MTFS. In response, the government has attempted to square the circle by maximising borrowing through non-bank sources (gilt sales, National Savings), and this was an important factor in the increase of nominal interest rates in the early years of the present administration.

Moreover reductions in the PSBR appeared as a soft option in a situation when the authorities' influence over the other counterparts via interest rates appeared tenuous, to say the least. Net external flows to the government purse and the private sector tend to respond perversely to interest rate changes, for the high interest rates designed to choke off bank lending at home attract overseas funds into bank deposits and reserves in the UK, thereby increasing the money supply. Similarly, it is not evident that high nominal interest rates did, in effect, moderate bank lending to the private sector, since the response of corporate borrowers to interest rate increases appears to have been to maintain or even increase borrowings: they borrow in order to pay the interest.

The preceding discussion has dealt with problems of market control of the money supply in a situation where the authorities have retained and used discretionary control over short-term interest rates, even if the situation is now to allow interest rates to be determined more by market forces. Instead of allowing the authorities to control interest rates, some monetarists have proposed an alternative method of market control over the money supply. This is called monetary base control, which in its extreme version would require interest rate movements to be determined completely by changes in the monetary base (notes and coin and bankers' deposits with the Bank of England), thus eliminating the Bank of England's discretion in this respect. Control over the monetary base – the banks' reserves of cash – can be employed as a lever over the banking system, for the system needs cash to operate the payments mechanism, to meet withdrawals of deposits and to meet obligations in the event of committed but unused credit facilities like overdrafts being drawn down. As such, the supply of cash constrains the expansion of banks' non-cash assets (mainly lending) and so on operates as a quantitative market control over banks' balance sheets. This is thought to be an effective method of control since the authorities exercise a monopoly over cash in the banking system, but opponents have pointed to its likelihood of excerbating interest rate volatility as well as producing unacceptably high interest rate levels.

The City's view of the high interest rates resulting from domestic and overseas monetary control policies was equivocal. Some banks, particularly the High Street clearing banks, profit considerably from high rates because they increase their profit on lending while the money deposited with them in current accounts, being interest-free, costs them no more. This fact has made it appear that the City's support of monetarism is a matter of crude self-interest – the attempt to control the money supply can appear as an excuse for high interest rates with consequently high bank profits.

But the City's attitude to high interest rates is, in fact, more ambiguous. Their high level under Mrs Thatcher's regime was accompanied by volatility; for, in accordance with the promotion of *laissez-faire*, demand and supply in the credit markets were increasingly left to their own devices with less 'smoothing' by the Bank of England. For those banks that do not have a large base of current account deposits but, being wholesalers of credit, have to borrow large amounts themselves at market interest rates, a sharp rise in rates increases their costs, and in some circumstances their cost of borrowing may outpace the yield on their loans. Moreover, those parts of the City that do business with British industry – those bankers, for example, who lend to industrialists – are threatened by high interest rates, which transform the firms to which they lend from prime assets into potentially bad debts. The clearing banks said, in 1980, that they 'know only too well from contact with their corporate customers that the current level of interest rates is imposing a considerable burden on the profitability and cash flow of many industrial companies'. And the Bank of England, fearful for the effects of high interest rates and depression upon the bad debts facing the banks, increased the activities of its industrial department.

The City, therefore, was not wholly in favour of market control of the money supply if it involved high interest rates, any more than it would have been in favour of direct controls to hold down the stock of money. Apart from anything else, the political unpopularity of high interest rates, the effect of which spreads to every borrower from giant firms to young house-purchasers, makes the City sensitive to accusations that it is profiteering from others' misfortunes. It was in favour of monetarism as long as control of the money supply was achieved by cutting state spending (deflationary fiscal policy), and as long as the government promoted *laissez-faire* in the markets for foreign exchange and credit; and there is no doubt that on this basis some parts of the City actively pushed for monetarist policies to further their perceived interests.

The earliest propagandists for modern monetarism in Britain

were Professor Harry Johnson and the group he built at the London School of Economics in the late 1960s, and Peter Jay, whose platform was *The Times*. But the constituency that actively took up their views comprised some economists who wrote stockbrokers' newsletters, some bankers and fund managers and, especially the dealers in money, bonds and the foreign exchanges. The dealers wholeheartedly embraced the basic theoretical propositions underlying monetarism – the idea that government borrowing leads to an increase in the money supply which, in turn, causes inflation – because, whether accurate or not, their simplicity meant that quick decisions could be made to buy or sell according to the state of some simple indicators such as the latest statistics on the money supply or public sector borrowing.

That constituency gives some justification to the claim that monetarism was the product of the City's actively arguing for it, but it would be wrong to identify monetarism with the City's interests. We have seen that City support for control over the money supply was conditional and qualified. At the same time, support for *laissez-faire* in the financial markets was far from unequivocal. While bankers and fund managers were wholly in favour of the abolition of exchange controls, which from 1979 gave full freedom to export capital and credit, the volatility of interest rates and exchange rates produced by the free operation of market forces was not wholly welcome. Dealers can make large profits from such fluctuations, but the risk of large losses too is unavoidable, and traditional City people find the unpredictability of such a regime uncomfortable.

Thus, instead of the completely unfettered market forces demanded by monetarist purists, a powerful City current favoured a stabilization policy under which the authorities would step in to buy (sterling on foreign exchange markets or bills on the money market) wherever speculators were selling and vice versa. Moreover, although the City was united in its support for the policy of cutting government borrowing, even that was, in some sense, against its own interests, for the City's strength is founded partly upon the large, risk-free and profitable lending to the British state: historically, this lending has been the bedrock on which its other operations have been built.

The City's pursuit of monetarist policies was, therefore, equivocal, and the conflicts between City and Whitehall over how they were to be operated came to a head two days before Christmas 1982, when Mrs Thatcher's decision effectively to sack the Gover-

nor of the Bank of England and appoint a successor more
sympathetic to her monetarism was announced. The Governor is
the spokesman for the City, or, more accurately, a marshaller and
former of City opinion, and as such Mr Richardson and his Bank of
England had several times been out of alignment with government
policies, while Mr Leigh-Pemberton was appointed as something
of a City outsider but a political trustee of the monetarist party
within the government.

The evolution of the financial markets

Although Mrs Thatcher's monetarism was not the simple product
of the City actively pursuing its interests, it was the City's policy in a
more subtle way. There is no doubt that the way the City's markets
operate, particularly the way they evolved in the 1970s, set the
conditions that put monetarism on the agenda and made it appear
to some as both necessary and feasible.

In earlier chapters we outlined two of the principal developments in financial markets, the growth of the institutional investors
(pension funds, insurance companies and trusts) on the one hand
and the growth of Eurodollar banking on the other. Both meant
that vast sums of highly mobile private money were able to dominate financial markets. Institutional investors and the banks that
advised them or managed their funds controlled previously
unimaginable sums generated by British savings, which they could
switch in and out of government bonds to affect their interest rates
and (before as well as after the 1979 removal of exchange controls)
into and out of sterling, affecting the exchange rate. The Eurodollar banks controlled literally immeasurable sums of international
money, which they could switch into and out of sterling and into
and out of British bills and bonds.

Whereas governments between 1945 and 1971 had adopted
Keynesian policies of trying to stabilise exchange rates and interest
rates, subsequent administrations found it increasingly difficult to
adhere to such policies because of these two phenomena and the
general growth of multinational corporations. If a government of
the 1970s tried to stabilise the exchange rate by selling foreign
exchange (buying sterling) when speculators, banks, institutional
investors and multinationals were selling sterling, the weight of the
money on the other side would have been impossible to balance
without seriously eroding the foreign exchange reserves. Indeed, in

the months before Mr Callaghan's 1976 speech repudiating Keynes, the authorities had been shaken to find that their attempts to stabilise the exchange rate by buying sterling had been swept on to the beach by the force of this swollen tide of Eurobanks' liquidity rushing away from sterling. The enormity of the authorities' task is borne out by the fact the foreign currency transactions of a single large multinational may exceed those of the Bank of England. Similarly, if the authorities had attempted to stabilise interest rates by buying bills at lower rates when Eurobanks and institutional investors, convinced that interest rates should be higher, were selling them, they would have faced a daunting task. Indeed, because of their size, the large pool of funds did create several embarassing incidents when the authorities, in selling government debt, tried to outguess the institutions' and banks' expectations.

The size and mobility of market funds in the 1970s made it difficult for any government that wanted to use the markets to stabilise interest and exchange rates; monetarism's promotion of *laissez-faire* in financial markets became a necessity rather than a policy choice, given the City's growing international role. These developments also meant that no such government could avoid attempting to control the money supply or avoid a deflationary fiscal policy. If governments could not stabilise exchange rates or interest rates by buying and selling against the market, they could attempt to influence them to some extent by influencing the opinions, and hence the purchases and sales, of market operators. Since the City's bars, newspapers and dealing rooms believed that they should sell sterling and government bonds whenever the money supply or government borrowing grew too fast, a government that wanted to prevent falls in the exchange rate or rises in interest rates had to deliver the requisite sacrifices. It had to restrict the money supply and government borrowing to produce favourable opinions in the market. There was no god-given law compelling market operators to believe in those particular indicators – if everyone believed that money supply and government borrowing were irrelevant to the exchange rate, for example, then they would be irrelevant – but as long as they did, governments felt forced to respect them.

For some monetarists, the way that the City markets operated was so influential that they based their policies on the assumption that the whole economy worked in the same way. In the early stages of Mrs Thatcher's monetarism, several in the government believed that, if the growth of the money supply were cut, inflation would fall without a significant rise in unemployment. Their optimism was not just wishful thinking but was supported by the theoretical models developed by economists such as Professor Minford and his Liverpool University team. The idea was that, if the government announced that it was going to control the growth of the money supply, and if everyone believed the old theory that says that prices and money are directly linked, the announcement (such as that contained in the 1980 medium-term financial strategy) would lead immediately to expectations that inflation would fall. In particular, it was argued, workers and employers would immediately recognise that prices were going to be more stable and would rapidly settle wage negotiations at a lower level than they would otherwise have done. With the ensuing wage moderation, companies would be happy to employ their existing workforce and would not create redundancies.

The crucial element here was the theorists' assumption that workers and unions would *believe* the theory and would instantaneously adjust their expectations of inflation (and, hence, their actions) in response to an announcement of future control over the money supply. But in fact, the people who did exhibit such fundamentalist faith in the theory and such dazzling speed of decision-making were the sharp young dealers on the financial markets and their City clients; it is remarkable that some economists have been so influenced by the *modus operandi* of those markets as to think that trade union and employers' wage negotiators, schooled in a rather different market place, would work in the same way.

Thus, the way the City worked in the 1970s set the conditions and climate for monetarism in several ways. However, it was not wholly a new policy, for it sought to mimic in some ways the financial conditions that obtained in the days when London stood at the centre of an Empire and controlled the web of financial links spun by the gold standard.

Parallels with the gold standard

Monetarism and the gold standard are associated with diametrically opposed international standings of the British economy. On the one hand, the gold standard in the nineteenth century was synonymous with success, being linked with both the apogee of the British Empire and the hegemonic world role of the City during the period between 1870 and 1914. On the other hand, monetarism is associated with the hastening de-industrialisation of the British economy in the current recession, despite the undiminished pre-eminence of the City in the Euromarkets and other international financial markets. Nevertheless, the operation of the gold standard serves to remind us that monetarist policies are not the twentieth-century brainchild of Milton Friedman or Friedrich von Hayek but can be traced back to at least the beginning of the last century, even if some of their detail or institutional setting differs.

The 1870–1914 period was co-terminous with the operation of the international gold standard proper, and since the gold standard enjoyed a brief revival from the mid-1920s to the early 1930s, its operation coincided with two great world depressions. This, just as monetarism is associated with the current world depression, consti-tutes one link between monetarism and the gold standard. But if Britain was not the first country to adopt monetarist policies in recent years, its lead in establishing a gold standard is undisputed. Britain had been on a *de facto* gold standard from as early as 1717–97 and, following the Napoleonic Wars, on a *de jure* standard from 1821.

How did the gold standard operate? In 1717 Isaac Newton had established gold's price at £3 17s. 10½d.; the pound was fixed at that price to gold and to other currencies on the gold standard. At this fixed price the Bank of England (which then was still a private company) was willing to buy or sell gold in exchange for notes, which were convertible into gold. Gold coin circulated freely, and gold bullion could be freely imported or exported. In other words, the gold standard ensured that British money (sterling) was anchored to a fixed international standard. Moreover, it con-stituted an international system that was effectively orchestrated from the City of London, given Britain's leading world military and economic role.

In addition to their mutual association with slumps, both the gold standard and monetarism share some of the same objectives. One objective of the gold standard was the removal of discretion from fickle governments in the operation of economic and espe-cially monetary policy. The rationale behind it derived partly from an alleged association of wide government discretion in economic management with an erosion of individual freedom, which many regard as the ultimate objective of *laissez-faire* policies. In fact, it derived from a suspicion that discretion over monetary policy exacerbates the movements of the trade cycle and, as Sayers

(1957a) argues, from the long British tradition that tampering with the monetary unit implies a fraud on debtors or creditors. In constraining governments' discretion, monetary targets such as those of the MTFS are favoured by some in the City in the 1980s because they are seen as the contemporary equivalent of the gold standard of the nineteenth century.

Throughout the nine decades following the resumption of cash payments in 1821, the gold standard acted as an external force which circumscribed the discretion of the enacting authorities. Under it, governments had to subordinate their economic policies to the need to maintain the fixed rate of exchange between the pound and gold, and the money supply was determined by the 'automatic' international inflows and outflows of gold. Likewise, the Conservatives in the 1980s hoped that the MTFS, with its overriding target for the money supply and public borrowing (rather than the exchange rate), would operate as an internal standard having a similar effect. But Mrs Thatcher's medium-term financial strategy was bedevilled by disagreement over how the money supply should be defined; for setting an overriding target for the growth of this item proved to be a weak discipline if there was uncertainty over what it comprised. Should the money supply include, for example, deposits with building societies and other deposit institutions as well as bank deposits?

The fact that the question was posed and that there was no satisfactory answer (the authorities in the end eclectically watching on one hand a measure including building society deposits and on the other one excluding them) reflected the changes that were going on in Britain's financial system, and the fact that bankers in the City were apprehensive of direct controls over the money supply. The most important financial change in this respect was the fact that, as we saw in chapter 7, building societies and banks had become increasingly alike by the beginning of the 1980s. The bankers' apprehension was that control of a money supply that was defined to include mainly bank deposits would restrict their freedom and competitive position *vis-à-vis* the building societies.

These modern issues were similar to those that split the City into two bitterly opposed camps in the first half of the nineteenth century, the Currency School and the Banking School. The policy issues that divided them hinged on their different definitions of money, but beneath this was the question of whether the banking system should remain free from government controls.

The Currency School (of whom the most prominent was the

banker, Lord Overstone) viewed money simply as notes and coin or currency, as their name implies. Notes and coin, then as now, are simply a liability of the state or an asset for those (principally the banks) who hold them. The Currency School's leading opponents – Thomas Tooke and John Fullarton of the Banking School – criticised this definition for being too narrow and for excluding credit of various types. They recognised that credit, not notes and coin, forms a preponderant share of banks' assets, and should thus be incorporated in any meaningful definition of money.

In the event, the Currency School's narrower definition was enshrined the 1844 Bank Charter Act, which established a legal framework for the control of notes and coin as the responsibility of one section of the Bank of England, the Issue Department. Credit was left unregulated and nominally the responsibility of the other section of the Bank, the Banking Department. As early as 1847 the Act had to be suspended owing to the financial crisis, so the abandonment of the MTFS in 1982 by the Conservative regime has a historical precedent.

With the benefit of hindsight, we can see that the definition-of-money controversy hinged on an understanding and measurement of the role of the credit system, which in turn is underpinned by the banking system in capitalist economies. This is recognised in contemporary debates, where *all* definitions of money include some measure of banks' liabilities and deposits (recall that the Banking School focused on banks assets or credit), as well as notes and coin. M1 adds 'sight' deposits (mainly current account deposits) to notes and coin, while sterling M3 adds all sterling deposits of the UK public and private sectors. And the broadest possible definition of money, Private Sector Liquidity 2 (PSL 2), includes not only all the deposits of all deposit institutions (banks, savings banks and building societies), but also other money market instruments and certificates of tax deposit. In their March 1982 Budget, the Conservatives set targets for the growth of these three definitions of money, namely M1, £M3 and PSL 2.

The differences between the Currency and Banking Schools over the definition of money were related to differences over whether the state should regulate the banking system to ensure that the money supply obeyed the rules of the gold standard. The gold standard was meant to exert a powerful external constraint upon politicians, but the Currency School thought the legislation would have to force the banks into the appropriate mould, for otherwise they would expand credit at will, thereby exacerbating the trade cycle and, *in extremis*, causing a financial crisis. Thus, for bankers on that side there was a conflict between control of the money supply (in order to maintain a system that controlled the politicians) and state regulation of the banks to ensure that the latter did not circumvent that system.

This was a forerunner of the modern conflicts between monetarism's objectives of controlling money while promoting *laissez-faire* in the City. The Currency School thought to resolve it by turning control of the monetary system into a type of constitutional principle, a principle enshrined in the constitution of the Bank of England under the 1844 Act; but as the failure of that Act showed, the state could not be kept simultaneously in and out of monetary affairs by such devices. The Banking School, by contrast, saw the banking system and credit as essentially passive. Bank lending merely responded to the needs of trade, and bankers could not precipitate an over-expansion of money and credit. Hence there was no need for state regulation, and the gold standard could be left to itself. The modern Conservatives sought to resolve the contradiction between money control and *laissez-faire* by enshrining publicly announced money supply targets in their MTFS, with control to be exercised principally via existing market mechanisms. The fact that the MTFS has been jettisoned almost as rapidly as the 1844 Bank Charter Act was first suspended would seem to suggest that modern monetarists have made little headway in resolving what historically has remained the principal contradiction of monetarism.

Conclusion

The monetarist policies pursued by Mrs Thatcher's government were the policies of many City buffs and commentators, but they cannot be said to be wholly the result of the City explicitly fighting for monetarism in pursuit of its own interests. For the three elements of monetarism – promotion of *laissez-faire*, deflationary fiscal policies, and control of the money supply – often conflicted with each other and with the interests of one section of the City or another. In particular, control of the money supply by the state contains a potential threat to the freedom of banks, a form of *laissez-faire* the City is anxious to preserve; while an absence of the state even from indirect operations in the financial markets permits a volatility of interest and exchange rates that is distinctly uncomfortable for some City institutions.

These contradictory pressures on opinion in the Square Mile reflect the fact that for Britain's financial community monetarism is essentially about the construction of a system that limits the economic power of the state (but does not limit it so much as to generate instability which threatens it). Hence, the City had little difficulty in supporting one component of monetarism – cuts in government spending (deflationary fiscal policy) – and approved limits to the money supply if they were achieved by such cuts and a consequent reduction in government borrowing. It was for policies of that nature that City interests have been identified as monetarist, and it was for the pursuit of similar deflationary policies that the bankers earned notoriety in the interwar period. Then, instead of having the monetary targets of the medium-term financial strategy with which to beat the disciplinary drum, they had the supposedly immutable constraint of maintaining the gold standard and the exchange rate of sterling with which to force governments to cut spending. And with that tactic in 1931 they broke the Labour government and captured the handsome Ramsay MacDonald, the hero of the anti-war left of a decade and a half previously, for their own.

Quite apart from the question of whether the City actively foisted the whole panoply of monetarism upon Britain or whether, while supporting cuts in state spending, it was more contradictory on the other elements, the monetarist stance of Mr Callaghan's government after 1976 and Mrs Thatcher's after 1979 owed much to the changed financial world that the City had brought about. The ways in which the financial markets operated made monetarism almost inescapable for any government unless it was willing to go the whole hog towards full control of the financial system. If the state was not to go to that extreme, the sheer weight of mobile, privately controlled funds meant that it could not intervene in the markets by merely buying and selling on its own account but instead had to go to the extreme of monetarism, the attempt to create *laissez-faire* in the financial markets.

In that sense, the *laissez-faire* element of monetarism was the policy of the City, the result of the way the City markets operated, just as deflationary fiscal policy was the result of an actively articulated City view. Moreover, from that perspective control of the money supply had to follow, for if there were to be *laissez-faire* in the financial markets there could be no fixed target for the exchange rate. 'Support the value of sterling' could no longer be a watchword with which to control politicians who wanted more government spending or workers who pressed for higher wages without delivering higher productivity; and a new disciplinary standard, the limits to the growth of the money supply, had to be put in its place. If the money supply was being controlled, politicians had to restrain their profligacy and workers would realise that, if they bid for higher wages, the money would not be there to pay them all. The only problem for the bankers was whether the attempt to control the money supply would reinforce the power of the state, rather than reduce it, by encouraging politicians to control bankers.

10

Nationalise the City

In 1982, as the nation, or at least its newspapers, began to speculate on the date of the next general election and the possibility of a Labour victory, Alan Watkins, the political columnist of the *Observer*, wrote about the causes of previous Labour governments' failure to keep their promises. He claimed that Labour leaders in general were reluctant to discuss the problem:

> Mr Benn at least has talked about it, and deserves credit for that, but he has come up with the wrong answers, notably a hostile Civil Service and a disposition to 'treachery' by Labour Ministers. Ever since 1931, this last has been a popular accusation among Labour activists. The solution he and his friends have proposed is 'accountability'. But how do you make the International Monetary Fund accountable to anyone? Or the little men in Switzerland? On these questions Mr Benn is silent.
>
> Yet previous Labour Governments have failed not because of hostile civil servants, treacherous Ministers or a general lack of accountability (whatever that may mean in practice), but because of runs on the pound. This was so in 1931, in 1964–67 – even though Labour won the 1966 election – and in 1976. If Labour wins the next election, or forms a Government as the party holding the largest number of seats, there will be a run on the pound once again, however reasonable and moderate Mr Foot and his colleagues may appear. To predict this is not to be hostile to Labour but to be realistic.
>
> And yet, what would Mr Foot and his colleagues do about it? They do not seem to have considered the matter seriously or even at all. They are proceeding on the assumption that with North Sea Oil, a healthy balance of payments and an allegedly overvalued pound – all factors that were absent in the 1960s – the outside world would be content to treat a Labour Government much as it does a Conservative. Past experience suggests that this would not be so. [*Observer*, 14 November 1982]

Now, that observer's views are striking: Watkins is claiming that finance and financial interests have greater power than Parliament, and are more likely to undermine a party and programme chosen by the voters than is the civil service. He implies that a Labour government could not bring these forces to heel, for how could the gnomes of Zurich or the Washington-based officials of the IMF be made accountable? But that is to miss half or more of the point; for the runs on the pound that undermine Labour governments originate in the Square Mile of the City of London as much as elsewhere. The question that would have to be faced by politicians concerned to assert the power of Parliament, or at least the power of governments to carry out the programmes on which they were elected, is first of all whether the City can or should be made accountable.

The Labour Party itself has debated the question particularly vigorously since it lost power at the end of the 1960s. In 1971 its conference resolved to consider future proposals 'for the public ownership of all the banks, insurance companies and building societies', and in 1976 its National Executive Committee proposed the nationalisation of the top seven insurance companies, the Big Four clearing banks and one merchant bank. Nevertheless, Labour governments have rejected proposals for nationalising financial institutions and they have also been opposed by unions whose members work in the City.

As we write, in 1983, the Labour Party does not have a programme for nationalising the financial system, or significant parts of it, and there is no immediate prospect of its adopting one. Nevertheless, the question of nationalisation is unavoidable when we consider how the City can be made accountable.

Our conclusion, based on the view of the City presented in this book, is that major financial institutions, including the leading banks and insurance companies, should be nationalised, as too should pension funds, although they are not privately owned corporations like banks.

Previous arguments for nationalisation have pointed to one or other particular failing of the City. Some have pointed to the factors that Watkins identified in the quotation with which this chapter opened, the power the City has over the economy and left-wing governments through its influence over the foreign exchanges. Others, the most notable recent example being Richard Minns (1982b), have argued that the City should be taken over principally because its failure to provide the requisite finance has hindered industrial expansion. The first damns the City for its sins of commission, the second for its sins of omission. In each case nationalisation is the means for expurgating the particular sin. However, the approach we have taken in this book sees the City as a whole, with interconnections and links between every aspect of its operations. Accordingly, policy towards the City has to be judged according to its impact upon the whole rather than upon one problem or another. Seen in that light, the argument for nationalising some of the leading City institutions has much in its favour; although it is not unequivocal, it has more pros than cons in the balance.

Nationalisation of the main banks, insurance companies and pension funds can achieve nothing by itself, for it is merely a change in their *ownership*. If there is a need for a change it is because of the City's *operations*, so nationalisation has to be judged as one element in a package that also includes a change in the way finance operates. Mitterand's socialist government in France nationalised 30 per cent of the (commercial) deposit banks and the two great financial–industrial banking trusts of Paribas and Suez in 1982 but their operations were hardly affected: after all, another 50 per cent of the deposit banks had been state-owned for many years without showing any appreciable difference from privately owned banks. Certainly, the government did issue directives to grant credit to specific industries, but issuing directives proved to be only marginal. Nothing was done to change the role of finance in the economy, so the role of finance did not change: nationalisation, which absorbed great political energy, had little point to it.

Nationalising financial instititutions in Britain has to be seen as an element in radically changing the City's position and role in the economy if it is to mean anything. What is that role at present? What is it now, and towards what can it be altered on the basis of nationalisation?

The role of the City

The City is very private but its role is very public. It is private because private ownership is the order of the day. The institutions within it that are state-owned (some foreign banks) or are legally the property of their members (such as building societies and pension funds) operate in much the same manner as private bodies. The building societies and the private commercial banks have been pushed by their mutual competition to become more alike, while pension funds operate in the same way as the private insurance companies (with rather less accountability). The City's role is public because it affects every member of the public directly and indirectly. Its pervasiveness stems not from the hunger for power that demonologists often ascribe to financiers, but from the key position that finance has in an economy like Britain's.

It is tempting to see our economy as the sum of its various parts. Foreign trade and overseas investment is one area that sits in the limelight at one time; the problems of industrial production and investment in the modernisation of industry is another such area, and the ability of the economy to deliver the necessities of life such as housing is yet another. Such individual parts are in fact different aspects of the economy as a whole, and none can be understood fully without seeing the whole. The labour force has a clear connection with every development and issue in the economy, and the public's focus on questions of wages and labour productivity is a recognition that this aspect provides a window through which the economy as a whole can be viewed. Less well recognised is the fact that finance, too, has a connection with all the apparently distinct parts of the economy. The financial aspects of the three areas we have mentioned – foreign trade and investment, industrial regeneration, and housing – were the subject of earlier chapters, and are linked by the fact that credit and funds are mobile and flexible. Although there is no fixed pool of money to be shared out, each use of funds has to compete with the others and a rise in interest rates affects every area of the economy.

This aspect of finance, its universality, gives the City a special role. The financial system is not just another industry, just one sector of the economy, like engineering, agriculture or hairdressing; the expression that has become fashionable in recent years, 'the banking industry', is misleading. The financial system stands above and over all other economic activities. Its superior position stems from the fact that it is the source of the stuff that all industries need, credit and financial capital; it is the means by which all sectors deposit their surplus funds to produce interest and dividends; and within the City are contained the banks, money markets and foreign exchange markets that handle the cheques, bills of exchange and currency deals that are thrown up by the buying and selling in factory estates and shopping parades throughout the 'real economy'.

The universality of finance does not necessarily mean that the

City exercises power over the economy. The financial system certainly must reflect conditions within the 'real economy', but that is not the same as saying that finance controls those conditions. Indeed, in chapter 5 we saw that the long-term investing institutions with an inescapable stake in industry have done little to exert the power this could confer; nevertheless their accounts have been squeezed as a reflection of the unemployment and redundancies thrown up by the problems of the 'real economy'. But although the key position of finance does not automatically bestow power, the City has acquired a formidable strength on the basis of it.

The twin fulcra of its power are the exchange rate and interest rate. These two rates, the price of foreign exchange and the price of credit, are determined on markets within the City's domain, but they affect the whole economy. The ups and downs of the exchange rate, affecting the prices of imports and exports, disturb both the conditions faced by industrial firms and the standard of living of ordinary people. And the ups and downs of interest rates can push firms, dependent on credit, to bankruptcy while changing the cost of living for every mortgage-holder. Compared with the factors that industrial firms, merchants and trade unions determine, exchange and interest rate changes have an unrivalled immediacy and pervasiveness. For example, if trade unions take the view that, as a result of inflation, wages have got out of line with the cost of living, the actions they can take for an increase in wages are protracted, piecemeal and uncertain; if they do result in a general rise in money wages the effects are widespread, but they are far from uniform and far from immediate. On the other hand, if the City's money dealers take the view that inflation is causing the exchange rate to be out of line, their view – a lack of 'confidence' in sterling – is translated immediately into a mass of selling orders, which promptly produces a fall in the exchange rate with its pervasive effects.

The exchange rate and interest rate are the levers of the City's power; they are measures of its pivotal role in the economy. But power is not something that necessarily is consciously wielded. The power of finance makes itself felt in several ways, and especially through the day-to-day operations of dealers who are interested only in a quick profit: they have no consciousness of the power they share. When dealers judge that inflation, the rate of growth of the money supply, or the government's spending plans are inconsistent with the existing level of the exchange rate, they do not mark the pound down (and their clients do not sell) in order to exert power

over the government or the economy: they do it in order to make a
quick profit or avoid a loss, and each trader follows the others
immediately to avoid the danger of loss that comes from being left
behind. With similar factors operating on interest rates, these
beliefs and actions are what determine the day-to-day movements
in exchange rates with their impact on the rest of the economy.
Even when there are major events that push governments off
course – the sterling crises that throughout much of this century
forced governments into attempts to cut their spending, impose
wage controls and so on – the turmoil on the markets arises as much
from this profit-seeking as from any conscious attempt to force the
hand of the state.

However, the City is not a political eunuch; it has leaders and
representative bodies who speak for it and a direct connection with
the state and with policy-making. Its power is wielded consciously
as well as through its everyday operations. The Bank of England is
the principal channel for this, although not the only one, and the
direct access its Governor has to the Prime Minister is its symbol.
Joe Haines, a Downing Street 'political' adviser under Harold
Wilson, imagines a typical scene when the financial markets'
opinion pushes a Labour government towards cutting its spending.
The Governor of the Bank of England would be 'sitting in his car
with engine running and bonnet pointed toward Downing Street'
while 'the Prime Minister, on his return from a Whitsun week-end
in the country, would have been greeted by the Chancellor of the
Exchequer with the news that large overseas holders of sterling
were about to withdraw their deposits because of the falling
exchange rate; that confidence had to be restored at once; and that,
the only way to regain that confidence would be further drastic cuts
in public expenditure.' But in his account of his Downing Street
days Haines also pointed to the other political channels through
which the power of the City is wielded at such times, in particular
the City insider, who is privy to the operations that the City
shrouds in mystique but is also an insider within the government;
the financier politician, such as Harold Lever was in the reign of
Harold Wilson, who is in a powerful position to convey City
views.

Haines's image of the Governor sitting in his purring car with
bonnet pointed west, while the confidence of the dealers – seeking
profits rather than power – needs to be bolstered, was written as
'faction', neither quite fact nor quite fiction, and it was applied to
the events of 1975 and 1976. But it does correspond to the reality of

several crises. The autumn of 1931 is judged by the Labour Party even today as the most awful autumn and the most decisive for its twentieth-century prospects, because it was then that Ramsay MacDonald and his followers split off to form a National Government. Those events were the outcome of exactly the combination of a market loss of confidence in sterling and an intervention by the Bank of England and other leading bankers to press for cuts in government spending. It was the bankers' man that delivered to the Cabinet the crucial assessment of financial markets' 'confidence'. According to Richard Sayers's history of the Bank of England, the members of Ramsay MacDonald's Cabinet broke up with some 'imagining they were being dictated to rather than merely informed' by the City's representative (Sayers, 1976, vol. 2, p. 399). And the King was dining with highly political and highly placed City men when he asked MacDonald to form the National Government that would carry through the economic policies for which the financial markets had voted. In the twentieth-century parables told by Labour's left wing, the City had voted without the rigmarole of ballot boxes: it voted with its pounds, selling them in a flood over that summer; and, finally, it voted with a word in the right ears at the right moment. According to the parable, as often happens when only one party has access to the means of expressing its vote, the City won.

The purpose of power

The position of finance in the economy – its immediacy, pervasiveness and indispensability – is the basis of the unconscious power exercised by the financial markets and of the conscious interventions, given weight by disorder on those markets, of the Bank of England's Governor and other City politicians. Because of the role of finance, the market fluctuations affect the whole economy directly, and political interventions have the ability to change the direction of governments' economic policies. It is not simply a question of the City dictating the economic policy of socialist governments; in chapter 9 we argued that it had a role in ensuring that the 1979 Tory government adopted monetarist policies. But in what direction is this power exerted? What are the City's aims?

Just as the City's power arises from the very character of finance, so too the directions in which that power exerts its influence result from the fact that it is in a sense above the rest of the economy.

Financiers are as self-interested as anyone else and their power is exercised to further their own and their institutions' well-being; for those at the top of the hierarchy, the City's interests are always judged in ways that reflect upon the national economy as a whole and the world economy.

First, because the raw material of bankers and brokers in foreign exchange dealing is the money of different national economies (pounds, dollars, francs and so on), the pursuit of short-term profits forces the dealers to make judgements on what is happening to the economies in which those currencies are used. If they believe that the key feature is an economy's level of state spending (too much state spending indicating weakness), then to make profits they will sell dollars when the US budget deficit rises and sell pounds when the UK government expands its spending. And because the markets' judgements are made on the basis of such singleminded indicators of the national economy, the results have an impact on the economy.

Although dealers do not sell sterling (or buy it) in order to influence governments' economic policies, the actions they take in the pursuit of profit inevitably do push policies into conformity with their views. As a result, it was common, and still is, to hear ministers and pundits claiming that the money supply (or government spending, or whatever happens to be the market's favourite indicator) cannot be expanded above a certain rate if the exchange rate is to be steadied.

Second, standing above the rest of the economy means that the profits of some financial operations depend very directly on the health of the 'real economy'. Because of this, those who speak for the City have to take a view on what would be good for industry and commerce as a whole. And here there is an inescapable tension. The City's influence has time and again been exerted on the side of discipline: the long-term strength of industry depends, in the City's customary view, on there being sufficient competitive pressure upon it to hold down wages and to press industrialists to rationalise, reduce employment and raise productivity. Thus, as commentators from G. D. H. Cole and J. M. Keynes onward have noted, the City has a deflationary bias: if a choice has to be made between unemployment and inflation, the City presses for the former as a necessary but regrettable medicine. However, when there is a major economic crisis, like the depression of the early 1980s, that policy is not without problems; for the suffering of industry (whether or not it is only short-term) brings danger to the financial system, too. Increasing proportions of banks' profits are eaten up by having to make provisions to cover the potential bad debts of industrial bankrupts. And pension funds' new receipts suffer from the fact that their members are joining the dole queue in increasing numbers.

Third, and most significantly, the City's leaders have always brought their influence to bear to strengthen the City's international standing, its competitive strength *vis-à-vis* other financial centres. A consistent objective has been to ensure that London rather than New York (or, at various times, Paris or Zurich) is the world's main centre for international finance. It is an objective that is pursued side by side with the City's aims for British economic policy, at times coinciding and at times clashing, but it is inevitable that the City has both international and domestic objectives because, as the previous chapters have shown, the City's character is inseparable from both its international and its domestic business.

The financial community's policy towards devaluing the pound between 1964 and 1967 illustrates well the way in which domestic and international objectives combine. Many economists believed that at $2.80 the exchange rate was too high in the sense that it was harming industry, and there is now some evidence to suggest that a lower exchange rate would, indeed, have assisted industrial profits in the short run; but the City policy, articulated and promoted by the Bank of England, was to maintain the exchange rate rather than devalue (Coakley and Harris, 1982b).

By 1967 devaluation was inescapable, but in the meantime the City's objectives were to defend the pound in order not to 'betray' the trust that overseas holders of sterling had placed in Britain; and the importance of sustaining that integrity was such that bankers thought that their ability to attract international business depended upon foreign banks', governments' and firms' willingness to invest in sterling (although subsequent experience, the growth of Eurodollar business, belied this). Second, a dear pound was a necessary discipline upon British industry and workers; it might cause immediate difficulties for industry, but it would have a salutary long-term effect as a result.

A more recent episode is a more ambiguous illustration of the relationship between the international and domestic faces of the City's power. The abolition of all exchange controls in 1979 was a City policy greatly welcomed by the leaders and institutions that wanted to enhance their world role, but it is widely claimed that the resulting outflow of funds has harmed British industry by depriving it of the long-term finance it needs to modernise and re-structure its operations and to launch new ventures. If the claim is true, the City's objectives of building its international competitive strength in this case clashed with its objectives for British industry.

The validity of the claim sometimes appears self-evident: as we saw in chapter 2, the abolition of exchange controls led to a flood of money overseas from pension funds and insurance companies, the very institutions that are best placed to have used the money for providing industry with long-term finance. But some of the City's pundits and journalists maintain that the lifting of exchange controls actually did industry a favour, because the outflow of funds helped to keep the exchange rate lower than it would otherwise have been in the years following 1979. However, if a lower exchange rate had been needed it would not have required foreign investment by pension funds to bring it about: an increase in government spending on health or education would, by increasing state borrowing and affecting market sentiment, have obtained the same exchange rate. Nevertheless, the argument that the export of capital has starved industry of appropriate finance is far from proven. Since it is often presented as a reason for nationalising City institutions, we shall examine it as part of the wider question concerning the character of finance for industry under a publicly owned financial system.

We have seen that the role of the City gives considerable power to the financial system's operators and to the leaders of the City as a whole, and that City interests pursue policies with respect to both international and domestic finance. If nationalisation of leading banks, insurance companies and pension funds is to have any impact, it has to change those roles, and in doing so it would change the objectives and policies of the City.

The nature of a state-owned financial system can be judged sensibly only in the context of much greater state intervention throughout the economy. The economic strategy that was discussed throughout the labour movement and partly adopted by the Labour Party in the early 1980s envisaged intervention of several types, particularly in the planned growth and modernisation of industry and the planned development of foreign trade and investment.

Substantial industries were to be nationalized or subject to planning agreements and thereby linked to national plans, while overseas trade, regulated through import controls, was to be expanded as the economy grows and by negotiation. Although nationalising parts of the financial system was not included in the Labour Party's programme, it would only arise in the context of such a strategy for the economy as a whole and it should be judged in that context.

New directions in financing industry

A nationalised system of banks, insurance companies and pension funds would provide the industrial finance to match the development plans that the industrial giants agree with the government; one of their responsibilities would be to ensure that money is available for the re-structuring of British industry in an agreed pattern. That is not to say that the City has so far failed to provide industry with the finance it needs; but its needs will be much greater if British industry is to be fundamentally reconstructed, as European and Japanese industries were after the Second World War, and the City's conventional ways of allocating funds will then be quite inadequate. Just as the European countries and Japan took a crucial lead in coordinating the finance to back their countries' industrial miracles, so government coordination of finance and industry will be necessary in Britain.

But why? Why not rely on the City's traditional ways of financing industry? And if that is not adequate, why is nationalisation, rather than government direction of independent banks and investment institutions, necessary? Does not the argument of many left-wing activists, that nationalising financial institutions would be an exhausting diversion from the main task of rebuilding the 'real' economy, hold water?

Richard Minns (1982b) expresses the view, shared by many, that we cannot rely on the City's traditional methods because these have failed in the past. Whereas the City's advocates claim it has performed well in financing industry, Minns claims that for industrial strength 'the sort of finance needed is long-term capital: most lending in the UK is tied to assets and security, and therefore has a short-term perspective, and generates a tendency to emphasise the . . . liquidation potential of companies rather than their long-term production and trading prospects' (Minns, 1982b, p. 61). In other words, the finance for industry has not been of the right type; and, moreover, both its form and its total quantity have been restricted by the City's tendency to export capital instead of investing in British industry.

There is, in fact, no evidence to support the claim that overseas investment (or investment in real estate and other 'non-productive' speculative bolt-holes) has caused a shortage of funds for industry. The Wilson Committee reported in 1980 that they found no general shortage of funds: 'we have examined the contention that real investment in the UK has been unnecessarily constrained by shortages in the supply of external finance.' Wilson's conclusion cannot be the final word, for the Committee's basic concept of the financial system was faulty and, apart from that, there is no simple empirical method of confirming or refuting the existence of a general shortage. But there is no *evidence* to suggest that there has been a general shortage. Equally, there is no evidence to support the view that the financial system itself has been the cause of the concentration on short-term finance.

It is too simple to argue that the City has failed British industry by not making sufficient finance of the right (long-term) type available for investment because demand for such finance has not been forthcoming: as Minns notes *both* industry and the City must change.

Historically, industry in Britain has had at its disposal a pool of internal finance, principally retained profits and depreciation allowances, out of which it could choose to finance investment. Over the 1960s and 1970s the proportion of investment capable of being financed from these sources has averaged 98 per cent. This may be the result of a distinct preference by firms for relying on their own resources to finance investment; for the evidence given to the Wilson Committee by industry's representatives was consistent in its theme that in forward planning firms deliberately aim to finance the growth of their plant from internal resources. The availability of such large sums of internal finance, compared with French and German firms, for example, which could have financed, respectively, only 61 and 80 per cent of investment from their own funds, appears to result partly from firms' preferences rather than from the shortcomings of the financial system. There is no reason to think that, if the City had provided more funds of a different type, industry would have invested them in greater and more modern plant; the complex causes of both industry's low investment and the character of industrial finance in Britain cannot be reduced to a single factor, the City's propensities.

Nevertheless, nationalisation relates to future policy rather than the past. It is not a question of 'what would have happened if . . .' but of 'what type of system will be necessary to ensure the finance of a planned growth of the "real economy"?' The traditional practice of industrial finance is inappropriate to this because of the features to which Minns and others have pointed. It is true that bank finance for industry has been predominantly short-term instead of a commitment for the 10- to 15-year period that an investment project may take to show its full returns. And it has been true, although it is decreasingly so, that bank lending has been tied to the value of the collateral, the security the bank would get on a company's liquidation, rather than to a careful, exact study of the company's strength as a going concern.

We discussed these aspects in chapter 6. It is also true, as we argued in chapter 5 that the investment institutions that are the repositories of long-term funds facilitate the long-term finance of industry only very indirectly. The funds that they do not invest overseas or put into property, fine art or government bonds are invested in the shares of companies (not all of which are industrial companies), but these are principally existing shares bought from other investors rather than newly issued shares raising new capital for firms. At best these purchases of second-hand shares may make it easier for companies to raise new capital by issuing new shares at a higher price than would otherwise be the case, but that is a very indirect effect and not sufficient to exonerate the institutions from the charge of failing to provide long-term finance; even the opening of the Unlisted Securities Market for small firms to raise capital has not significantly changed this situation.

Because the financing of industry has traditionally had these characteristics, the very large industrial investment programme that is required for regenerating the British economy cannot rely upon the City's traditional methods of finance. A systematic and comprehensive link between long-term investment, production and financial strategies is required, but why is nationalisation a necessary prerequisite for it?

Privately owned banks and insurance companies and independent pension funds do not consider the development of the national economy (or the amelioration of world poverty, or any similar matter) in disposing of funds. There is no reason why they should, for it is not their business to do so. They are in business to make a return on their assets (formally, on behalf of their shareholders or their members), and for any *individual* institution there is no reason to think that they will make a better return by taking the risk of, say, a long-term commitment to an industry's development plans than they will by doing what they have always done. (Although writers such as Minns argue that pension funds *as a whole* may benefit their members by taking a long-term perspective and investing in industrial regeneration instead of seeking quick financial gains). Financial institutions can be required to change their role – to take the risks involved in financing a major restructuring of industry, risks very different from those, involved in short-term market operations and short-term lending – only if they have the backing of the state; and the state can give full backing and take full responsibility only if it owns and controls the institutions.

Nationalisation is not the only way for the state to affect the investment policies of the City, but it is the only effective way. Without it, it is possible for the state to exert a negative constraint, but not to give a positive impetus to the direction of industrial finance. Negative constraints have been brought to bear before, most notably with the controls over capital issues that restricted firms' ability to raise new equity capital during and after the Second World War, and they can be effective if applied rigorously (although the financial system devises legitimate means to circumvent controls wherever loopholes exist); but there can be no effective way that private financial institutions can be positively directed towards an expansion of lending in particular directions if they are to retain the autonomy that goes with their private standing. Public ownership of the financial institutions would permit such a positive policy, a reorientation towards financing long-term investments in partnership with industry and under the aegis of a national plan.

Nationalisation would not *automatically* lead to a change in the financial system's direction; one recent reminder of this came from France, where, after M. Mitterand's government extended and completed the public ownership of French banking, it directed them to lend to the leading enterprises that the state was restructuring and met with a great deal of opposition from the bankers, struggling to maintain their old way of doing things. But, although no panacea, nationalisation is a precondition for achieving the changes.

It could also be said that, if the financial system needs state backing in order to take on the new kinds of risks, it needs guarantees rather than public ownership. In fact, the financial system already has a considerable amount of state backing in the form of both formal and informal guarantees, but it has not led to any changes in the City's orientation. At the formal level the banks have built a large, profitable and risk-free business upon Export Credit Guarantees provided by the state; but these have merely reinforced (as they were intended) the City's traditional function of financing trade, smoothing the flux and reflux of money from the movement of commodities, rather than financing long-term industrial development. More generally, the state (via the Bank of England, which in this respect was an organ of state long before it was nationalised in 1946) has guaranteed the viability of the banking system as a whole by acting as lender of last resort. The major banks, at least, have known for a century that if they are hit by a shortage of liquidity the Bank of England will lend to them to prevent a panic. Moreover, the City rests on a strong cushion of shock absorbers in the form of the national debt. Government borrowing over the centuries has created a large volume of state bonds which are held by the financial institutions as assets that are as good as gold: 'gilt-edged' bonds or, for short, 'gilts' is an appropriate name. In the preceding chapters we have seen that banks, insurance companies and pension funds all hold these investments, and they do so in the certain knowledge that Britannia will not default on her bonds. Yet this guaranteed cushion has done nothing to encourage the City to branch out into the tougher world of long-term industrial financing.

In fact, it can be argued that the existence of a large state debt and other forms of guarantee has encouraged the financial system to take the soft options. Public ownership would entail its taking the hard options instead, as part of a state strategy designed to face the future. One of the options the City has traditionally taken has been that of international expansion; by placing those chapters first in this book we have emphasised the fact that in many respects it has taken priority. If City institutions were to be nationalised and were to be incorporated in a new economic strategy, what of that international business?

New directions in international finance

If at home it makes sense for finance to be harnessed to the planned development of the economy, overseas it makes sense for it to be directed towards supporting the trade and investment flows that are the planned counterparts of that reconstruction programme. By a combination of selective import controls, export promotion and negotiated trade treaties, governments have the power to influence the pattern of Britain's trade with other countries, and to do so in such a way that it matches the needs of a growing economic base. And by a combination of controls and planning agreements with multinational corporations, the pattern of flows of capital into and out of the country can be brought into conformity with the overall economic strategy. The City's role would be to finance the trade and investment patterns that are chosen.

The idea is straightforward enough, but it is very different from the City's present international role, and because it involves radical changes it can be carried out only by nationalising the financial institutions. At present the City finances trade and investment flows in the only manner it recognises: in ways that bring it a profit rather than take heed of a wider economic interest. Thus, to take the major part of the City's business, its borrowing and lending of Eurodollars (and other Eurocurrencies) has grown to a point where it dominates the markets, but it has little connection with financing the trade generated by the British economy or the international investment associated with Britain's development. Nor, despite the claim that London's Eurodollar markets effectively 'recycled' the money accumulated by oil-exporting countries in the last decade, can it be said that this aspect of the City's business furthered development on a world scale. A financial system with a dominant publicly owned core, orientated towards the trade and investment flows of planned economic growth, would have no role as the world's centre of Eurodollar banking and lending, and that would be a very big change indeed.

Let us be clear about a withdrawal from the City's offshore role. We do not mean that Britain should not borrow Eurodollars or lend them; all advanced countries have to borrow and lend foreign currencies in order to finance trade and investment, and Britain can be no exception unless it returns to a primitive autarky. But borrowing and lending Eurodollars to support a planned pattern of trade and investment is quite different from the City's present role, which is to act as the centre for the world's Eurodollar markets as a whole. It is the creation of Eurodollar credits *sui generis*, the transactions to generate profit by multiplying credits, by foreign currencies being borrowed and lent without any connection to Britain, that would be changed. It would not be easy to do this, for apart from the British banks and institutions in London the market includes four hundred foreign banks within the City, and there is no real prospect of nationalising them; but a change of policy by the British banks combined with stiff regulations over the foreign banks would effectively run down this part of the City's work, since its very existence depends on relative freedom from regulation.

Why should such a dramatic change be carried through? London's Eurodollar business brings in profits that contribute to the balance of payments (although the importance of these should not be exaggerated, for they are partly and, in some years, wholly outweighed by outflows from the City). And it does not directly cause the runs on the pound that Alan Watkins, in the article quoted at the start of this chapter, identified as an index of the City's power. Because the Eurodollar business largely depends upon borrowing foreign currencies and lending them, rather than upon transferring money from sterling to other currencies (an operation that also occurs), it does not directly affect the exchange rate of the pound, although its growth has, as we noted in chapter 3, indirectly influenced the volatility of all major exchange rates. So why should London's business as an offshore centre be cut down? There are two reasons. First, the growth of Eurodollar markets has greatly contributed to the danger of a banking crash which would have an impact throughout the world economy, and as we suggested in chapter 4, there are severe limits to the extent to which state supervision or the supra-national actions of institutions like the International Monetary Fund can overcome the danger. Second, Eurodollar business is a central element in the whole ensemble of financial operations the City engages in, and if its role is to be changed the links that hold the whole together at present have to be re-strung. Let us explain.

Nationalising City institutions will not, of itself, change the way they and their people work. It will not even automatically ensure that they are subject to Ministers' directives. When the Bank of England was nationalised in 1946 it was formally brought under the control of the government; but in fact it has remained an independent power centre, in the state but outside it, vying with the Treasury and other centres for influence over economic policy and with virtually complete autonomy regarding policies for the City itself. There is no reason to think that the nationalisation of other financial institutions would be any more effective in challenging their independence; their day-to-day operations would remain unchanged unless there were an explicit and determined policy to eliminate whole elements of it. Unless the Eurodollar business is explicitly run down, the banks and investment institutions will continue to weigh their lending to industry or the state, and their financing of trade in the balance against the possibility of reaping management fees and interest yields from this offshore business. Since the latter consists of a pyramid of pure finance whose ultimate links to the real economy are rather distant for most of its operators, it and similar business is always a tempting prospect compared with the more 'involved' finance that the 'real economy' needs.

In the same vein, running down the City's offshore business blocks one of the directions in which its power has been exercised. The policy-makers at the top of the City hierarchy give London's international competitiveness as a financial centre a top priority, and as long as its predominance in that world remains at the heart of its business, the pursuit of that aim will continue to dominate its counsels. If the City were to continue to be the world's leading Eurobanking centre, its leaders and representatives in Westminster and Whitehall would judge financial policies according to whether they strengthen or hinder that business. If, for example, the aim of ensuring that finance for industry was adequate led to the general imposition of interest rate ceilings, they would be opposed by bankers, fearing that such ceilings would affect their ability to compete on the Eurocurrency markets (in the way that interest rate ceilings hindered the growth of New York's international role in the postwar decades). If, on the other hand, the banks' participation in these markets had been run down, such opposition would be defused.

Controlling the foreign exchanges

Some would hope that nationalisation would have another effect on Britain's international economy: it would enable the exchange rate to be taken firmly under control, thereby preventing the runs on the pound, the sterling crises, or even the over-valuations of the pound that have been held responsible for many of Britain's economic problems at various times this century. But although nationalisation would give some support to exchange rate policy, it would not solve the problem by any means, and this could not be the main aim for nationalisation.

The exchange rate's pervasive effects upon the economy mean that any government attempting to plan a programme of economic growth has to have a policy dealing with it; there has to be a target exchange rate or a band within which the government aims to maintain it. The historic problem is that the exchange rate is set by the balance of demand and supply for pounds and other currencies on the foreign exchange markets, not by government decree, and no future government can escape that fact however *dirigiste* it is. Nationalisation of the banks and investment institutions can play some role in affecting the balance of demand and supply, but not a major role.

Firm influence over the exchange rate requires full exchange controls, like the system that operated in Britain during the Second World War. It requires a system under which Britons and British firms require permission whenever they buy foreign currency, whether it is to pay for imported goods, to take on holiday to the Costa Brava or to buy shares or a villa abroad. Exchange controls themselves will be difficult to operate without nationalising the banks. Whereas in the 1940s the banks operated them on behalf of the government, now there is no wartime patriotism to support such cooperation, and since the banks' business is now so inter-meshed with untramelled foreign exchange dealings, it is extremely unlikely that they would again willingly act as government agents. Their implementation of exchange controls on behalf of the government could be gained only if they were publicly owned.

But full exchange controls backed by nationalisation would not give full control over the exchange rate. Foreign exchange markets in other countries and the dealings of non-residents of Britain would determine its 'unofficial' rate even if British banks, firms and individuals were able to be effectively restrained. The most that could be gained would be partial control. Nationalisation of the banks (which operate the foreign exchange markets and deal in them) and of the investment institutions (whose overseas invest-ment drained funds abroad when the last of the exchange controls were abolished) would assist that partial control, but it could only be a side benefit of public ownership rather than its principal rationale.

A concentration of power

The financial system's position in the economy gives the City great economic and political power. That power takes several forms and is exercised for several different ends, but within the City itself it is highly concentrated in the hands of a few institutions. The banks, merchant banks and commercial banks represent a great concentration which has marked them out for special attention when nationalisation is on the agenda. Richard Minns (1982b) has pointed to their concentrated control over the accumulated invest-ments of the pension funds as an argument that nationalisation of the banks alone would indirectly give the state effective control over much wider sectors of the economy. Rather more weakly, the Wilson Committee, while rejecting nationalisation, thought that, given the clearing banks' near-monopoly of the payments system (the system of cheque clearing and other transfers), it could be worth considering the public ownership of that system to increase its efficiency. But irrespective of the special position of banks, the concentration of power in the City as a whole makes the arguments for nationalising its leading institutions compelling if a democratically elected government is to succeed in directing the economy on a new path.

The words 'democratically elected' are at the heart of the matter for the politicians. The major episodes of financial policy in the twentieth century have created the impression for left-wing politicians that the City competes with the state for the power to govern in one important area, the governance of the economy, and that when the conflicts become acute the City wins. Their argument for nationalisation is wider than the improvement of Britain's economic performance. Like the argument for the Alternative Economic Strategy as a whole, it is a claim for greater democratic control over the economy; for, whatever its virtues, no one can claim that the City is democratic. The power of the City is exercised without any of its leaders being elected at the ballot box and without anyone being accountable for it. Except for the formal responsibility of the Bank of England to the government, the only accountability in the City is the accountability for making profits.

Nevertheless, no one can claim that the nationalisation of leading City institutions would be easy. One major problem will be to decide which institutions should be nationalised; should all British banks be taken over, and what of the 400 or so foreign banks in London? Should the assets and liabilities of every small pension fund be vested in the state? And almost as immediate is the problem of exactly how publicly owned financial institutions are to be administered and operated; how to ensure that they are under the control of the democratically elected government and that they do not simply follow their old paths.

The greatest difficulty in carrying out effective nationalisation is the very flexibility and universality of finance, which has always underlined the power of the City and other financial centres. The nationalisation carried out by the French government in 1982 exemplifies the difficulties, and we quote one example as a warning. One of the main targets of nationalisation was a trust called Paribas, a modern exemplar of the type of finance capital described by Hilferding; but the international power and flexibility of finance enabled a large part of it to get away.

The Paribas group, under M. Pierre Moussa, contained banks and industrial enterprises and had expanded rapidly and strongly, particularly in its foreign operations. It was seen within the Socialist Party as a 'state within a state', so that its nationalisation was a political necessity to consolidate state power. However, with the aid of its foreign associates, the Paribas group was reconstructed under the nose of the French government. Interlocking shareholdings were switched around to ensure that a sizeable part of the group's assets was taken over by a hitherto-unknown Swiss company beyond the reach of the French government. The *Financial Times* summarised the outcome the day after the complex transaction was completed despite the government's protestations:

> The battle . . . has been between a group of international financiers who saw the nationalisation of Paribas, with which they were closely involved, as damaging to their interests and who then organised themselves to thwart it and an inexperienced Socialist Administration which in the euphoria of taking office failed to see the pitfalls of taking over multinational companies and banks. [*Financial Times*, 23 October 1981, p. 29]

The lesson to be drawn from the difficulties the French experienced in taking over banks is not that nationalisation is impossible, but that it carries with it difficulties for which preparation has to be made.

Bibliography

Aaronovitch, Sam and Smith, Ron with Jean Gardiner and Roger Moore (1981), *The Political Economy of British Capitalism*. London: McGraw-Hill.

Adam, G. (1975), 'Multinational Corporations and Worldwide Sourcing', in Hugo Radice (ed.), *International Firms and Modern Imperialism*. Harmondsworth: Penguin.

Aglietta, M. (1982), 'World Capitalism in the Eighties', *New Left Review*, no. 136, 5–41.

Artis, M. J. and Lewis, M. K. (1981), *Monetary Control in the United Kingdom*. Oxford: Philip Alan.

Bagehot, W. (1873), *Lombard Street: A Description of the Money Market* (1962 edn). Homewood, Illinois: Richard D. Irwin.

Bain, A. D. (1981), *The Economics of the Financial System*. Oxford: Martin Robertson.

Bank of England (1980), 'Corporate Insolvency', *Bank of England Quarterly Bulletin*, 20 (4), 430–436.

Bank of England (1982), 'The Supplementary Special Deposits Scheme', *Bank of England Quarterly Bulletin*, 22 (1), 74–85.

Barratt-Brown, M. (1970), *After Imperialism*. London: Heinemann.

Berle, A. A. and Means, G. C. (1932), *The Modern Corporation and Private Property* (rev. edn 1968). New York: Harcourt, Brace and World.

Boddy, M. (1980), *The Building Societies*. London: Macmillan.

Bottomore, Tom (ed.) (1983), *A Dictionary of Marxist Thought*. Oxford: Basil Blackwell.

Building Societies Association (1979), *Mortgage Finance in the 1980s*, Report of a Working Party under the Chairmanship of Mr. Ralph Stow. London: BSA.

Building Societies Association (1983), *The Future Constitution and Powers of Building Societies*. London: BSA.

Cain, P. V. and Hopkins, A. G. (1980), 'The Political Economy of British Expansion Overseas 1715–1914', *Economic History Review*, second series 33(4), 463–90.

Cleary, E. J. (1965), *The Building Society Movement*. London: Elek.
Coakley, J. and Harris, L. (1982), 'Evaluating the Financial System', in D. Currie and M. Sawyer (eds), *Socialist Economic Review 1982*. London: Merlin.
Coakley, J. and Harris, L. (1983), 'Industry, the City and the Foreign Exchanges: Theory and Evidence', *British Review of Economic Issues*, 4(10), forthcoming.
Committee to Review the Functioning of Financial Institutions (1980), *Report and Appendices*, Cmnd 7937. London: HMSO.
Donaldson, J. A. and Donaldson, T. H. (1982), *The Medium-Term Loan Market*. London: Macmillan.
Friedman, M. and Schwartz, A. J. (1963), *A Monetary History of the United States, 1867–1960*, NBER Studies in Business Cycles 12. Princeton: University Press.
Gamble, Andrew (1981), *Britain in Decline: Economic Policy, Political Strategy and the British State*. London: Macmillan.
Goode, R. M. (1982), *Legal Problems of Credit and Security*. London: Sweet & Maxwell.
Gough, T. J. (1982), *The Economics of Building Societies*. London: Macmillan.
Gough, T. J. and Taylor, T. W. (1979), *The Building Society Price Cartel*, Hobart Papers. London: Institute of Economic Affairs.
Harris, Nigel (1982), 'The Road from 1910', *Economy and Society*, 12(4), 347–62.
Herman, E. S. (1981), *Corporate Control, Corporate Power*. Cambridge: University Press.
Hilferding, R. (1910), *Finance Capital: A Study of the Latest Phase of Capitalist Development* (1981 edn). English translations by M. Watnick and S. Gordon; edited with an Introduction by Tom Bottomore. London: Routledge & Kegan Paul.
Johnson, C. (1981), 'Banks to the Rescue', *Lloyds Bank Economic Bulletin*, no. 20 (June), 1–4.
Johnston, R. B. (1982), *The Economics of the Euro-Market: History, Theory and Policy*. London: Macmillan.
Karn, V. (1983), Mortgage Arrears, *Roof*, 8(1), 11–14.
Kotz, D. M. (1978), *Bank Control of Large Corporations in the United States*. Berkeley: University of California Press.
McRae, H. and Cairncross, F. (1973), *Capital City: London as a Financial Centre*. London: Eyre Methuen.
Mandel, E. (1975). *Late Capitalism*. London: New Left Books.
Mather, L. C. (1966), *Securities Acceptable to the Lending Banker*. London: Waterlow.
Mendelsohn, M. S. (1939), *Money on the Move: The Modern International Capital Market*. New York: McGraw-Hill.

Minns, Richard (1980), *Pension Funds and British Capitalism: The Ownership and Control of Large Shareholdings*. London: Heinemann.

Minns, Richard, (1982a), Management of Shareholdings in Large Manufacturing Companies', Social Sciences Working Paper, Open University.

Minns, Richard, (1982b): *Take Over the City: The Case for Public Ownership of Financial Institutions*. London: Pluto Press.

Minsky, H. P. (1978), 'The Financial Instability Hypothesis: A Restatement', *Thames Papers in Political Economy*, London: North East London Polytechnic.

Olle, W. and Shoeller, W. (1982), 'Direct Investment and Monopoly Theories of Imperialism', *Capital and Class*, no. 16, 41–60.

Overbeek, Henk (1980), 'Finance Capital and the Crisis in Britain, *Capital and Class*, no. 11, 99–120.

Plender, John (1982), *That's the Way the Money Goes: The Financial Institutions and the Nation's Savings*. London: André Deutsch.

Radice, Hugo (ed.) (1975), *International Firms and Modern Imperialism*. Harmondsworth: Penguin.

Redaway, W. B., Potter, S. T. and Taylor, C. T. (1968), *Effects of UK Direct Investment Overseas*. Cambridge: University Press.

Reid, M. (1982), *The Secondary Banking Crisis, 1973–75: Its Causes and Course*. London: Macmillan.

Revell, J. (1973), *The British Financial System*. London: Macmillan.

Rowthorn, B. (1971), 'Imperialism in the 1970s – Unity of Rivalry? *New Left Review*, no. 69, 31–51.

Savage, D. (1980), 'Some Issues of Monetary Policy', *National Institute Economic Review*, no. 91, 78–85.

Sampson, A. (1981), *The Money Lenders*. London: Hodder and Stoughton.

Sayers, R. S. (1957a), *Central Banking after Bagehot*. Oxford: Clarendon Press.

Sayers, R. S. (1957b), *Lloyds Bank in the History of English Banking*. London: Oxford University Press.

Sayers, R. S. (1976), *The Bank of England 1891–1944*. Volumes 1, 2 and Appendices, Cambridge: Cambridge University Press.

Sinclair, A. (1981), *Corsair: The Life of Pierpoint Morgan*. London: Weidenfeld & Nicolson.

Stewart, M. (1977), *The Jekyll and Hyde Years: Politics and Economic Policy since 1964*. London: Dent.

Thompson, Grahame (1977), 'The Relationship between the Financial and Industrial Sector in the United Kingdom', *Economy and Society*, 6, 235–83.

Versluysen, E. L. (1981), *The Political Economy of International Finance*. London: Gower Press.

Wilson Report (1980): see Committee to Review the Functioning of Financial Institutions (1980).

Index

Wood R K Gn. cony. 521163
Chri Morgan.